Klabund: The Gravedigger
and Other Early Plays

KLABUND

THE GRAVEDIGGER

AND OTHER

EARLY

PLAYS

Translated by Jim Doss

LOCH RAVEN PRESS   SYKESVILLE, MD   2025

Printed in the United States of America

Cover Art: Cover photo is Klabund in 1928
  Back cover photo is Klabund seated next to Kathi Kobus,
    owner of "Simplicissimus."

Cover and book design: Jim Doss

ISBN 979-8-9905505-6-8

Loch Raven Press
140 Milrey Drive, Suite L
Sykesville, MD 21784
www.lochravenpress.com

Table of Contents

Klabund: The Gravedigger
and Other Early Plays

Biographical Sketch

1. Introduction: Klabund's Place in German Literature

Alfred "Fredi" Georg Hermann Henschke (1890-1928), known by his pen name Klabund, occupies a unique position in the annals of early 20th-century German literature. His works, characterized by lyrical expression, stylistic innovation, and an ever-present exploration of existential themes, reflect the complex socio-political environment of the time. While other literary figures such as Thomas Mann and Bertolt Brecht gained greater international fame, Klabund's contributions as a poet, playwright, and translator have left an indelible mark on German cultural history.

Klabund's distinctive voice is particularly significant in the context of German Expressionism, a literary and artistic movement that emerged in response to the rapid modernization, political upheaval, and existential anxieties of pre- and post-World War I Europe. His works, while rooted in the Expressionist tradition, often ventured beyond the confines of the movement, incorporating influences from Eastern literature, historical narratives, and personal reflections on mortality.

This brief biography aims to outline the life of Klabund, touching upon his evolution as a writer and intellectual, his engagement with contemporary literary movements, and the personal struggles and health issues that helped shape his worldview.

2. Early Life and Formative Years (1890-1910)

Klabund was born on November 4, 1890, in Crossen an der Oder at 1:00 a.m., a small town located in what was then part of the German Empire (now Krosno Odrzańskie, Poland). Crossen was a small Prussian garrison town with around 7000 inhabitants, loyal to the emperor, provincial and conservative. His family belonged to the middle class. His father, Dr. Alfred Henschke (1858-1936), was a pharmacist at the Adler-Apotheke which was located at Dammstrasse 344/45, and was appointed to be of the magistrate in 1893, a position he remained in until 1930. He was also elected to the unpaid position of first deputy mayor in 1907, which he held for seven years. His mother, Emilie Antonie (1867-1945), a housewife, ensured the household ran smoothly. His upbringing was comfortable yet provincial, and from a young age, Klabund displayed both intellectual precocity and physical frailty.

Despite the relatively ordinary circumstances of his early life, Klabund's childhood was marked by a deep emotional sensitivity, an acute awareness of life's fleeting nature, and a fascination with literature. By the age of twelve, he was a young gifted pianist with larger than average hands and already engaged in writing poems, although at the time, he had no idea that this early passion would shape his entire life. Klabund's delicate health also became a key part of his formative years. He suffered from recurring bouts of illness, particularly high fevers and bilateral pneumonia, which caused him to be hospitalized in Crossen for six weeks in 1907, and would later be diagnosed as "closed tuberculosis" and dominate his adult life. A 1912 letter is the earliest written confirmation we have that Klabund knew he had tuberculosis. Up until the middle of the twentieth century, a diagnosis of tuberculosis was roughly the equivalent of receiving a death sentence that would be carried out at some unknown, unpredictable time in the future. In the early 1900's, there were primarily two ways to fight this disease, and both were rarely successful. The first technique was to attempt to mobilize the patient's immune system through long climatic cures in wooded highlands, through a "healthy diet" and by avoiding strenuous activity. With the second technique, following the research of Berlin doctor Ferdinand Sauerbruch, doctors tried to defeat tuberculosis surgically: through a resection of the ribs. By means of a "pneumothorax," whose noisy effects Thomas Mann so mockingly described in his "Magic Mountain," part of the lung was shut down. This second option was not viable for Klabund since both of his lungs were affected and he could potentially experience a dramatic deterioration in his condition at any time.

His father, a stern but loving figure, expected Alfred to follow in his professional footsteps. Pharmacy, like many middle-class trades of the time, was viewed as a stable and respectable career. However, Klabund's early schooling revealed a different trajectory. His teachers recognized his literary talent, and he excelled in subjects like literature, history, and philosophy, even as his physical health continued to decline.

In 1909, upon completing his early education, Klabund moved to Munich to study medicine, largely due to the expectations of his family. Munich at the time was one of the intellectual and artistic hubs of Europe, home to a vibrant community of writers, artists, and thinkers. The shift to Munich exposed the young student to a broader world of artistic and literary experimentation. Here, he first encountered the currents of modernism that were sweeping across Europe.

Despite his initial dedication to medicine, his attention quickly shifted toward literature and philosophy. He began attending lectures on philosophy, philology, and history, further cementing his interest in these intellectual pursuits. His time in Munich also allowed him to engage with Expressionist artists and writers, whose works reflected the growing sense of existential crisis that pervaded European intellectual life at the dawn of the 20th century.

By 1912, Alfred Henschke had officially abandoned his medical studies in favor of a full-time literary career. This period also marked the adoption of his now-famous pen name: Klabund. As Klabund explains it: "I created the name Klabund one day in a mood of serious self-parody, but I gave it so much of my blood that it began to live alongside and above me, becoming a reflection of my art and worldview... Klabund emerged from Klabautermann – the mischievous sea ghost that appears to sailors on foggy nights as a harbinger of doom – and from Vagabund. The name points to the vagabond-like days of my early student years..." The symbolic weight of this name is significant – it reflects Klabund's itinerant spirit, his status as a wanderer through both physical landscapes and the realms of human thought as evidenced by the many themes and settings within his literature.

> The It of things to which I've pledged my being
> Softens into the You of reverie.
> I will love my soul unceasingly,
> In its peace, in its frenzy.
> Beloved, eternal upon my lips:
> I am and was and will always be Klabund.

As "Klabund," the young writer fully embraced the bohemian lifestyle of the avant-garde literary circles in Munich and Berlin. He became a part of the burgeoning intellectual community that included figures such as Frank Wedekind (1864-1918), Heinrich Mann (1871-1950), and the young Bertolt Brecht (1898-1956). Klabund's work from this time was heavily influenced by Expressionist themes of alienation, urban chaos, and the search for spiritual meaning in an increasingly industrialized and dehumanized world, with the expectations of war and social conflict between the classes always looming large.

3. Expressionism and Early Literary Output (1910-1914)

Klabund's early works – primarily poetry – were deeply rooted in the Expressionist movement, which sought to reject the materialism and realism of the late 19th century in favor of more subjective, emotional, and often apocalyptic visions of modern life. His first major poetry collection, *Morgenrot! Klabund! Die Tage dämmern!* (Dawn! Klabund! The Days are Breaking!) (1913), embodies the key elements of Expressionist aesthetics: intense emotions, vivid imagery, and an exploration of existential anxiety.

In 1912 Klabund wrote to Walter Heinrich, an occasional writer and bank clerk in Crossen who went by the pen name Unus: "To impress you a little, here are a series of numbers and titles. I have written 597 poems, 29 novellas, 13 one-act plays, 1 novel, a collection of aphorisms, as well as fragments and collections of material for dramas and novels of the highest style (Don Juan, Nausicaa, Adam and Eve, etc.), essays, etc." While only Klabund knows if this was a bit of an exaggeration or not, it demonstrates the type of productivity Klabund would maintain throughout his literary career.

In the winter of 1912, inspired by the writer Villon, Klabund sent some verses to the theater critic Alfred Kerr (1867-1948), who published them in the magazine *Pan.* These poems, written in a coarse and cheeky style, caused a bit of a public stir. The Imperial Censorship Committee found grounds to charge Klabund with "the dissemination of obscene literature." They heard the opinions of Frank Wedekin, Max Halbe (1865-1944), Erich Mühsam (1878-1934), and Richard Dehmel (1863-1920), who objected to these charges which also implicated Kerr by arguing the poems had artistic merit. The trial lasted from September 1913 to January 1915. The judiciary ultimately fined Klabund 50 Reichmarks, only to have the verdict overturned a year later.

This period also marked Klabund's growing fascination with death and the ephemeral nature of life, themes that would persist throughout his career. His lifelong battle with tuberculosis, coupled with his intellectual engagement with Expressionist thought, made him particularly attuned to the fragility of human existence. His poems often meditate on impermanence, mortality, and the disillusionment of the modern age.

In collections such as *Morgenrot!*, Klabund's poetic voice expresses a mixture of despair and wonderment. The natural world, in his work, is often a place of both beauty and terror, filled with fleeting moments of grace that contrast sharply with the bleakness of urban life. For Klabund, the modern city represents a place of alienation, where individuals are disconnected from one another and from the natural world. Yet, even in this disenchanted landscape, he seeks moments of transcendence, whether through love, art, or spiritual reflection.

Klabund reflects on the book *Morgenrot!* that: "I have absolutely nothing: no paper, no money, no profession, not even a proper apartment. As a bait for credibility, rhymes are accompanied not by 'hot' but cheerful 'sexual distress,' ensuring that something primal and vivid is not missing from this lyrical portrait of Samuel Klabund – by himself."

Klabund was also heavily influenced by German Romanticism, particularly the works of Friedrich Hölderlin (1770-1843) and Heinrich Heine (1797-1856). Like these earlier poets, Klabund imbued his work with a sense of longing for a lost ideal – whether a spiritual utopia or a pre-modern world untouched by the corruption of modernity. His use of lyrical, often musical language, as well as his interest in myth and folklore, connects him to this Romantic tradition, even as he critiques the very notion of romantic ideals in a modern context. In 1913 Klabund came into contact with Alfred Kerr's Magazine *PAN*, though he continued to publish in the magazines *Jugend* and *Simplicissimus*. Beginning in 1914 he contributed to *Die Schaubühne* (Show Place), which later changed its name to *Die Weltbühne* (The World Stage).

Klabund completed the manuscript of his first novel – *The Ruby – Novel of a Young Man* in May of 1914 and sent it to his mentor Walter Heinrich in Berlin. The novel was intended to be published by the Erich Reiß Verlag, but disputes between the author and the publisher and the outbreak of World War I prevented its release. *The Ruby* was eventually published posthumously in 1929 by Phaidon in Vienna.

By this point in time, Klabund was destined to live up to the "vagabond" part of his pen name as he frequently changed his place of residence from Crossen to Munich to Berlin to Locarno and other cities, and when his tuberculosis began to severely impact his health he sought healing in the Swiss spa town of Davos.

4. World War I and Changing Attitudes (1914-1918)

The outbreak of World War I in 1914 marked a turning point in Klabund's life, both personally and professionally. Like many intellectuals and artists of his generation, Klabund initially greeted the war with a mixture of excitement and patriotic fervor. He saw the conflict as a way for Europe to purge itself of its decadence and moral decay, viewing it through a lens of romantic heroism. However, this initial optimism would quickly give way to a more complex and critical perspective as the war dragged on, exposing the futility and horror of modern warfare.

Due to his poor health, Klabund was unable to serve on the front lines, in spite of his repeated efforts to enlist, but he followed the war closely and responded to its events in his writing. His early war poetry, while still somewhat idealistic, began to take on a darker, more cynical tone as the scale of the destruction became clear. In works like *Kriegsfibel* (War Primer), a collection of war poems written between 1914 and 1918, Klabund grapples with the senseless violence and the moral degradation that accompanied the conflict.

Kriegsfibel (War Primer) stands as one of Klabund's most important wartime works, capturing his evolving disillusionment with the war. The poems in this collection are characterized by their stark realism, eschewing the romanticized depictions of battle that had characterized his earlier works. Instead, Klabund presents the war as a grotesque and meaningless spectacle, in which human life is reduced to little more than fodder for machines and bureaucracies. Klabund's shift from early enthusiasm to deep cynicism about war culminates in his 1918 novel *Bracke*. The novel is a scathing critique of the social and political structures that led to the war, as well as a meditation on the personal toll of violence and destruction. *Bracke* is one of Klabund's most explicitly political works, and it represents his growing disenchantment with both the war and the nationalist ideologies that had initially fueled it. The novel's central character becomes a kind of anti-hero, whose moral confusion and emotional detachment reflect the broader sense of disillusionment felt by many in post-war Germany.

It would take almost three year before Klabund recognized the senselessness of the war and on June 3, 1917 published on open letter to Kaiser Wilhelm II (1859-1941) in the Neue Zürcher Zeitung (New Zurich Newspaper) urging the Kaiser to abdicate with passages like: "Be the first prince to voluntarily renounce his fictitious rights and bow to the Areopagus of human rights. Your name will then be mentioned among the truly great in the new books of history, where the history of humanity will no longer be written in terms of coalitions but in terms of the history of the human spirit. Then you will establish the people's kingdom of the Hohenzollerns on rock; whereas it is now only a cloud formation that, if you do not recognize the time, will soon be vanished in the rising storm." Many believed his future wife influenced his transformation toward pacifism. Needless to say, this letter did not go over well with all citizens, and cause much resentment and hard feelings toward Klabund. In September 1917, Klabund addressed the controversy of his earlier war poetry to Munich journalists: "These poems were written three years ago at the beginning of a horrific war – when no one knew where it was heading, and when everyone was deceived about its goals. I have greatly changed my opinion about the war; my 1915 Chinese war poetry, more like the pack wagon, and later Moreau, show the path that leads to absolute pacifism, on which ground I now stand."

On a personal note, in 1918 Klabund married Brunhilde Irene Herberle (1896-1918) on June 8th, whom he had met in a sanatorium for lung patients. She was a passionate pianist who loved to play the music of Schumann and the tubercular Frederick Chopin. Larngeal tuberculosis also occasionally rendered her voice nearly inaudible. He calls her Irene in his poems because to him that word meant peace. Klabund described her in a letter: "I am married: to a woman who is entirely animal, entirely child, entirely butterfly, like those beings around us." Rumor was that she was pregnant at the time of their marriage. On October 17th she gave birth to daughter Irene Fiete Anny after a seven-month pregnancy, and was operated on due to complications. Klabund's wife survived until October 30th. On February 17, 1919 the daughter also passed away. Klabund sent a telegram to his friend Walter Heinrich: "Irene has called her child to her today." Klabund wrote several books of poetry dedicated to his first wife, such as *Small Verses for Irene*, and *Sonnets to Irene*. Klabund blamed himself for Irene's death.

I was your death. I murdered you.
I am guilty that chaos, like a crater,
Bursts open and spews its fire. I am the father
Of anarchy, red and overflowing upon us.

I was your death. I murdered you.
In vain the pious father warned me;
I desecrated you, dolorous mother...
I killed you with my own child.

The rule you wielded with the lily,
I overthrew in the fever of my caste.
You smiled. You blessed. You loved.

I glared darkly. Threatened. Cursed. Hated.
And while you sifted gold from dust,
I ran to debauchery, bellowed, drank, and reveled.

5. Postwar Work: Cultural Exploration and the Search for New Forms (1919-1928)

In the aftermath of World War I, Klabund entered a period of intense creative output. The political, social, and economic chaos that followed the war deeply influenced his work during the 1920s. Yet, even as he engaged with the traumas of the war and its aftermath, he also began to explore new forms of artistic expression, venturing into drama, historical fiction, and cultural translation.

In early April 1919, Klabund received a telegram that a friend from his Munich student days, Erich Mühsam (who would later be incarcerated at Fortress Niederschönenfeld with Ernst Toller), had been arrested, and Klabund was asked if he could help him. However this raised suspicions about Klabund and the possibility that he might be part of the Munich insurgents so he was taken into "protective custoday" from April 17th to April 26th in the Straubing prison. The "anarchist" Erich Mühsam was one of the leading figures of the Bavarian Soviet Republic. He was arrested by the counter-revolutionary troops of the Reichswehr and sentenced to fifteen years of fortress imprisonment. Klabund became a victim of his own efforts to help his friend, and was himself accused of participating in Spartacist activities. The political ideologies of socialism, democracy and revolution in reality meant little to him. He was merely committed to trying to help a friend. In the end his "help" achieved nothing, and his ten days of incarceration were documented in his book *Tagebuch im Gefängnis* (*Diary in Prison*). Upon release, Klabung writes: "Free! Outside again! Alive again! I am still too agitated and nervous to contain the waves of emotions coursing through me... Today, I plan to visit Nuremberg, the Hirschvogel Hall, and Hans Sachs. At the Hans Sachs House, I will tip my hat for the first time in nine days and pay reverence to the Germany I love."

During this time, Klabund also became active in the cabaret scene in Zurich and Munich at the Cabaret Voltaire, the Bavarian Cabaret, The Beautiful Bird, and other venues. There he met fellow writers such as Bertolt Brecht, Hugo Ball (1886-1927), the founder of Dadaism, his wife Emmy Hemmings (1885-1948), and other German writers and performers. Klabund was an occasional performer and his ballads of love, murder, alcohol and other frivolities made him a popular performer as he shot a few mocking arrows at both himself and the audience, but he didn't come under the Dadaist influence and remained true to his own poetic instincts. During his time in the cabarets, Klabund also met Maria Kirndörfer (1893-1981), aka Marietta di Monaco, about whom he wrote the novella *Marietta – A Love Story from Schwabing*. Marietta became known as the poet's muse and famous through her close friendships with poets like Joachim Ringelnatz (1883-1934), Frank Wedekind, Fred Endrikat, and Klabund. She recited their works on stage.

Like his health, Klabund's finances were on a constant rollercoaster ride with dizzying highs and depressing lows. As a bestselling author of the time, money would come into his pockets based on the popularity of his books, but then it quickly evaporated again as the poet helped those in need and usually picked up the tab at parties and celebrations. He also would occasionally support penniless students until he himself was in need of help again and had to call on his friends.

One of the most distinctive aspects of Klabund's postwar work is his deep engagement with Eastern literature, particularly Chinese and Persian poetry. This fascination with non-Western cultures set Klabund apart from many of his contemporaries, who remained focused on European literary traditions. Klabund's translations and adaptations of classical Chinese poetry, particularly his translations of the Tang Dynasty poets, introduced German readers to a new literary form that emphasized simplicity, natural beauty, and philosophical reflection.

In addition to Chinese literature, Klabund was also deeply influenced by Persian poetry, particularly the works of the Sufi mystic Rumi. His fascination with Eastern spirituality reflected his broader search for new forms of meaning in a post-war world. For Klabund, Eastern literature provided an alternative to the disillusionment of modern Europe, offering a vision of inner peace, harmony with nature, and a transcendence of the material world.

In the 1920s, Klabund began to focus more intensively on drama, producing several important plays that would secure his reputation as a major figure in the German theater. His most famous play, *Der Kreidekreis* (The Chalk Circle), was first performed in 1924 and became an immediate success. Based on an ancient Chinese folk tale, *Der Kreidekreis* tells the story of a legal dispute over a child and the wisdom of a judge who determines the child's true parentage.

Der Kreidekreis was notable not only for its narrative structure but also for its fusion of Eastern and Western dramatic traditions. Klabund's play would later serve as the inspiration for Bertolt Brecht's *The Caucasian Chalk Circle* (1944), one of the most important works of 20th-century theater. Klabund's use of the chalk circle as a metaphor for justice, loyalty, and truth resonated deeply with audiences, and the play was praised for its universal themes and innovative staging.

In addition to *Der Kreidekreis*, Klabund wrote several other plays during this period, including *Karfunkel* (1923) and *Xantippe* (1920), both of which reflect his continued interest in history and myth. His plays, much like his poetry and prose, were marked by a lyrical style, a fascination with moral ambiguity, and a desire to explore human relationships in the face of societal collapse.

6. Personal Struggles: Illness and Relationships

While Klabund's literary career flourished during the 1920s, his personal life was increasingly dominated by his struggle with tuberculosis. The disease, which he had contracted in his youth, worsened as he grew older, forcing him to spend long periods in sanatoriums, primarily in Davos. His experiences with illness and isolation are reflected in many of his works, particularly his later poems, which often meditate on the themes of suffering, death, and the passage of time.

In 1924, Klabund met celebrated actress in Berlin's theater scene Carola Neher (1900-1942), who would later become one of Brecht's most famous collaborators, on a streetcar in Munich near the Café Stefanie. Klabund keep staring at her until she whispered to him: "If you want to stare at me without any shame, you have to go to the theater. I'm playing Hugenberg in Frank Wedekind's play *Pandora's Box* at the Kammerspiele tonight." After the play, he waited for her by the stage exit, hands her his business card and insists on another meeting. In the spring of 1925, severe blood poisoning forces Carola Neher to spend several weeks in the Breslau Friederici Sanatorium, where she must be operated on immediately after admission. On May 7, 1925,she and Klabund were married in the sanatorium. Their relationship was passionate, but troubled, largely due to Klabund's deteriorating health in combination with the demands of their two artistic professions which requires Carola and sometimes Klabund to move to the various cities where the theaters are located for her parts. Klabund writes to Herman Hesse (1877-

1962): "I live, blown here by fate, still in Breslau, the (bulwark of the East), a damp, unfriendly place in Prussian Siberia. How often I long for the warm, tender Ticino." Neher is cast in Klabund's play *The Chalk Circle*, and he creates parts in subsequent plays for her such as *The Burning Earth* and *XYZ*. On May 30, 1928, Carola Neher and Klabund depart from Gottfried Benn's (1886-1956) apartment for their trip to Brioni. For Carola Neher, it is a holiday of one and a half months before starting rehearsal work as "Polly" in the premiere of Brecht's play *The Threepenny Opera*, and for both, it is their last holiday together. During this trip, Klabund completed work on *Borgia*, his last novel. In July, Klabund contracted a fever again, and needed to return to Davos immediately, where the patient, critically ill, arrived exhausted in the middle of the month. The doctor diagnosed pneumonia once again. On the evening of August 13th, Klabund's life began to fade away. His doctor had not expected the end so soon. Carola, the doctor and a night nurse stood by Klabund's bedside, hardly recognizing him, as he gently passed away on August 14th at 4:30 a.m. Klabund described his wish to be cremated: "I would like my ashes to be scattered over the sea. Then I will end up like Jonah in a whale's belly, or a flounder will swallow me, and one day, a fat gentleman from Königsberg will invite me to dinner. But perhaps I will reach the bottom of the sea safely, yes: perhaps I will reach the bottom of all being." The burial took place in Crossen at the Bergfried Cemetary on September 9, 1928 with the poet Dr. Gottfried Benn delivering the eulogy for his deceased friend.

In his eulogy, Benn said: "I knew him in the times when he was nothing, and in the times of the brilliance of his name. The best years were probably those when, shortly after the war, he lived in a small street in southwest Berlin, in a small room with only one window and no bed; he slept on a sofa, and when you visited him in the morning, he was lying on that sofa, completely covered with manuscripts, newspapers, letters, and journals, working tirelessly and feverishly, as he did his whole life. These were the years of the second period of his poems, his novels, and the years when the thought of the 'Chalk Circle' came to him. They were also years of illness, and I often went to him as a doctor. Sometimes I called him in friendship 'Jens Peter,' which were the first names of the great Danish novelist Jens Peter Jacobsen, to whom he resembled physically, and who suffered from the same illness and died. I often saw violets in his room, Chopin's favorite flowers, his other companion in illness. Once we read together the last words of Chopin, which he wrote on his day of death: 'My attempts are completed according to what was possible for me to achieve' – the farewell words of a true artist who had experienced the fragmentary nature of the individual, words of silence and restraint, as Klabund could have written them too, whose fundamental characteristic throughout all the years was one of deep, brotherly modesty."

Years after Klabund's death Carola Neher married Anatol Becker in 1932 and left Germany following Hitler's ascension to power in 1933. She first emigrated to Prague, where she worked at the New German Theater, but went on to the Soviet Union in 1934, where she met Gustav von Wangenheim and worked with him at his cabaret Kolonne Links. In 1936, during the great purge both she and her husband were denounced as Trotskyites, resulting in their being arrested on July

25, 1936. Becker was executed in 1937, while Neher was sentenced to ten years in prison. She eventually died of typhus at Penal Colony No. 6 of the Federal Penitentiary Service of Russia in Orenburg Oblast.

7. Conclusion: Reassessing Klabund's Legacy

Klabund's early death cut short a brilliant literary career, leaving many to wonder what further contributions he might have made to German literature had he lived longer. Despite his relatively short life, Klabund left behind a significant body of work that continues to be studied and appreciated today – 25 plays, 14 novels, numerous short stories and books of poetry. His poetry, plays, and translations are admired for their emotional depth, stylistic innovation, and cross-cultural reach. Klabund's ability to bridge the literary traditions of East and West, his exploration of human fragility, and his engagement with the existential crises of his time make him a vital figure in both German literature and the broader tradition of European modernism.

In recent years, there has been a renewed interest in Klabund's work, as scholars and critics have sought to recontextualize his contributions within the broader framework of modernist literature. His unique blend of Eastern and Western influences, his engagement with existential themes, and his lyrical mastery make him a key figure in the literary history of the early 20th century.

While his works may not have achieved the same widespread popularity as those of Brecht or Thomas Mann (1875-1955), Klabund's legacy remains significant. His ability to capture the emotional and intellectual turbulence of his time, coupled with his desire to seek new forms of artistic expression, continues to resonate with contemporary audiences.

Ultimately, Klabund's life and works offer a powerful testament to the enduring human struggle for meaning in a world marked by uncertainty, impermanence, and suffering. His voice, though often melancholic, is one of hope, suggesting that even in the darkest moments, there is beauty to be found in the fleeting and the fragile.

Part One:

A World-Historical Event

Written in 1903. Typewritten copy in: "A Book for Young People about Klabund" with illustrations, originals, letters, cards, and advertisements. Edited by Sylvia von Harden. Unpublished typescript, 1926/1927.

A World-Historical Event

Figures:

Napoleon, Emperor of France
Count of Metternich, Austrian Statesman
Berthier, Prince of Neufchatel, Marshal of France
Rustan, Napoleon's Black Valet
Maret, Duke of Barzano

Scene One

Setting: Dresden, June 28, 1813

NAPOLEON (*seated in an armchair in front of his desk*) Dreams are foam. I have just conquered a powerful enemy in my thoughts, and before me lies the bitterest reality. (*after a short pause*) I was never a dreamer (*rising and striding toward the window*), so away with all fantasy! Why feign night when it is day? (*Pulls back the curtain so that light enters the room*) – (NAPOLEON *extinguishes the burning candles, saying*) As miserable and wretched as these flames flicker towards the bright day, all the castles that man builds appear just as wretched in the air on the bright morning of happiness, or when sorrow and worry knock at his door.

Scene Two

The front door opens quietly and RUSTAN *enters*

NAPOLEON (*calling to him*) What is it?

RUSTAN Monsieur Niort asks to be admitted, Sire.

NAPOLEON (*Angrily*) He may wait or come again.

RUSTAN He already received that answer yesterday, Sire.

NAPOLEON Today he must be content with it again.

Scene Three

NAPOLEON *paces restlessly back and forth in the room.* RUSTAN *leaves and soon returns.*

RUSTAN Monsieur Niort has some very important information to give Your Majesty.

NAPOLEON (*peevishly*) These gentlemen call everything important, in which they play a role, and exaggerate every event, no matter how insignificant, into a world-historical event! I expect Monsieur Niort this evening. Until then, I'm fully occupied. (RUSTAN *bows and disappears*)

Scene Four

Napoleon goes to his desk and processes letters and dispatches.
Maret appears in the study.

Maret Count von Metternich requests an audience, Sire.

Napoleon (*hastily rising and ringing Rustan. He appears*)

Rustan What do you wish, Your Majesty?

Napoleon Give me my hat and sword.

Rustan (*obeying*)

Napoleon (*gesturing to Rustan to leave*)

Napoleon (*to Maret*) Your Excellency, please approach.

Maret (*moving away*)

Scene Five

(The door to the anteroom remains open; we see Berthier and
Count of Metternich

Berthier (*to Count of Metternich*) Well, are you bringing us peace? Be reasonable, let's end this war, which we too need.

Count of Metternich (*shrugs his shoulders and approaches the imperial cabi-
net*)

Scene Six

Napoleon (*Allows Count of Metternich to enter and then locks the door*) Are
you finally here, Herr von Metternich? If peace is what we want, why are you
delaying and coming so late? We've already lost a month, which prevented
us from destroying the Prussians and Russians. I know very well what's
going on in Vienna and how they're flirting there. Is this the thanks I get
for restoring the throne to Emperor Franz three times and for making the
mistake of marrying his daughter? You act like people who are ready to
raise the sword in war. Well then, declare yourself: do you want war with
me? I have beaten the Russians and Prussians. Now are you longing for your
turn again? Well, it can be done! See you in Vienna.

Count of Metternich (*in a cold, polite tone*) We certainly do not want to declare
war on you, Sire, but we must put an end to a situation that has become
unbearable for Europe and threatens us all with annihilation.

Napoleon Well – what do you want, what do you demand of me?

Count of Metternich A peace, an absolutely necessary peace that secures your
position and ours. Emperor Franz is of the opinion that if you, Sire, desire
peace, you must return Illyria and Italy, restore Prussia, dissolve the Duchy

of Warsaw, and allow the Pope to return to his Papal States; release Spain, Switzerland, and the Netherlands, as well as the Hanseatic cities and the area between the Elbe, Weser, and Ems. It is also desirable that you withdraw behind the Rhine.

NAPOLEON (*in extreme anger*) So you demand that I surrender Saxony to the Prussians without a sword stroke? Is that why my father-in-law sent you here, sir? But before you achieve that, you will have to raise millions of soldiers and shed the blood of generations, only to be able to negotiate peace with me at the foot of Montmartre. (*Pausing for a moment*) Ha, Metternich, how much did the English pay you to say such shameful things to me and play this role towards me? (*Both pace up and down in agitation. The emperor's hat falls to the ground.*)

NAPOLEON (*after a few seconds*) I cannot agree to their demands, for I am a soldier and need honor and glory.

COUNT OF METTERNICH Then these wretched wars must never end. And yet, Sire, your nation, in particular, needs peace so much. Where have your greybeards gone? Your soldiers, Sire, are children. You conducted premature conscription and called a barely grown-up generation into arms. If they too have perished, do you want to call up even younger recruits?

NAPOLEON (*no longer in control*) Sir, you didn't live in a camp and learn to despise the existence of others as well as your own. I... I spit on the existence of 200,000 people!

COUNT OF METTERNICH Let's open the windows and doors right now so that all of Europe can hear you!

NAPOLEON (*running around the room with long strides, angrily kicking his hat into a corner*) So you want to declare war on me?

COUNT OF METTERNICH (*completely calm again*) Not at all, Sire, we want to mediate peace between you and your enemies.

NAPOLEON (*laughing mockingly*) Aha, so you're sticking with your desire to prescribe laws for me. Well then, you shall have war. See you in Vienna! (*Running around with long strides*)

Scene Seven

COUNT OF METTERNICH (*Leaving the anteroom door open as he leaves*)

BERTHIER Are you satisfied with the Emperor, Your Excellency?

COUNT OF METTERNICH Yes, I, for one, am satisfied. Your master has put me on the spot and, I swear to you, he has lost his mind. (*He hurries away*)

    The curtain falls

Part Two:

Alcestis

Written in 1909. The text of the play comes from a copy in the possession of Ernst Heinrich of Nienburg – Walter Heinrich's son.

Alcestis

Dramatis Personae:

Apollo – Eumelos – Another Old Man – Death –
Alkestis – Young Maidservant – Heracles – Chorus –
Admetus – An Old Man – Old Maidservant

Scene: In front of the palace of Admetus.

APOLLO I must leave this house, which has long welcomed me, the god Apollo. Zeus forced me to serve a mortal because I slew the Cyclopes so harshly – (but I only took revenge because Zeus burned my son from this earth with his lightning.) –

Faithfully I served Lord Admetus as a shepherd, and drove the woolly lambs to pasture each morning – it was hard work, had not my flute playing gently carried me high to the wind and eagles, far from the world that bleated from the lambs, yet I grew to love King Admetus, for I, a human being, served human beings. Never did he wielded a whip of command, never did rage fly from his wide-open eyes, never did his whip crack on the backs of slaves – he wrote barbarian letters on a white tablet in red and blue. –

He was just and gentle, a true king. – I loved him as his people loved him, and pondered how to show God's gratitude to him. Nothing is more dear to man than his life, uncertain death is hateful to him, because gray chains bind his winged existence to decay and the dead of night, banishing him forever from the beloved light. –

And I went to the Fates, who spin destiny, and begged for eternal life for Admetus. –

Their answer was a guarantee — but they demanded that another selflessly sacrifice themselves for him,

freely and of their own will — and Alcestis, his own wife, offers herself for him there. –

The king regrets his rash question – trembling with aguish, he clings to her body –

In vain – death's soft footsteps are already approaching, and barn owls perch in the rafters. –

But I am leaving this house, farewell, the proximity of death easily dishonors the god.

Exit.

ALCESTIS Apollo has gone — the god who brought ruin, hiding its black glow in a golden bowl. –

YOUNG SERVANT Mistress, why do you stare into the sacrificial flame, your gaze so clouded with tears?

ALCESTIS She lives! Kore, she lives! And every day the watchman comes and piles up the logs so that she will not go out.

Give me the mirror that Admet gave me, spun from sea glass – which acts so strangely, as if it were alive – and draws the viewer into itself, so that he becomes another person.

The YOUNG SERVANT hands her the small amber-framed mirror

ALCESTIS Trembling, I weigh the small mirror in my hand, which was once my happiness, for it praised my beauty anew every day — and yet all beauty was only valuable to me because of him — Kore, did you see Admetus?

YOUNG SERVANT I saw him weeping.

ALCESTIS Why is my lord weeping? Beautiful women are as countless as the fruits of summer harvest — and the branches bend low to the ground, easily within reach of those who pick them.

YOUNG SERVANT Those who once bore the apple of the Hesperides cannot be lured to cherry and peach trees.

ALCESTIS Look at this hair, I grasp it wildly, it flowed black through our nights of love, lust swam on its blue waves. I don't trust these strands. Are they still there? Doesn't my hand move through air or dream? Is my skull not bare and devoid of flesh? And aren't two gruesome, dark worms crawling out of the eye sockets? Kore, I'm afraid. I pull at my breasts. Are they not slack? They were firm and soft, when Eumulus sucked life from them and Admetus still slept upon their hills.

YOUNG SERVANT Mistress, the fear within you speaks falsely. You are as beautiful as ever.

ALCESTIS Does compassion seize him before another's youth? No — I will not have the dry hangman's pity. Let him come — he will find me armed and adorned to tread the path that leads to Hades, for it also leads to those bright eyes where Admetus frolics in eternal strength. Oh, if only I could sometimes approach that life where Admetus frolics in eternal strength, as a falcon that plucks leaves around his sleep, as a starry eye that beholds him happy. Hush, there's a sound.

YOUNG SERVANT I can't hear anything –

ALCESTIS Kore, why didn his old, decrepit father not give himself up for him? He is half-blind and witless. Why does he drag his life around here like a sack of dry brushwood that is good for nothing?

YOUNG SERVANT With this brushwood he warms his days, and until the last stump burns out, he doesn't escape, but crouches by the ashes, warming his shivering, cold limbs.

ALCESTIS That's how people are — should I be any different? Admetus, he's alive: Why the cowardly lament! I sense his steps; (*EUMULUS goes with him*) Is that you, Admetus?

ADMETUS, with the boy EUMULUS at his side.

ADMETUS Alcestis, stay with me! Look at the child, how his gaze and arms fly to his mother.

Now in the future he will look into emptiness; the ball thrown from his playful hand will fall uncaught into the sand.

ALCESTIS No Eumelos. Who will be the mother? Perhaps a woman devoted to finery and trinkets, who will call you, her stepson, a beggar.

ADMETUS I swear these words to Alcestis as an oath: I will never touch a woman again.

ALCESTIS My dear, let me feel your head once more, so that its shape will forever etch itself into my hand and soul.

ADMETUS Alcestis, I have long since cursed my own question.

ALCESTIS And by the shadows that Hypnos flees from, I have your image and with my fingers I continually redraw the features that I love so much. And I have a lock of the child's hair in this silver capsule. No ghostly hand will often stroke it or seek to snatch it.

In vain: this hair is more real than I.

EUMULUS You have tears in your eyes, Mother. Let's go play; that will make you happy.

ALCESTIS Throw me the ball – like that – catch it now – if you miss, you'll have to learn to do it better, Eumulos.

EUMULUS Now, whoever can throw the highest, you throw it, mother, until it reaches the clouds and soars into the sky...

ALCESTIS Quiet – a clattering is breaking against the pillars (*she holds the ball*). With steps of bronze – it dances closer, closer – suddenly: A vulture flies into my view – Admetus. Someone grabs me around my waist – his nails dig deep into my flesh like daggers – Now he crawls in front of me, eyeing my ball, (*she throws the ball away*) There – catch it, but let me go –

EUMULUS Mother, the ball –

ALCESTIS He leaps at my neck – he wants to kiss me, Admetus has kissed me – and no other man. Help me, Admetus – what a foul, hot breath – he bites hard – (*she collapses into* ADMETUS'S *arms*)

ADMETUS Alcestis...

EUMULUS Mother, are you sick?

OLD MAN Bring a bier, the Shadow King is wrestling for her. We mustn't be near her, the breath of pestilence that his lustful mouth exudes could poison us. – At the sacred pond outside the city! Let Hades woo him, the most beautiful woman who ever entered his gloomy chamber.

> *Two young men bring a bier.* ALCESTIS *is laid out. She is gently torn from* ADMETUS.

ADMETUS Apollo – as you appeared to me – instead of eternal life I was awarded eternal death of the soul.

EUMULUS What are you doing with my mother? Where are you carrying her?

> *The funeral procession forms and moves off to the left, accompanied by muted flute music.* ADMETUS, *holding* EUMULUS'S *hand, follows him, and lastly a* CHOIR.

CHORUS Rarely has a god come to earth in physical form to thank us. Zeus courted our women. Apollo blinded the king's will so that he forgot himself and broke free from his bonds. The god intended good. But Fate reigns supreme over his salvation. She is the mighty mistress of them all and all of us.

> *Exit. The stage remains empty for a few moments.*
>
> *After a pause,* HERACLES *enters*

HERACLES Hey, is there no one here? A stranger seeks lodging and drink. Hey, open up. Is this not the palace of King Admetus?

OLD SERVANT Who cries out into this house and blasphemes (*comes out of the palace*) the silence sacred to the dead?

HERACLES What are you grumbling about, old hag? I am Heracles, son of Olympus, and I am traveling to King Diomedes. Tonight I will sleep here with you.

OLD SERVANT With us...

HERACLES (*laughing*) No, not with you. That, by Charon, would be a firm bed for me, made of nothing but bones and tanned hides.

OLD SERVANT Unholy one.

HERACLES Call the king himself to me.

OLD SERVANT I cannot.

HERACLES Why?

OLD SERVANT He's in the field.

HERACLES In the field? Is he plowing the footpath? It's not autumn, is it? The berries are hanging gray-green on the trellis. When will he return?

OLD SERVANT I don't know.

HERACLES Well then, he won't stay outside. The night bears a cool and feverish air. – Meanwhile, bring me a drink – and unmixed. Thirst makes my throat raw and sandy, and a boy shall serve it to me, with broad hips and a ripe mouth, I will pluck berries from his lips, for one suffers much on a journey. She will weave a wreath of fresh leaves around my forehead like the victor in the pentathlon – I will sing of her too, even if she is as unyielding as Pentelic marble –

OLD SERVANT Don't speak so loudly, the gods are angry with us – Death reigns here.

HERACLES Death? I'm not afraid. Life twitches and sparkles in my fibers. – Is a slave girl perhaps lying sick by her child's bed? A new life wants to come into the new light? A rotten trunk perishes, an old man dies, eh?

OLD SERVANT Horrible.

HERACLES Not as horrible as you, but now I'll fetch the drink myself, you're worse than your crippled feet and gout. (*pushes her aside.*)

Let me in. (*goes into the palace, the old woman follows him, whimpering. HERACLES can be heard singing.*)

After a while, ADMETUS and his entourage.

OLD MAN What evil spirit rages in the palace? It triumphs as if it were a celebration of joy or a wedding feast?

A SECOND As if Silenus were celebrating a drunken feast.

HERACLES This to the gods — and this drink to the king. (*Steps out of the palace, cup in his fist*) You are Admetus, I know you from the crowd. The king's face bears the halo of saints. The graces at birth weave the meaning of fate and purpose into each one's living garment. Yes, they weave the meaning of fate and purpose. Parthenius smiled upon your cradle with his gracious grant. The protector of wisdom, justice, and strength.

ONE (*quietly*) The knave mocks the king's pain.

ANOTHER Who is it?

ADMETUS Who are you, stranger, who thus disturbs my soul, pregnant with all torments?

HERACLES I am Heracles –

ALL Heracles –

HERACLES Sent by King Eurystheus after Diomedes' man-eating horse. My path leads through your castle – so welcome me.

ADMETUS Practicing hospitality is the first duty. I have never knocked the smallest one off his horse. – And now you, Heracles – command me – and all that our house can offer – is yours. And though I am surrounded by pain as by swarms of gray-winged locusts — speak, and the dancers shall move gracefully in their rounds, and the flute-girls shall play. But forgive me one thing – seek another drinking companion, not me. My mouth is sealed against jokes and drink.

Off to the palace.

HERACLES Just be carefree, King, (*watches him go*) Heracles drinks even without companions.

(*recollects*). He's so strange. Did his favorite horse die?

OLD MAN His life was lost, Heracles, because he now lives forever.

HERACLES A foolish word: how so?

OLD MAN His wife, Alcestis, died.

HERACLES Died — his — wife?—(*startled*)

OLD MAN She is still alive, but death is certain for her. Because she sacrificed herself for Admetus, who lives forever. Outside at the sacred pool, she gave birth.

HERACLES Thus I have desecrated this place with my lascivious and reckless behavior.

With my Bacchic roar, I wounded the king in his pious grief.

OLD MAN (*thoughtfully*) Where is the path that leads to her?

OLD MAN You want —

HERACLES Tell me.

OLD MAN Go after those poplars, you will not miss them.

HERACLES Heracles loves life — and life loves him. So I will wrestle with death for my prize. (*quietly*) I will bring back the king's wife, as atonement for my rude misjudgment. Alcestis lives: Heracles will protect her... (*exit*)

Scene at the sacred pond. ALCESTIS lies in state. HERACLES enters.

HERACLES Is she still alive? – She lies as soft and white as a nymph slumbering under the moon. I place this feather over her mouth – -The down stirs. Death has touched her only lightly – and lurks behind the bushes to carry her off. – What a bright name,
Alcestis! If I sing it to her ears, will she understand it? Alcestis – Alcestis – does she hear me? Alcestis! – No – (*he bends over her*) – Like tiny daggers, her eyelashes pierce my gaze, preventing me from contemplating her lovely eyes, which rest closed, glowing shudderingly in invisible depths. If I follow the body's delicately curved rhythms, my youth echoes within me. And my roughness melts in her body's burning light. Now all longing is only as it

once was, when need had not yet overcome me, when a gray purpose had not disturbed my dreams, but made them sparkle golden and bolder. (*he bends over her again*) If I wished for a lovely sister, she would have to be like you: so lightly cradled in this life, touching our difficult days with the tips of her fingers, longing from eternity to eternity, to force the god into our sight, and advancing our battle in song. As my wishes expand, most beloved my heart has ever beheld, I will save you — will I save you for Admetus? May I fight for your new life?

DEATH (*steps out of the bushes*) The new life, Heracles, is me. I heard your hymns of love with delight. You enchanted her dreaming soul, yet you labored only for me.

HERACLES I, I live, Death!

DEATH I only live for women like Alcestis, for men, Heracles, like you: that people like this one and that one, and that one and this one die off, it almost disgusts me when their carrion stinks around me, and their burden already weighs on my shoulders. They never lived right and never die right, and are like mist that palely surrounds the red glowing core. You burn, Alcestis, you, Heracles, burn in flames that eternity has kindled. On them I want to test my strength: be Alcestis, grant me that I may be!

HERACLES Heracles exists, grant her life!

DEATH When this hand moves her eyelids, Hades takes her into his shadows. And her (*mockingly*) eternal beauty is scattered, vanished like a cloud in the sea.

HERACLES O Nafr! O Death! Alcestis lives — in me! Gouge out her eyes: I have long carried them as stars within my breast. Shatter the deceptive synchronicity of her being. It still resonates within me after eons. Crush her body beneath the moss. I know of it! Enough, it lives!

DEATH Then I tear your heart from your breast. You die, so Alcestis also dies within you!

HERACLES O Death! O Fool! Alcestis lives and lives on! And lives in everyone who from afar only sensed the gentle sun of her gaze, whom her hand greeted as if from Olympus!

DEATH So would I do to everyone! If I kill humanity, I kill Alcestis.

HERACLES Death! You do not kill one to whom the gods swore eternity, do not kill Admetus!
Alcestis belonged to him (*painfully*). How can Alcestis then die in his soul?

DEATH Admetus is human. A human forgets so easily.

HERACLES The gods' blessing created Alcestis for us! (*simply*) Alcestis must live forever in them! (*Pause.*)

DEATH No man has defeated me, a word has, and words are more dangerous than deeds, living ones, who trust in the mind of the gods! – Alcestis lives! So love lives forever! And death and love are fierce enemies. I am leaving. (*Departs.*)

HERACLES Go ahead, (*laughing*) farewell!
> ALCESTIS *slowly, awakening.*

ALCESTIS Someone went,... who... hurt me.

HERACLES Someone remains whom you hurt, and you don't know it. – You shouldn't know it.

ALCESTIS Does... death... speak... to... me?

HERACLES You live, Alcestis, open your eyes!

ALCESTIS A man...

HERACLES You do not know him!

ALCESTIS Though he may have a shaggy beard and hair, he is kind to me! – How strange that I'm alive! Why doesn't Admetus approach, why doesn't Eumulus break free from his stalks when his mother calls him! – (*Funeral music is heard – A procession slowly approaches from a distance. HERACLES and ALCESTIS listen*)

ALCESTIS Who are they carrying in the funeral procession?

HERACLES Me... let me cover you again with the veil, so that your fate may finally be mine! – (*does so*) – (*The funeral procession has arrived. ADMETUS, EUMULUS, etc.*)

ADMETUS Horrible man, why do you not let her rest?

EUMULUS What does this stranger want? Is he to blame for my mother being taken from me? Tell me, man, did you steal my mother? Give her back!
> HERACLES *opens the veil, extends his hand to* ALCESTIS, *and raises her up*

HERACLES Alcestis lives!

ALCESTIS Admetus!

ADMETUS Alcestis!

EUMULUS Mother!
> *They stand tearlessly embracing.*

HERACLES Farewell, Admetus.

ADMETUS And my thanks, I cannot give him in words or deeds –

HERACLES I thank her because she is so beautiful, (*to a flute player*) Child, give your flute (*the player drops it, startled*) – My heart is swollen with music... Farewell, Alcestis!
> *Exits, playing the flute.*

ALCESTIS Don't let him go before I see his eyes and express my gratitude to him. Call him back. Who is it, Admetus?

ADMETUS Heracles!

ALCESTIS Heracles? Heracles?! (*calls*) Heracles! (*brings them together*)

EUMULUS Heracles!

ADMETUS Heracles!!! (*collapses – The flute tones fade into the distance*)

CHORUS Seldom has a god come down to earth in bodily form to earn our thanks. Zeus courted our women. Apollo clouded the king's will, so that he forgot himself and broke free from his restraints. The god meant well. But Fate, mighty in its pursuit, reigns supreme, the immense mistress of them and all of us.

(Curtain.)

Part Three:

The Young Hetaera

Based on the Greek of Lucian. Autographed manuscript,
undated, probably around 1910.

The Young Hetaera

Mystification

(after the Greek by Lucian)

Characters:

Bion
Glycia, a young Hetaera

BION It wasn't long ago that you escaped the guild of your virgin sisters?

GLYCIA Three months ago, Leukoderme, the old procuress — whose skin is no longer white at all — picked me up at the Sunian gate. And by evening, I had lost my flower, but gained 40 blooming denarii. I would have imagined the loss to be worse. I soon got over it — the wound healed quickly — and I like to see denarii and darics: they are a useful remedy.

BION How old are you?

GLYCIA Fifteen times Persephone has come up into the light for the harvest on my behalf.

BION But you have not yet ripened, because you still haven't found your sun. Your abundant beauty is worthy of a fertilizing sun. But your youth and inexperience are very great. What do you consider your profession: an art or a craft?

GLYCIA I believe it should be art.

BION It should be art. – Now, an artist must know his tools, the sculptor the chisel, hammer, and marble, the poet the soul and rhythm of language. Do you know your body?

GLYCIA Your question is bewilderingly simple. Doesn't everyone know their body? Can't they contemplate it sufficiently in front of the mirror and in the beautiful eyes of the opposite sex, can't they feel it, grasp it with their hands, and kiss their hands again with their lips?

BION To touch one's body only means knowing that a body exists, not how and what it is for.

GLYCIA I love my body because its skin caresses itself like the fur of a young cat. Arante, my servant, sometimes has to caress it. She has delightful hands.

BION Let the joy of your body be your virtue. You must put your entire soul into its lines and gestures. Just as the artist works on internalizing forms, you must work on externalizing your soul. Of course, it must be the soul of a woman, not that of a streetwalker or mere lump of flesh. I found too few who practiced that virtue, too many who knew nothing of it. For some, it is innate: you, Glycia, for example. But remember, virtues must be nurtured.

28

GLYCIA When I step into the bath, I kneel down and slowly, gently lower my breasts toward the surface of the water until they and their reflections kiss.

BION How do you continue to care for and protect your body?

GLYCIA What are you asking, Bion? Don't you know almost better than I do about the dressing table and the makeup and powder pots, the bottles and flasks, the sticks and knives of the smiling Aphrodite? Every day, Arante rubs my entire body with rose essence, puts fragrant oils in my hair, and fragrant powders in my armpits and pubic area. The scent of my breath is pure; it needs no help. I also only wear makeup on my eyebrows and under my eyes. The red of my lips is fresh, you learned that, Bion.

BION Yet I discovered, Glycia, that you lack one thing for perfection: training in the artifice of love.

GLYCIA Please explain what you mean, Bion.

BION You are very young, and youth lies clumsily. But your art demands subtle deception. Just learn it early.

GLYCIA Then give me, beautiful teacher, a lesson. I listen willingly.

BION You must rehearse your movements, your body, your laughter, so that they can respond differently, yet always correctly, to the slightest amorous idiosyncrasies of your various friends. Let everyone believe that you exist only for them and are only their companion. If you call yourself an artist of love, they may demand this belief of themselves, and confirmation of this belief from you. May the mechanics of love remain forever far from us! The age and people who have made it this far are crude, barbaric and dull. They have no culture of the senses. What do they know of Zeus, Apollo, love, and life? If you follow my suggestions and strive to be a pliant lover to everyone, not simply throw yourself with your legs spread wide on the pillows, you will bring it to the truth in all the variety of your lies. For what is truth but the plus and minus of several lies that cancel each other out?

GLYCIA I sip your speech like warm amniotic fluid.

BION One more thing, Glycia – money is a tiresome matter. It spoils so many people's dreams of love. Never speak to me about money – as little as of witless ribaldry, if you wish to seem truly witty, you may tell it. But few can present indecent things with decency. I will send you a silver bowl through Alexander, my slave – he is a handsome fellow, Glycia. You shall place it in your anteroom. Into that I shall entrust my votive pennies. Farewell now, sweet Glycia.

GLYCIA Farewell, Bion, my life – and do not keep the silver bowl and — Alexander waiting too long!

Part Four:

Cecil

"Cecil" is likely one of the largely lost plays
from his early work prior to 1911.

Cecil

A Scene
To my friend Cecil.

Characters:

Colmar
Margot

A room in lilac. There is a door in the middle of the background and another on the right. COLMAR, resting in an armchair, smokes a cigarette. MARGOT is standing before him in hat and coat.

MARGOT I know when you changed completely!

COLMAR Well?

MARGOT Since you started smoking cigarettes and lying in the armchair whenever I arrive, not lifting a finger to help me out of my jacket.

COLMAR Well??

MARGOT And you get bored when I'm around...

COLMAR Well???

MARGOT Ever since Cecil appeared on the scene.

COLMAR Really?

MARGOT I know it for sure!

COLMAR Really??

MARGOT You treat him as if he were a human being...

COLMAR Really???

MARGOT Even better.

COLMAR That's how it should be.

MARGOT Better than me!

COLMAR That's only your fault.

MARGOT (*shouting*) And yet he's a dog!

COLMAR That's his honorary title.

MARGOT A dog!

COLMAR Please don't shout like that, he might hear. He's lying sick in the next room.

MARGOT Probably ate too many sweets... your darling.

COLMAR He had the attack after you were last here. I think you gave him poisoned cake.

MARGOT Oh — so you want to make me responsible for the illness of the stupid animal?

COLMAR Certainly.

MARGOT That... that... is... outrageous.

COLMAR Why? You were the one who dragged the dog into the house. It's your fault that he got sick.

MARGOT You!

COLMAR If the dog weren't here in the house, he wouldn't be sick. That's obvious.

MARGOT I want to hate you.

COLMAR Dogs have likes and dislikes... like humans... and, on top of that, a finer sense of smell than they do.

MARGOT Is my perfume perhaps overpowering? You accuse me of that, when you even perfume your ink!

COLMAR I suppose it depends on the perfume. And Cecil simply can't tolerate yours. Even though you probably attracted him with it in the first place... that night...

MARGOT And because of that, you want me out of the house, so as not to offend the sensitive nose of the sensitive animal.

COLMAR (*stands up*) I have a nose too.

MARGOT Colmar... tell me... do you love the dog?

COLMAR I inherited the... fondness for the dog from you. Back then.

MARGOT (*sobbing*) That night!

COLMAR (*telling his story, staring blankly ahead*) One morning, around five o'clock, we were walking home from a celebration. The streets lay empty and yellow like hollowed banana peels. You linked arms with me, I walked along, lost in thought, not even aware you were there, sending my soul wandering into tired dreams — when suddenly I heard a step behind me, keeping double time with ours, that is, we took one, he took two steps. I asked you: Who's that behind us? You got flustered, trembled, said: No one.

MARGOT Oh, if only I had said his name back then!

COLMAR I didn't want to turn around, let the soft, quick steps follow me all the way to my front door. When I unlocked the door, a dog stood beside me, nervously lifted his right front paw, and looked at me from swollen eyes, as though he had cried a lot. His white coat was covered all over in dirt stains. He stood there the way many women stand in front of the door you're meant to open... and you're not quite sure...

MARGOT It's laughable...

COLMAR You didn't laugh then, when I asked you: Shall we bring the dog into the warm room with us? – The dog's eyes fixed with cool determination, first on you, then on me. That's when I knew you had brought the dog.

MARGOT I wanted to... test you!

COLMAR A dangerous test! – Inside the living room I lit the lamp, and he jumped on a chair.

MARGOT From then on, you didn't see me anymore!

COLMAR We sat there for hours across from each other, and the deeper I looked into his eyes, the more human they revealed themselves to me... no... better than human.

MARGOT While I lay alone in bed, tearing the pillows with my teeth.

COLMAR In the morning... we had sat facing each other for so long, almost motionless... and the early sun cast the dog's silhouette on the wall as if on a gold background... I loved him.

MARGOT Like... a woman...

COLMAR No... more! Because we had no questions or answers for each other... we were both one.

MARGOT The dog... your brother!

COLMAR Women always have questions to ask you: What will tomorrow bring? What was yesterday? And they even question today by putting a question mark after it: if today is already like this, what else could it be like? When I say "today," I mean it...

MARGOT Did the... dog say that too?

COLMAR Oh, that's the wonderful thing about him: he doesn't speak, he doesn't need to speak. – If women didn't speak, but only smiled, they'd be perfect.

MARGOT (*mocking*) And Cecil... smiles.

COLMAR No... He cried once before he came to me. Now he can no longer smile, only... look. Do you want to look into his... eyes? They've changed since they stopped resting on you. They no longer shimmer erratically. They gaze!

MARGOT (*fearfully*) I... I... don't... know. What... you... are... planning.

COLMAR Why are you suddenly trembling like that? Are you afraid of... the... dog?

MARGOT Yes... that is... (*pulls a revolver from her pocket, hides it from Colmar*) no!

COLMAR The vet comes twice a day. He says Cecil's condition has significantly improved and the seizure won't recur. Says the vet.

MARGOT Can I... see Cecil? I want to apologize to him.

COLMAR He's lying here on the right side of the room in a basket on cotton wool. (*Opens the door to the right. Both look into the other room. The revolver trembles in Margot's hand.*) – Do you see him?

MARGOT Not... yet...

COLMAR He's opening his eyes...

MARGOT Now! Now!

COLMAR You have to pull yourself together if you're going to stand up to them.

MARGOT Oh God! (*Wants to raise the revolver.*) I... I... can't.

COLMAR Cecil!

MARGOT (*raises the revolver at Cecil. It almost mechanically turns on herself. She fires. A shot. She collapses on the threshold*) He bit... through my throat.

COLMAR Margot... (*Bends over her.*) She's dead, Cecil. She couldn't bear you, Cecil... my dog.

Part Five:

The Servant in Red

"The Servant in Red" was probably written in 1911-12
and published in 1913.

The Servant in Red

Characters:

Lilly
Bertold
Arved
A Servant in Red

The room must be kept completely dark. Only a yellow-lit table in the center with chairs, accessories, etc. remains visible. A window to the right. A door in the middle of the background. When it opens and the servant enters, he brings light from outside. The SERVANT is dressed in red. When the curtain rises, ARVED and BERTOLD stand facing each other on the right. ARVED has his hands behind his back.

ARVED Well?

BERTOLD Left!!

> *ARVED places his left hand in front of him and opens it.*

BERTOLD Black!

ARVED You!!

BERTOLD (*leans on the table*) Give me... the... ball. – (*ARVED hands BERTOLD the ball. BERTOLD examines it. Goes to the window. Looks out.*)

BERTOLD Oh... The first snow...

ARVED Yes, winter is arriving very early this year.

BERTOLD Eight days ago we were still sitting outside, in the Isar Valley.

ARVED Lilly was wearing a white blouse and laughing a lot.

BERTOLD She crumbled the cake into small pieces and fed it to a lame crow that had come limping from God knows where.

ARVED I think it was tame, but Lilly claimed it fell from the poplar into her lap and broke its wings and legs out of pure love for her.

BERTOLD The unreasonable animal! Why was it sitting on a poplar? I've never heard of crows sitting on poplars.

ARVED Not usually. But when Lilly wants them to.

BERTOLD And she has no will at all! She works just by being there. And drives people to commit the greatest follies.

ARVED As many examples prove.

BERTOLD It's blissful for her to be out of her mind.

ARVED And to leave her fate to the roll of the dice.

BERTOLD (*looks at the black ball again*) Do you think this ball could also decide her... fate?

ARVED I would like to... believe it...

BERTOLD Over there in the first trees... sits a crow...

ARVED Perhaps it's the one from the... Isar Valley...

BERTOLD She's freezing... wait, I'll throw the black ball at her.

ARVED But she won't fall into a friendly lap if you hit her.

> BERTOLD *has opened the window and throws the ball out.*

BERTOLD No, at most onto the pavement.

ARVED She'll fly away!

BERTOLD But only as far as the next tree. The beast is bugging me. Where did you... the... white ball?

ARVED I don't like giving it away... from me. (*Takes it out of his pocket.*)

BERTOLD You're superstitious?

ARVED No. But one shouldn't be tempted.

BERTOLD Give me the ball!

ARVED There... (*Hands the ball to* BERTOLD.)

BERTOLD (*Throws the cue ball; jubilant*) He's falling from the tree. The cue ball hit him.

ARVED My ball...

BERTOLD Do you think it's dead?

ARVED It's whipping the pavement with his sick wings.

BERTOLD I'll send the servant. He shall bring it up to us. (*Rings the bell.*)

> *The door opens. The* SERVANT *enters.*

BERTOLD Go down to the square and bring up the sick or dead bird that's lying under the linden tree.

SERVANT (*bows*) Very well, sir. (*Exits.*)

ARVED I would like to have a servant like that: so quiet, so... honest.

BERTOLD And above all, so deaf to things that don't concern him — you can have him, I'll bequeath him to you.

ARVED If he doesn't resign.

BERTOLD Why?

ARVED You had a clear conscience!

BERTOLD And you?

ARVED Then I'll have him. He'll damn well keep reminding me of you.

BERTOLD You're right. Perhaps it would also make Lilly uncomfortable to see you tormented with memories.

BERTOLD And herself with the present!

BERTOLD How easily, then, the servant becomes the future! (*The SERVANT enters with the bird.*)

SERVANT Sir, the bird.

BERTOLD Put it on the table.

SERVANT Very well, sir.

BERTOLD Is it dead?

SERVANT I don't know, sir.

BERTOLD You can go! (*SERVANT leaves.*)

ARVED It's broken both legs.

BERTOLD It's not even warm anymore. (*Touches the bird.*)

ARVED What do you want to do with it?

BERTOLD You could have it stuffed and Lilly worship it in my name as a parting gift.

ARVED Lilly would kill him again.

BERTOLD Maybe this time with the black ball. (*SERVANT enters with tray, glasses, and Rhine wine.*)

BERTOLD What do you want?

SERVANT I'm just bringing the wine the gentleman requested.

BERTOLD Why didn't you knock?

SERVANT I thought, sir, I no longer needed to knock just to bring wine. (*Exits.*)

ARVED Your servant even has wit.

BERTOLD But he only shows it the way a stubborn patient calls for the doctor — in critical moments.

ARVED Rhine wine?

BERTOLD Of course.

ARVED (*pouring*) Allow me...

BERTOLD (*painfully*) Yes, right, you're the host from now on.

ARVED (*shocked*) Forgive me.

BERTOLD But why! You're right. Let's toast. To Lilly.

ARVED (*clinking glasses, looking each other in the eye*) To Lilly!

BERTOLD Tell me, when did you first meet her? And how?

ARVED Two years ago, in winter, I was walking one afternoon in the English Garden. Suddenly, by chance, I saw the footprints of a woman walking carelessly across the field next to me on the lawn, probably trying to shorten her journey. I followed her and met Lilly. And you?

BERTOLD One day I was playing tennis with a lady I hadn't met before, at the club. We were rallying. Suddenly, I realized we were only moving our rackets mechanically, that there was no ball between us anymore, and we were playing with our eyes. The lady was Lilly.

ARVED The lady became Lilly.

BERTOLD But not through our strength! They always say that women are soft and delicate. That's not true. They can't be shaped. They're hard. Like glacial boulders. You can't carve statues out of them either. Women are like boulders in general. Carried to us by the glaciers of a distant, bygone world. Their chill and icy air still cling to them. And no sun warms the atmosphere women exude.

The SERVANT enters.

BERTOLD (*irritated*) What do you want again?

SERVANT Sir, I'll bring the revolver.

BERTOLD Why don't you knock?

SERVANT The door opened on its own... before the revolver, sir.

BERTOLD Put the revolver on the table.

SERVANT (*does so, puts it next to the bird*) It's already loaded and the safety is off, sir. Two bullets, if needed, sir.

BERTOLD I don't need your advice. Go.

SERVANT I didn't mean to advise you, sir.

ARVED Then go. You're unsettling me.

SERVANT Servants are meant to unsettle — because they always seem to become people at just the wrong moments.

BERTOLD Go.

SERVANT Very well, sir. (*Exits.*)

BERTOLD How much time do we have left?

ARVED (*looks at his watch; startled*) Five minutes!

BERTOLD We've used our time well. We've talked about her.

ARVED And about the servant!

BERTOLD (*playing with the revolver on the table*) What do you have against him now?

ARVED He suddenly became too lively for me with his deed.

BERTOLD You can drive him out once he's your servant.

41

ARVED With what?

BERTOLD For example: with this revolver.

ARVED The one he brought.

BERTOLD Dear friend, someone else always brings the revolver. And it's usually already loaded. (*The SERVANT enters.*)

SERVANT Sir, a lady wishes to speak to you.

BERTOLD (*looking at his watch*) If she can present her matter in two minutes, show her in.

SERVANT Sir, it won't take that long. (*Opens the door: LILLY enters.*)

LILLY Good evening, Bertold! Good evening, Arved! (*Firmly, slowly.*) Who wrote this letter?

BERTOLD I did, Lilly.

ARVED And I.

BERTOLD It wasn't supposed to arrive until tomorrow morning.

SERVANT I put it in the mailbox one post earlier than I should have.

ARVED You're still there?

SERVANT As you can see. And I hope to participate further in the affair.

LILLY (*reading*) "One of us can only live in the world with you. We know you love us both, and we'll make your choice easier by making it ourselves. With the help of the black and white balls." — Who has the white ball?

SERVANT (*steps forward*) I do! (*Opens his fist and shows the white ball.*) I found it with the dead crow.

LILLY (*to the servant*) Then I belong to you.

SERVANT (*slowly*) The revolver has two bullets, but only two black ones.

LILLY You don't need to shoot yourselves, Bertold, Arved. I'll spare you the childishness. You're already dead, since you made yourselves look ridiculous in my eyes.

SERVANT : Sir, shall I re-engage the safety?

> ARVED *stands paralyzed at the table.* BERTOLD *collapses into an armchair, broken.*

BERTOLD (*groaning*) Turn off the light. It's blinding.

SERVANT (*into the wings*) Let the curtain fall!

> *Curtain.*

Part Six:

Poor Kaspar

"Poor Kaspar" is a folk play in twelve scenes
and published in 1912.

Poor Kaspar

A Scene
A folk play in twelve scenes. Set at any time.

Characters:
The Farmer – The Farmer's Wife –
The Farmer's Daughter, called The Young Lady – Kaspar
The Maid – The Sexton – The Doctor – A Maid – Another Maid
Servants – The Bright Figure – The Dark Figure – The Judge
A Witness – The First, Second, and Third Defendants
The Jailer – A Prostitute – A Prisoner – A Young Prisoner

First Scene: In the Field

FARMER It's time to go home, Kaspar.

KASPAR Yes, sir.

FARMER What are you waiting for?

KASPAR I don't know, sir. The evening star smells like an elderflower.

FARMER I didn't know that you could smell and taste the sun, moon, and stars like rhubarb puree and apple blossom.

KASPAR The stars are blossoms on the celestial tree. That's why they shine day and night. For the stars shine even during the day, even if we can't see them with our humble eyes. I read it in a book.

FARMER You're clever, Kaspar.

KASPAR But the earth can no longer shine from within itself. It's extinguished. It borrows all its light from the sun and moon. It is a worm-eaten, rotten fruit that fell from the celestial tree one September night.

FARMER Do you want to come with us or are you staying in the field, Kaspar?

KASPAR I'll stay, sir.

FARMER The farmer's wife will put milk and bread in the cupboard for you.

KASPAR Yes, sir.

FARMER Good night, Kaspar.

KASPAR Good night, sir.

> *FARMER leaves*

KASPAR The sun has set. My forehead feels chilly. I don't know anything. I can do nothing. Oh, poor me.

> *MAID comes.*

MAID I know you're still staying in the field, pondering. Keeping yourself company. It's going to be a hot night. Lightning is flashing everywhere.

KASPAR What do you want from me?

MAID You — I want you!

KASPAR You don't have much when you have me.

MAID A lot — a lot — everything!

KASPAR Don't believe it.

MAID I swear.

KASPAR Don't burn your finger when you swear. There was a flash.

MAID My squirrel.

KASPAR You're making fun of my red hair!

MAID Spitfire.

KASPAR I feel good when you kiss me. I lie quite still beside you. Don't upset me.

MAID Kaspar – did you see the shooting star? Did you make a wish? What was it?

KASPAR It wasn't a shooting star. It was lightning that flashed right through my heart.

MAID You – do you love the young lady, Kaspar? Is it true or not?

KASPAR I love no one. No human being nor animal.

MAID That's not true. You're not that godless. You make yourself worse than you are. You secretly go to church, I've seen it often.

KASPAR It's quiet in the church. And it smells different than in the goat shed. And the windows are brightly painted. And the saints painted on the windows are completely transparent. They are red, blue, and gold. The light passes through them, and they can't play hide-and-seek with soul and body. They can't lie or pretend like we dark beings, around whom the light veers: but it doesn't enter us. They are clear and true. But we are in twilight.

MAID You are pious, Kaspar. You take off your cap before every crucifix.

KASPAR Because there, on the wood, hangs a poor man whose hands and feet have had nails driven through his feet and who is suffering greatly. I take off my cap before everyone who is in pain. Before every woman who is carrying a child. She bears double the pain.

MAID Kaspar?! I'm having a child with you: you know. I'm in my third month.

KASPAR Anyone who fathers a child is a murderer.

MAID You seduced me in the hay.

KASPAR That's not true. I didn't seduce you. You didn't seduce me. It was the night.

MAID Don't forget to order the banns. I won't wait longer longer than five months for the wedding. It was a disgrace.

KASPAR Now — there's a lightning flash again. And now it's thundering. The storm is approaching. Like a hot woman approaching you. Kiss me. Let the sky collapse above us. Now it's raining castles. It's going to be a wild night.

MAID Oh you!

Second Scene: Farmhouse Parlor

FARMER Hey there!

MAID Leave me alone, farmer.

FARMER Well, don't be so standoffish. We're both human: you and I.

MAID Go to bed with your wife. Do it with her.

FARMER But I'd rather do it with you. You have firm thighs and firm breasts. The farmer's wife is spreading out like a pancake.

MAID (*laughing*) You shouldn't have broken the eggs.

FARMER Cow!

MAID Quiet: the young lady is coming.

MAID leaves

YOUNG LADY Father!

FARMER Child!

YOUNG LADY I'm so restless all day. All these days. I go here and there. I can't find peace.

FARMER Should I call the doctor —

YOUNG LADY (*smiling*) Oh, the doctor — what's he going to do? I always know what he'll say before he does. The weak chest, of course. And the young lady must have rest, and drink milk, and eat eggs. And sleep, lots of sleep. Before meals, after meals: always sleeping. — (*Pause*) I love to sleep. — Where's Kaspar? Yesterday he put a forest herb in my soup, and I slept like in a fairy tale.

FARMER Kaspar is out in the field.

YOUNG LADY He's strong. He turns over the whole earth.

FARMER He brings me joy and support. He's grateful I picked him up off the street.

YOUNG LADY He is an orphan. But I think he never had a father or mother. He fell down to earth from a star.

FARMER Kaspar doesn't look so heavenly, so star-like. He has paws like a tiger. And he can probably chop down the thickest tree in the forest all by himself.

YOUNG LADY Where is mother?

FARMER In the barn with the cows. Milking. Then off to the fields, bringing the hands and maids their afternoon meal.

YOUNG LADY I'll go look for her in the field, Father. Today I feel like running a thousand miles, flying, soaring.

FARMER Butterfly!

Third Scene: In the Field

FARMER'S WIFE Kaspar.

KASPAR Farmer's wife.

FARMER'S WIFE Put the spade aside for a moment.

KASPAR It's not time for vespers yet.

FARMER'S WIFE I'll pardon you. Do it anyway.

KASPAR You are kind to me.

FARMER'S WIFE Come... here to me... into the shade. Sit with me.

KASPAR It's a terrible heat.

FARMER'S WIFE (*pulls him toward her*) Don't you want to love me?

KASPAR I've always loved you, farmer's wife.

FARMER'S WIFE No one can see us here by the haystack. I'll lift my skirts, and you be quick. Fiery love is the sweetest.

KASPAR I'd gladly please you, farmer's wife, but the maid would take it badly. I'm promised to her.

FARMER'S WIFE Once doesn't count. And the maid won't find out.

KASPAR But there's someone else before whose eyes I couldn't stand if I had sinned with you. And those eyes are like the eternal stars, and I would die if I saw them pale because of me.

FARMER'S WIFE Who is it?

KASPAR The young lady. – (*The YOUNG LADY enters*)

YOUNG LADY Mother, I'm happier today than I've been in weeks. I picked forget-me-nots by the stream on the way and wove a wreath and sang while doing it. I'll place it on your brown hair.

FARMER'S WIFE I'm not worthy to be crowned — place the forget-me-not crown on Kaspar.

YOUNG LADY Kaspar already has a golden crown. That's how his hair shines in the sun. Good day, Kaspar.

KASPAR Good day, Fräulein. I'm glad you're so cheerful.

YOUNG LADY It's summer after all — the birds are singing, the flowers are blooming, and people — are in love.

KASPAR Show me how you do it, how you love every creature.

YOUNG LADY Like this. (*Takes his head and kisses him on the forehead.*)

KASPAR (*startled*) Fräulein!

FARMER'S WIFE Girl, you're not right in the head. You'll drive Kaspar mad.

KASPAR I'm only a servant of the lady, farmer's wife.

YOUNG LADY Kaspar, when you've finished your work, you must come to the stream and carve me a willow flute. You must sing me to sleep. Music and sleep — they are my dearest siblings.

Fourth Scene: By the Brook

KASPAR I've caught you a toad for you, Miss. Would you like to play with it?

YOUNG LADY Show me, Kaspar. – It sits in my lap fearless and calm, looking at me with its amber eyes like – like – like you, Kaspar.

KASPAR I wish I were a toad, Miss.

YOUNG LADY Being a human isn't bad either. It's all the same: whether you're a human, a toad, a cloud, or a tree.

KASPAR I'm a brook. I run away. I flow off.

YOUNG LADY I'm a birch. I sway ever so slightly.

KASPAR You take root – everywhere. I am rootless.

YOUNG LADY You've taken root in my heart, Kaspar.

KASPAR Miss.

YOUNG LADY Sing me a song, Kaspar.

KASPAR I'm going – where?
    I came from – where?
    Am outside and inside,
    Am full and bare.
    Born – where?
    Chosen – when?
    I slept on the straw
    With women and man.
    I love you
    And do you love me?
    I sadden you
    Do you sadden me?
    I stand and fall
    I will be
    I am a universe
    And I am alone.
    I was. I am.
    So easy. So difficult.
    I'm going – where?
    I came from – where?

YOUNG LADY The willow caresses my forehead. The sky smiles at me like a cheerful old man. I want to sleep. Play on the willow flute, Kaspar, then all the willow bushes will sing along.

> KASPAR *plays the same song on the flute he just sang*

YOUNG LADY I'm going – where? (*falls asleep*)

> MAID *sneaks in*

MAID Kaspar –!

KASPAR Be quiet – the young lady is sleeping.

MAID Kaspar: you're playing a cruel game. You betrayed me.

KASPAR Sweet girl, that's not true. I sang the young lady to sleep.

MAID Only a love fulfilled sleeps so deeply.

KASPAR The young lady is ill.

MAID Not so ill that she couldn't spread her legs.

KASPAR You insult the young lady. She is sacred like a saint.

MAID We're all sacred when we love. I love you.

KASPAR You love my weakness.

MAID I love your strength.

KASPAR What you love is when I hold you strongly in my arms and spend the night with you. The young lady loves me without sense, without senses, without aim – just as I love her. We are, and thus we love.

MAID Be careful, Kaspar, that nothing happens you and I might regret. I – hate the young lady. I'm healthy. She is sick. I am hard. She is delicate. She is good, I am wicked. Day and night do not go together.

KASPAR Go – go – the young lady is stirring. Don't disturb her dream.

Fifth Scene: In the Field

FARMER Where is the girl?

FARMER'S WIFE At the brook. Kaspar is with her.

FARMER Matchmaker.

FARMER'S WIFE Goat. Sneaking after the maid. I saw you once grabbing her breasts, and she slapped you in the face.

FARMER You old whore. You'd like Kaspar to mount you from behind like a dog. You're always in heat.

FARMER'S WIFE That's your fault. You can't manage without help anymore.

FARMER Why didn't you give me a son? An heir? What's the point of the bright farm? All the acres of land? Cow and ox in the stall, the chickens on the steps? Who's supposed to carry on the hunting and fishing rights after me?

Who'll guide the plow? From your bursting body came a sickly child, with death written on its forehead.

FARMER'S WIFE You should know what you picked up when you were with the soldiers in the big city. Sundays with the soldier wenches.

FARMER Lying woman.

FARMER'S WIFE Man!

FARMER You'll even soil my treasure, my sanctuary: my angelic girl.

FARMER'S WIFE Just now she wasn't good enough for you and you wished her dead.

FARMER I wish she'd never come — and yet I love her more than anything.

FARMER'S WIFE I love her no less than you. She's not a human like you and me. That's why she can lie with Kaspar by the brook without worry. I have no fear or doubt.

FARMER She – is – lying – with – Kaspar – by – the – brook?

FARMER'S WIFE So what? No man and no devil can take her innocence from her. She is the way I wish I were when I think of purgatory.

FARMER Sometimes I think Kaspar is my better self.

FARMER'S WIFE Give her to Kaspar as his wife, for as long as she lives. Then you'll have an heir for the farm right away. And maybe a grandchild too.

FARMER The maid's having a child by Kaspar, just so you know. He has to marry her. He's already gone to arrange the banns. Kaspar is a bull and my child is a butterfly. I have to watch out that no reckless hand dusts the powder from her wings.

FARMER'S WIFE Watch out for yourself, Farmer.

FARMER You're probably counting on my and her death, so you can marry Kaspar and enjoy yourself in your old age?

FARMER'S WIFE If you're thinking of such horror, it wouldn't be a loss if you dropped dead.

FARMER Monster!

The Ave bell begins to ring.

FARMER'S WIFE The Ave bell is ringing.

FARMER (*takes off his hat; both fold their hands and murmur*) O God, source of light, for your eternal love toward us we beseech you: enlighten our souls like altar candles, so that we may recognize how we have responded to your blessings on this day. Stir our hearts, so that we may sincerely repent of our known faults and make firm resolutions for the future. O God, heavenly Father, visit our home. O Jesus, Savior of the world, look down on us with mercy. O Holy Spirit, have mercy. O Mary, conceived without sin, pray for us. Holy Mary, pray for us. Mysterious rose, ivory tower, ark of the covenant, golden house — O Mary, pray for us.

The YOUNG LADY walks across the field on the horizon.

Sixth Scene: Village Church

HYMN You are the sweetness of life,
     Mary,
     You are the intimacy of life,
     Mary,
     You are immaculate,
     Lily of the valley,
     The Cherubim sing your praises,
     The Seraphim sing your praises,
     Salve, salve, Regina...[1]

> *The last tones of the organ fade away. The churchgoers leave the church: among them the FARMER, the FARMER'S WIFE, the MAID, the DOCTOR. When the people catch sight of the MAID: whispering and pointing fingers. KASPAR, his head buried in his hands, has remained seated on the church bench. YOUNG LADY is the last churchgoer to leave.*

YOUNG LADY *(to the SEXTON in the gallery)* Ah, sexton, good friend —

SEXTON You're still here? How can I serve you?

YOUNG LADY You must do me a favor, sexton, and I'll return it. You've always wanted to own the arias and cantatas by Bach and Handel. I'll give them to you.

SEXTON How can I thank you, miss?

YOUNG LADY Play me something —

SEXTON Gladly, young lady.

YOUNG LADY Just for me: a heavenly, blissful music — just for me.

SEXTON What shall it be? Something by Palestrina?

YOUNG LADY Then I'd have to sing along. That's far too tiring for me.

SEXTON O Sacred Head Full of Blood and Wounds?

YOUNG LADY Not a harsh, bitter, or painful song. Let the organ laugh, let the cadences skip — I want to be enchanted. Play me a minuet or a gavotte.

SEXTON *(shocked)* Consider, young lady — this is a house of God.

YOUNG LADY And I am a child of man.

SEXTON If His Reverence, the pastor, were to find out —

---

[1] Hail, hail, Queen...

YOUNG LADY I stand no worse with the good Lord than the pastor does. Play: I want to dance — for His honor.

SEXTON Forgive me, young lady, for correcting you: this is not a village tavern where they bow the bass and fiddle for a fair.

YOUNG LADY You're not to bow bass and fiddle: you're to play the organ for me.

SEXTON The meadow is the proper dance floor for you. Dance on the meadow.

YOUNG LADY Do you know the story of Our Lady's Dancer? Then let me tell it to you briefly. There was a juggler in France who entered a monastery and was accepted among the holy brothers. But since he didn't understand church Latin, nor how to sing or pray like the holy brothers, he honored the Madonna as best he could — with his art. He didn't kneel before her altar image: he danced and leapt before her, in her honor and praise. The divine Lady was so pleased with this service that she stepped down from her pedestal, reached him her ivory hand, and danced the figures with him.

SEXTON (*shakes his head*) I'll do it to please you, because I honor and respect you, and I know there's no evil thought in you. Don't betray me to His Reverence. He wouldn't understand. (*He plays a cheerful gavotte. The young lady dances lightly. KASPAR has raised his head and watches her. She suddenly breaks off, breathless, and clutches her chest.*)

YOUNG LADY Ah — the joy — hurts.

KASPAR The Virgin Mary in the niche smiled. The saints in the stained-glass windows knelt down before God's daughter. I wanted to kneel like them. But I'm too lowly even to kneel.

YOUNG LADY I danced — for you too, Kaspar.

KASPAR The doctor forbade you all excitement. You're not obeying him.

YOUNG LADY We must obey God more than men. When God says: dance — then I must dance.

KASPAR You rage against your beautiful young life, which brings so many people joy, as if it were an unruly colt.

YOUNG LADY I will die young, Kaspar — and that's why I want to die gladly, as I gladly lived.

KASPAR Do you know what day it is today?

YOUNG LADY A sunny day, Kaspar.

KASPAR And tonight will be a sunny night. The sun won't set this evening. Many suns will burn through the night on the hills. It is Midsummer Night. The farmhands will light fires all around.

YOUNG LADY You too, Kaspar?

KASPAR ((*shakes his head*) I'd rather extinguish all lights and all candles, so it would be dark like inside me.

YOUNG LADY (*strokes his forehead*) You have tears hanging in your lashes, Kaspar — why?

KASPAR (*lowers his head*) I saw the people pointing at the maid, because she's pregnant by me, and I can't change it.

YOUNG LADY Look, Saint Sebastian there in the church window begins to shine brightly despite all his torments and the arrows and swords in his body, because the sun has come out from behind the clouds. Everything will be all right, Kaspar.

Seventh Scene: Midsummer Night
Fires on the hills all around. Servants and maids in a circle

A MAID (*sings*) Ah mother, dear mother,
    I wish to go to sleep.
    I hear in my ears
    The evening winds blowing.

ANOTHER MAID Ah daughter, dear daughter,
    Go sit upon the garden bench.
    The music of ripe apples
    Will echoes in your ears.

A MAID Ah mother, dear mother,
    The cricket chirps so loudly.
    I lift my eyes upward,
    And can no longer sleep.

ANOTHER MAID Ah daughter, dear daughter,
    Leave the damp rain
    Go to your warm room,
    The lamp awaits you.

A MAID Ah mother, dear mother,
    Take this advice from me:
    I'll sleep in my own bed –
    My beloved sleeps with me.

    Laughter and cheering. Farmhands and maids form a chain. On the left the MAID, *on the right* KASPAR, *standing apart.*

FARMHANDS AND MAIDS (*singing*) We weave the St. John's wreath,
    Why do you stand all alone, little maiden?
    The fires blaze upon the hills,
    The lad must go to the dance.

    FARMHANDS AND MAIDS *exit, laughing.*

MAID You have no fire left, Kaspar. You're cold as stone.

KASPAR There's fire enough burning on the hills.

MAID Come behind the bushes – I'm burning.

KASPAR I am burnt out. Only ashes now. Scatter me in the wind.

MAID If you don't love me tonight, I'll cheat on you.

KASPAR Your pregnant belly will find lovers enough. No one needs fear making you a child.

MAID You mock me in my misfortune, when I trusted your word. Shame on you, Kaspar – you're not an honest man.

> *One hears harmonica music.*

KASPAR I'm leaving. I must be among people. I can't find my way alone. (*exits*)

MAID (*stays, then breaks into sobs. YOUNG LADY enters.*)

YOUNG LADY Why are you crying? Come, lay your head in my lap.

MAID Oh, miss, you are kind to me.

YOUNG LADY Not kind enough. I am too weak to do you good. Why are you crying? All are joyful on this night.

MAID Kaspar doesn't love me anymore. He's gone to dance with the other girls.

YOUNG LADY Kaspar loves you. He just doesn't know it.

MAID No, miss. He loves you. You alone. Only you. And who wouldn't love you? (*exits*)

YOUNG LADY Come, let's go to the dancing boys and girls. And if Kaspar dances with a stranger girl, then you must dance with a stranger boy. (*DOCTOR enters.*)

DOCTOR Miss —

YOUNG LADY What is it?

DOCTOR A word —

YOUNG LADY Well —

DOCTOR Three words —

YOUNG LADY Which are?

DOCTOR Miss — I — love — you.

YOUNG LADY God's law and man's command us to love one another: God the human, human the God, human the human, and every creature: beast, stone, tree, wind, and cloud.

DOCTOR You ignore the meaning of my words.

YOUNG LADY I see through them.

DOCTOR Through the words?

YOUNG LADY Through you too.

DOCTOR Am I made of glass?

YOUNG LADY Every human being is transparent. Each one like glass: more or less clouded.

DOCTOR You sadden me.

YOUNG LADY If only I could!

DOCTOR I make a good living.

YOUNG LADY And I will always get along well with you.

DOCTOR "Frau Doctor" — isn't that a title?

YOUNG LADY A fine one, too.

DOCTOR I'm forty years — but look me in the eye: am I not still young enough to be a husband?

YOUNG LADY Any woman would be lucky to be yours.

DOCTOR I could care for you, tend you —

YOUNG LADY You already do.

DOCTOR Will you be mine?

YOUNG LADY So far as I can be yours, I already am — more I cannot be. Dear Doctor: don't be angry — give me your hand. (*takes it, kisses it quickly*) Goodbye —

DOCTOR (*hides his face in his hands*) Veneris voluntas, suprema lex.[2] (*exits*)

> *One hears harmonica music. After a while, KASPAR returns with the YOUNG LADY.*

KASPAR Miss, I can't bear it any longer. You danced with me, and my head is thundering as if a thousand storms were let loose in it. Let me be trampled by a raging bull, throw a noose around my neck and hang me from the nearest tree, set me aflame like a dry haystack and let me burn alive, strangle me with your delicate hands, stab me in the belly with a knife: I know I'm not in the least worthy of the death you bring – but free me from the torment of my ignorant being, my dull heart, my pitiful savagery, my strength that sickens me. Make me weak, make me weak: make me gentle, quiet, tender, like you are: for only the weak are good. My hellish heart cries out to you, my heaven. I am the devil who loves you, angel, because you are all that he is not: because you are good, beautiful, still, gentle, tender – because you possess peace, eternal peace. But he is tossed about like a grain of dust in the wind. I stink like a fox. Don't come too near – my breath would poison you. My gaze defiles you. I howl like a dog. Place your foot on my neck and crush me.

YOUNG LADY (*kneels before KASPAR*) Kaspar, I am your servant. Do with me what you will. I kneel before your nameless torment in humility and devotion. You are damned, and you shall be saved – through me. For I am eternal

---

[2]The will of Venus is the highest law.

bliss. Call me Mary, and take me.

Eighth Scene: Parlor

DOCTOR I always told the young lady, kept reminding her of her conscience – after all, every human being has duties to their fellow human beings. People don't just have rights, as the youth try to demonstrate to us. In short, I warned the young lady again and again: no unnecessary excitement. Her weak lungs can't take dancing. One can get through life without dancing and jumping. Look at me: I have never danced a waltz or a polka step in my whole life. And I managed just fine. Did there have to be dancing on St. John's Eve? Couldn't these frivolities be left to the farmhands and maids? They're like Trakehner horses — seven hours of gallop won't harm them. But with the young lady, it's not just the lungs. Also the heart. Also the heart. Also the stomach. Only a light diet: a little chicken soup. A glass of red wine with egg for strength.

FARMER The girl felt so light, so cheerful these past days. She smiled constantly and floated almost bodiless through the room. She sang like a swallow.

DOCTOR Worrisome, highly worrisome. It seems to me this is the state science knows all too well: euphoria. That sense of well-being seems a highly suspicious symptom. The better a person feels, the closer they are to death. Est modus in rebus, sunt certi denique fines. Media in vita morte.[3]

FARMER'S WIFE God, how much love we still owe her. We did not make use of the time. It slipped away like a brook in the sand.

DOCTOR Carpe diem.[4]

FARMER She suffered – and still suffers.

FARMER'S WIFE Because of us.

DOCTOR Nemo ante mortem beatus.[5]

FARMER We go through life with dirty, earthy hands and filthy hearts.

FARMER'S WIFE She is innocence and purity itself.

DOCTOR Integer vitae scelerisque purus.[6]

FARMER She is the bride of God. We are the devil's creatures.

DOCTOR Omnia praeclara rara.[7]

FARMER I swear to you, All-Good, All-Wise, All-Powerful One, to have a mass said for you every day of the year, and three on the great feast days – if you

---

[3] There is a measure in things; there are, in the end, certain limits. Death lies in the midst of life. From Horace, *Ars Poetica*

[4] Seize the day.

[5] No one is happy before death.

[6] Upright in life and free from wickedness.

[7] All excellent things are rare.

preserve the girl for us, who bears the name of the Holy Virgin and is no less sacred than she.

FARMER's WIFE Mirror of Justice, Queen of the Most Holy Rosary, hear us, answer us... (*sobs*)

DOCTOR Est quaedam flere voluptas,[8] good woman. Let's go to the patient, feel her pulse. Is she coughing?

FARMER's WIFE A little.

DOCTOR Highly suspicious. Closed tuberculosis is a treacherous foe. Let's go. (*DOCTOR exits*)

FARMER Let us make peace at her deathbed.

FARMER's WIFE Lord, forgive us our trespasses, as we forgive those who trespass against us.

FARMER For thine is the kingdom —

FARMER's WIFE And the power and the glory —

FARMER Forever and ever —

FARMER's WIFE Amen.

FARMER I feel it – our happiness is dying, our soul.

FARMER's WIFE Our heart.

FARMER What remains is old age together.

FARMER's WIFE The quiet evening, when the birds have gone to rest and only the crickets still chirp.

FARMER But the stars shine on us: toward hope.

FARMER's WIFE Toward death together. (*KASPAR enters*)

FARMER Farmer's wife – Farmer –

FARMER's WIFE You look deathly pale, Kaspar.

KASPAR Farmer, how is the young lady?

FARMER Not well, Kaspar.

KASPAR I – am – to – blame – Farmer – for – her – suffering.

FARMER Don't speak nonsense, Kaspar. The young lady was always sick.

KASPAR I – am – to – blame – Farmer – can't – tell – you – I am – to – blame – Farmer – all – alone – I – alone – am – to – blame –

FARMER We are all to blame, because we were wicked.

FARMER's WIFE Because I lusted after you, Kaspar —

FARMER Because I fondled the maid's apron — because I saw the face of an angel

---

[8]There is a certain pleasure in weeping.

gleaming before me, and yet was as lustful as a billy goat.

FARMER'S WIFE And I was as wanton as a young hen —

KASPAR I – am – alone – to – blame – I – am – a – murderer – I – am – a – criminal – I – led – the young lady – into – the – dance – then – the – blood – burst – from – her – mouth – I – have – desecrated – the – Holy – Virgin – I – have – broken – the – mysterious – rose – I – have – defiled – the – vessel – of – devotion – by – pouring – my – filth – into – it – I – have – stained – the – Immaculate – toppled – the – Tower – of David – shattered – the – Gate – of Heaven – brought – grief – to – the – Comforter – of – the – Afflicted – unto – death – (*The Doctor returns from the room*)

DOCTOR Farmer's wife, Farmer, if you wish to see your child alive one more time – Ducunt volentem fata, nolentem trahunt. Non est ad astra mollis e terris via.[9]

> *Distant singing as if from above*

CHORUS You are the sweetness of death,
Mary,
You are the intimacy of death,
Mary,
You are immaculate,
Lily of the valley,
The Cherubim sing your praises,
The Seraphim sing your praises,
Salve, salve, Regina...

> FARMER *and* FARMER'S WIFE *exit into the room during the song.* KASPAR *remains motionless. The* MAID *enters*

MAID Kaspar, forgive me: I danced with the servant from Hafnerbauer's yesterday on St. John's Eve. We went into the woods – and – he forced me –

> *She collapses at* KASPAR'S *feet. A gentle call from the young lady from the room*

YOUNG LADY (*offstage*) Kaspar!

> KASPAR *rushes into the room without acknowledging the* MAID.

Ninth Scene: Morgue
It is night. Flickering candles. The YOUNG LADY *lies in state in a transparent glass coffin.* KASPAR *keeps watch*

KASPAR I stood on a high battlement
And looked down at the market,
There a beautiful sorceress
was being placed in a coffin by the gravedigger.

---

[9]Fate leads the willing and drags along the unwilling. There is no easy way from the earth to the stars.

Oh, dear gravedigger,
I beg you, stay here:
Let me see the sorceress once more,
The beautiful sorceress.

Oh, dear gravedigger,
I tell you these words:
I love the dead sorceress
And I will not leave her.

And if you want to bury her,
Lay me on the bier next to her.
The dead sorceress has
enchanted me completely.
(*He collapses*)

> *A dark figure on the left and a light figure on the right have simul-*
> *taneously stepped to the head of the coffin.*

THE LIGHT FIGURE Virgin of all virgins

THE DARK FIGURE You abyss of all whoredom

THE LIGHT FIGURE You faint scent of the white rose

THE DARK FIGURE You stench of decay

THE LIGHT FIGURE You child of God

THE DARK FIGURE You child of idols

THE LIGHT FIGURE You morning dew: bright and clear

THE DARK FIGURE You puddle water, green and yellow, muddy

THE LIGHT FIGURE You always knelt in prayer

THE DARK FIGURE You danced in the church

THE LIGHT FIGURE Enter into the eternal dawn

THE DARK FIGURE Sink into the eternal night

THE LIGHT FIGURE You wisest virgin

THE DARK FIGURE You foolish virgin

THE LIGHT FIGURE You kind virgin

THE DARK FIGURE You wicked whore

THE LIGHT FIGURE You honorable and praiseworthy, you faithful virgin

THE DARK FIGURE You unworthy, dishonorable, unfaithful one

THE LIGHT FIGURE You loved people, you loved humanity with the beauty of your
soul

THE DARK FIGURE You tempted people to lust and fornication with the beauty of your body

THE LIGHT FIGURE You bowed down to the least of all and were exalted by humbling yourself

THE DARK FIGURE You drew even the lowest down to you and coiled yourself around him: Snake, adder, be accursed!

KASPAR I hear your hissing voice, Satan. I see your grayish goat form with ram's horns. Your wolf's eyes shimmer greenish, and poisonous fumes drip from your ox-like mouth, hot as boiling lead. The room is full of newts and fire salamanders. Spiders rain down on my forehead, and woodlice and centipedes crawl up my feet. Now you stretch out your claws to steal the noblest, purest, sweetest soul: to convince God of the wickedness of even the best of men. You lie, you lie... (*lifts a tool, perhaps a hammer, from the wall*) Stand by me in battle, so that I may smash you... (*He swings the hammer at the black figure, which collapses*) Thank heaven, Madonna, that I may protect you, that you have blessed and chosen me as God's warrior...

THE LIGHT FIGURE (*standing upright to the right of the headboard of the coffin, strokes the dead woman's forehead*) Queen of Angels – be blessed.

> *The background dissolves: one sees heaven, where three holy virgins guard an empty golden throne*

THE LIGHT FIGURE This throne will be occupied by Mary, for the sake of her chastity...

CHANT OF THE THREE ANGELS You are the sweetness of heaven, Mary.
You are the intimacy of heaven, Mary.
You are the immaculate one, You are the lily of the valley.
The Cherubim sing your praises.
The Seraphim sing your praises.
Salve, salve, Regina...[10]

Tenth Scene: Court

JUDGE The witness in the robbery-murder trial F.... – Where is he?

WITNESS Here, Your Honor.

JUDGE Recite the oath. I recite it to you: I swear by God, the Almighty and All-Knowing, that I will tell the absolute truth, conceal nothing, and add nothing, so help me God. – Raise your hand to swear. Swear.

WITNESS I swear by God, the Almighty and All-Knowing, that I will tell the absolute truth, withhold nothing, and add nothing, so help me God.

JUDGE What do you have to say to that?

WITNESS (*One can only hear monotonous murmuring*)

---

[10] Hail, hail, Queen...

60

JUDGE That is sufficient. The ring of proof is closed. Witness expiration. (*Witness expiration*)

JUDGE Defendant –

1ST DEFENDENT Here, Your Honor. (*The 1ST DEFENDENT is handcuffed*)

JUDGE Seven years in prison. Lifelong deprivation of civil rights. (*The defendant groans*) Next. (*The convicted man exits*)

JUDGE Defendant, do you have anything else to say?

2ND DEFENDENT I did it out of dire necessity – my wife was in childbirth. The children were crying for bread.

JUDGE You confess?

2ND DEFENDENT (*nods his head vigorously*)

JUDGE Ten months in prison, three of which will be credited to his pre-trial detention. Next.

JUDGE Defendant –

3RD DEFENDENT Here, Your Honor – (*The defendant is heavily handcuffed*)

JUDGE Ah – I see from the way he's bound, a murderer?

3RD DEFENDENT ((*screaming*) I murdered, but the murdered man is to blame...

JUDGE In the name of the law. The court rules, in right and justice, as follows: Whoever kills shall be put to death. The accused is sentenced to death by hanging.

3RD DEFENDENT (*shouts out*)

JUDGE Next. (*Defendant exits*) – (*KASPAR enters*)

KASPAR Judge me, Your Honor. Judge me. I have sinned gravely.

JUDGE Where do you come from? Inquisitive one?

KASPAR From life. And I want to die. I was too cowardly to accept it voluntarily, as would have been fitting for me.

JUDGE What crime did you commit? Theft? Robbery and murder? Rape? Embezzlement? Forgery? Scheme A, B, C? There are only a very limited number of motives for acting. So?

KASPAR I did nothing of the sort.

JUDGE At least you're stealing my precious time. – Go away. Follow the prescribed legal process. Don't fall into the raised executioner's hand of justice. (Looks at his pocket watch) In the ten minutes you've been bothering me here, I could have easily sentenced five people to death. – You're innocent. Next.

KASPAR Sentence me to death. I am guilty – guilty as ever.

JUDGE I have never seen a person rush to judgment. For what and what should I condemn you to?

KASPAR I killed a person with my love.

JUDGE Nonsense. You kill: with a knife. With poison, Etc. But not with love. Love is not a weapon.

KASPAR I danced with the Blessed Virgin Mary –

JUDGE You are insane. I request an investigation into your mental state.

KASPAR I am not a human being. I am an animal. I defiled an angel with my embrace.

JUDGE Presumably defloration? Please spare me your private rebus sexualibus.[11]

KASPAR I am a thousand times more guilty than the poor thief who stole out of hunger, than the poor murderer who murdered out of desperation. I murdered out of the innate hatred of evil for good, of ugly for beautiful, of dull for clear, of impure for purity and integrity itself.

JUDGE Nonsense. Some people are good because others are bad. Some people are bad because others are good. The law of the scales, which Themis weighs in her hand, keeps the world in balance. The good are guilty of evil. And vice versa.

KASPAR I'm racking my brains. I don't understand you.

JUDGE The Creator is the murderer, the murderer has become the Creator. An executioner was the judge of the world. To prevent the blood ax from rusting, he slaughters people.

KASPAR I killed the young lady. The farmer's daughter.

JUDGE You accuse yourselves?

KASPAR Yes.

JUDGE Evidence.

KASPAR My word.

JUDGE Witnesses?

KASPAR The stars.

JUDGE (*rings a bell; a guard appears*) To be taken into custody until the matter is clarified. – Next.

>   *KASPAR leaves with the guard*

Eleventh Scene: Prison Cell
Moonlit night. KASPAR is asleep on the cot. Distant, faint music. Through the door, like a veil, the vision of the YOUNG LADY in her burial shroud drifts in

YOUNG LADY (*very softly*) Do you want to know who I am?
I am the Queen of Heaven.

---

[11] sexual matters

My white gaze is like a diamond,
The whole land is ablaze with fire.
I raise my hand and it ignites
The stars and banishes death and sin.
The firmament is set aflame
And every human heart ignites.
The flame burns, the flame rises,
Until it bows before God's throne.
Love destroys pride.
Love silences the chatterers.
Love burns like the sun, so intensely,
Love roars like a storm at sea.
Love strikes death down —
And love, love is everywhere.

Dawn. KASPAR waking

KASPAR I dreamt. What was it I dreamt again? The earth fell over me, as though I lay in a coffin, and someone cast the final three handfuls of dirt into the underworld over me. But then I suddenly felt light. So light that I shot up like a bird and landed on a cloud. I must have lived a thousand years there: I was hungry — and I was fed. I was thirsty — and I was given drink. When I grew tired, a gentle hand stroked my cheeks. The sun always shone. And I was always cheerful and content. I've now lived a year in this strange house. I bear it gladly. No: I don't suffer at all. I do penance. It is sweet, just to do penance. Is it summer again? I think I smell through the barred window above a whiff of the chestnut tree in the yard.

GUARD (*knocking on the door*) Get up, Kaspar, get up. Seven o'clock. (*He unlocks the cell and appears in the doorway, leaving the door open*) Chop chop, quick quick. Empty the bucket. Sweep the cell.

KASPAR (*rising from the cot. The GUARD folds up the bed, then leaves. KASPAR takes the bucket out into the corridor, returns, and begins sweeping the room*)

A PROSTITUTE appears in the doorway

PROSTITUTE (*singing*) In prison life is good,
That's my little room.
There's hot soup to be had,
And a cold enema too.

Heavens, I'll be so glad
Once I'm out of here.
If I were a flea,
I'd jump out of fear.

I went out walking,
Oh what a mess,

Then came the public prosecutor
And took me to bed.
(*leaves*)

A PRISONER *appears in the doorway*

PRISONER (*speaks*) I am a poor odd fellow,
Have neither house nor stall.
The forest is my home,
The air is my mate.

An old shirt is my skin,
The wind whistles through my legs.
Help me not to become
Just another hungry thief in hell.
(*leaves*)

A YOUNG FEMALE PRISONER *appears in the doorway*

YOUNG FEMALE PRISONER I, poor girl,
Am all alone.
I weep, oh, but no
Mother weeps with me.

She lies buried
Beneath the earth.
Just two feet deep,
A thousand fathoms...
(*leaves*)

The GUARD *appears*

GUARD Number 711 – you have a visitor.

KASPAR Visitor? From whom? I haven't heard a thing from the outside world for a year, and I haven't missed it. I'm enough for myself, and I don't want to hear or see anything or anyone from out there.

GUARD (*lets in the* MAID *with a child in her arms*)

MAID Good day, Kaspar. Aren't you happy at all? I got permission from the prison inspector to visit you. Don't you want to say hello to your child?

KASPAR Good day, woman. Good day, child. (*kisses the child silently*)

MAID I bring good news. You don't have to stay in prison anymore. There were terrible lies and slanders by wicked people, claiming you killed the young lady. The farmer, the farmer's wife, and all good folks testified for you, that you're a good man and not capable of such a crime.

KASPAR It — it's not as you say. The judge is mistaken. You're all mistaken. I'm guilty. Don't I feel it in the depths of my heart —

MAID Kaspar, one is always guilty toward another. Who knows how much. Who knows why. No one lives guiltless under the sun. Listen to the beat of your heart: Once you're free again, it will be the song of the nightingale. You are to live and act in life. The field awaits its sowing. The clods of earth steam. The oxen are already pawing at the plow in unrest, the goats bleat in the stall and the dog barks behind the lambs. Earth and sun await you, and the child of them both — this child — your child! (*Holds the child up to him ecstatically*)

KASPAR (*takes the child from her arms*) I feel the bloodstream of this being flowing into me, from me into this being. Yes: we are one.

MAID One and two and three. Come, do you hear the prison bell ringing? I've arranged with the priest to meet us in the prison chapel. He's to marry us — between door and threshold, between prison and freedom, between night and day: you and me. And he's to baptize the little one with your name and the name of the young lady. The boy shall be called Kaspar Maria. For he is her child, too.

KASPAR He will become a strong laborer.

MAID He shall become a master.

KASPAR Like Samson he shall strike the Philistines by the thousands with a donkey's jawbone.

Twelfth Scene: In Front of the Farmhouse

In the left foreground, the MAID, now Kaspar's wife, is playing with the child. In the background, KASPAR, still at some kind of work. Summer work

KASPAR (*in the background*) Whoever wants to look into a deep well,
Shall look into my eyes.
Whoever wants to blow like a storm,
Shall walk with my steps.

Whoever wants to see a living angel,
Must go to my wife.
Whoever wants to be in paradise,
Is invited to be with me.

KASPAR'S WIFE (*holding the child in her arms*) Rosemary and clove,
Who wants to be my beloved?
Sunflower and tulip,
My child wants to have a father.
White clover and red poppy - (*jubilantly*) It already has one -

KASPAR (has come forward, smiling) I was dull. Now I am clear. I was dark. Now I am bright.

KASPAR'S WIFE I am happy. Since I have been happy, I have been good.

KASPAR To whom do we thank our happiness?

A rainbow arches over the horizon

KASPAR Look – she is with us every day and every evening. The bridge arches from us to her, from her to us.

The Ave bell begins to ring

Arch yourself, colorful rainbow.
Bloom, mysterious rose.
Evening butterfly fluttering around our brows:
Bless, bless us.

Curtain.

Part Seven:

The Stranger

"The Stranger" was most likely written in 1912-13.

The Stranger

Characters:
Maria
Doris
The Servant
The Stranger

The scene is a room painted green and gold. MARIA, dressed in the elegant widow's attire of a distant time: black with purple silk, sits in an armchair by an arched window, gazing out at the moonlit landscape. A chandelier burns in the room. To the right is a sofa. Above the sofa are two pictures: depicting a boy and a man. DORIS stands at the center table, setting a lavish dinner table for three.

MARIA It is autumn again.

>*DORIS at the buffet*

MARIA Autumn...

>*DORIS at the table*

MARIA And the trees stand like bundles of twigs in the moonlight.

DORIS It's already very cold. And tonight there will be frost. Tomorrow morning the willow bushes will look as if they've grown catkins overnight and are bearing blossoms.

MARIA Many dead blossoms were blown down by the wind today. By day they lie there, brown and dirty. Now the moonlight silvers them. And a leaf that falls from the branch at night sounds silvery and metallic, like a note striking the ground.

DORIS (*still setting the table*) I so love the evening leaves when they glow red in dying.

MARIA They are like martyrs. Their color rejoices in destruction.

DORIS (*brief pause*) What wine would the gracious lady prefer?

MARIA Wait... his favorite wine... Magdalene's Tears.

DORIS Gracious lady... and for little Hubert?

MARIA (*smiling*) I almost forgot him a little bit — my Hubert. Give him a sweet wine, Doris, a Greek or Italian one. He does have such a sweet tooth.

DORIS Yes, gracious lady.

MARIA When life is around us, when husband and child play about us, we women are all mother — blossoming, giving. But the widow is one who longs, who receives, a lover searching for her beloved. That's the only reason I could forget Hubert for a moment.

DORIS But you still remembered to bring him a toy from the city today. It's still wrapped — shall I bring it?

MARIA Yes, bring it, Doris.

> DORIS *exits through the door on the left.*

MARIA The churchyard wall has been drawn so close by the moon. As if it were coming nearer and nearer. With steps. And feet. (*Groaning.*) As if it wanted to build itself tightly, ever more tightly, around my house.

> DORIS *returns with the wine bottles and a small package.*

DORIS (*hands* MARIA *the package*) Shall I uncork the wine?

MARIA What time is it?

DORIS Almost ten o'clock, gracious lady.

MARIA What time did they come last year, Doris?

DORIS At ten o'clock, gracious lady.

MARIA Then you may uncork the bottles. But don't forget (*she is busy unwrapping the package*) to set out a carafe of water for the boy. He always gets so thirsty, and sweet wine is not meant for quenching thirst. It would do him harm.

DORIS Certainly, gracious lady. His stomach is so sensitive.

MARIA How do you like this? (*She holds up a stuffed bear.*) Isn't he adorable? In his awkward grace?

DORIS And he has movable limbs too? Hubert will be so delighted!

MARIA Take down his picture from the wall. (*DORIS removes one of the pictures hanging to the right above the sofa. It is a blond boy of perhaps six years old.*)

DORIS Look, Hubert, what Mama brought you!

MARIA Will you be good for that, and no longer... make me sad... (*suddenly begins to cry*)

DORIS But gracious lady, don't cry — not today! Hubert will always be very good and never hurt Mama again, right, Hubert? (*Gently strokes the picture as if stroking a real person.*) And he won't run around in the wet weather anymore when Mama forbids it, catching a cold and pneumonia and... and... (*breaks into sobs*)

MARIA (*has stopped crying*) To die... what a word that is! Not melancholy at all, not sad. Just sharp, very sharp. Like... like pricking yourself with a thousand needles. Be still, Doris. Come. Take the bear. Set him on his chair. (*DORIS does so.*)

MARIA (*goes to the window*) I don't see them yet. But they must come soon. The moon shines so clearly. And the churchyard comes ever, ever closer. You know, Doris, last year... the weather was terrible. It had rained for ten days straight... endlessly... in long gray streaks... and the ivy rotted on the graves.

But at night the storm roared like a dragon around our house. And for a moment... I thought they wouldn't come, couldn't come, would never come again. Because, Doris, if they miss a visit once, they never, never come again. But it would only be our fault. Then we hadn't remembered them holy enough.

DORIS I think, gracious lady, the gracious gentleman looked quite displeased last year. As if he were angry at us for some mistake we had made. And he drank almost no wine.

MARIA (*reflecting*) I thought it was the awful road to blame. But you're right. Lukas was different. He didn't kiss me. And Hubert looked at me with such wonder. So wounded — I don't know why.

DORIS It was the first time last year, gracious lady, that you softened your mourning dress with violet ribbons.

MARIA I had to, had to — I had to be vain again, just once. — Doris...

DORIS Gracious lady...

MARIA Give me the mirror.

> *DORIS hands her the hand mirror from the table by the window.*

MARIA (*looks at herself*) This line... wasn't there before... nor this one... nor this... But my hair is still blond, Doris, all blond.

DORIS Not a single white hair, gracious lady.

MARIA (*steps into the moonlight, startled*) Yes, Doris... all of it... completely white... and my face green... like poison... like sulfur...

DORIS It's the moon, gracious lady...

MARIA No, don't speak to me of the moon, Doris. The reflection from the churchyard, from the churchyard wall makes me so white, so... dead.

DORIS Gracious lady, please, step here under the lamp. (*Holds the mirror for her.*) How beautiful you are, gracious lady, how beautiful, and your eyes shine more tenderly than ever. You are alive, gracious lady...

MARIA I live... (*Looks toward the window, startled.*) Doris... you must serve the soup now.

DORIS Yes, gracious lady. (*Exits left.*)

MARIA (*crouched at the window in fear*) Hubert... Lukas... (*Through the window, two shadowy figures appear — a boy and a man, hand in hand. They walk along the path from the churchyard toward the house. Suddenly, from the right, a man comes up behind them, overtakes them, walks as if through them; the shadows vanish.*)

MARIA (*cries out*) Lukas!

> *The man approaches... DORIS enters from the left with the soup. There's a knock at the back left door.*

DORIS It's them... (*Sets the soup on the table.*)

MARIA Open...

> DORIS *opens the door, recoils.* STRANGER *enters.*

STRANGER Good evening!

MARIA Good... evening...

STRANGER I see the table is set.

MARIA For... for... whom?

STRANGER For me.

MARIA (*pleading*) Doris...

DORIS Who gave you permission, sir, to enter here uninvited?

STRANGER I... I give myself permission. Go now. We won't need you as long as the soup is on the table.

DORIS Gracious lady...

MARIA Go, Doris, do as he says.

> DORIS *exits.*

STRANGER It's terribly cold... I'll have to stay the night. Or would you throw me out? Drive me back to town?

MARIA (*anxious, pleading*) No, stay.

STRANGER To a hotel with cold beds and a ridiculous table d'hôte — The table's set for... three?

MARIA Did you meet a gentleman... and a boy? Just outside the door?

STRANGER No. I saw no one.

MARIA Are you hungry?

STRANGER (*smiling*) Very! I rode the train for twelve hours... to see you.

MARIA (*smiling*) To me?

STRANGER To you! Without pause!

MARIA Sit here... no... let the bear stay on the chair... he won't harm you... sit here. (*She points to the chair at her right, where Lukas once sat, and serves him soup.*)

STRANGER How good that feels... after the long train ride... and the march through snowy fields...

MARIA Would you like more soup?

STRANGER Yes, please. (*As she serves him, he looks at her hands.*)

MARIA Why do you look at my hands?

STRANGER I love them. But you mustn't spoil them as you're inclined to!

MARIA Spoil them — with what?

STRANGER With handwork. It destroys the fine form of the hands, which are souls themselves.

MARIA You never work... or only rarely?

STRANGER Preferably never! I don't need to justify my existence by mechanizing my best powers. I'm meant for better things, by God.

MARIA Then what do you do in life?

STRANGER I live! Isn't that enough for you? (*Rings a bell. DORIS appears.*) Please, the fish! (*DORIS brings the fish. Exits.*)

STRANGER I see your attire — you are a widow. And beautiful. I made thorough inquiries in town!

MARIA You're beginning to... repulse me a little.

STRANGER That's the first sign of deep sympathy — you'll come to feel it. — What wine do you drink? Sweet wine? Fiery, inflaming?

MARIA No.

STRANGER Sweet wine??

MARIA No.

STRANGER Sweet wine?!?

MARIA (*weakly, softly*) Yes.

STRANGER See, now I like you. (*Pours two glasses.*)

MARIA (*smiling*) I'm glad you're pleased with me now.

STRANGER I am. Wait! The bear needs a glass too. (*Pours a third glass.*) So... a toast... to our friendship.

> They toast, including the bear.

MARIA You're quick with words.

STRANGER And with action too! (*Pulls her to him and kisses her.*)

MARIA (*jumps up and looks out the window*) I don't see them anymore.

STRANGER Who?

MARIA Lukas and... Hubert.

STRANGER You had a child?

MARIA (*softly*) Yes.

STRANGER (*steps close*) What is your name?

MARIA Maria.

STRANGER Don't you want to have a child again, Maria? Don't you want to be a mother again?

MARIA (*leans on his shoulder, sobbing*)

STRANGER Maria...

MARIA You?

STRANGER Shall I stay tonight?

MARIA Forever, forever!

STRANGER But you don't even know me yet. You might not want to keep me.

MARIA Oh yes, yes. (*Touches his head, his body.*) You — you are alive! I can touch you — and — kiss you. (*Kisses him.*) I've lived the past years with shadows. You've killed them.

STRANGER The dead don't die so easily. One must kill them again — with life.

MARIA You... murderer. See how calmly I can say that word? It doesn't even hurt.

STRANGER ((*rings, DORIS appears*) The roast, dear one. And champagne!

DORIS Gracious lady...

MARIA Obey the gracious gentleman, Doris.

STRANGER And take these pictures away (*points to the portraits of Lukas and Hubert*) and throw them into the junk closet. Wait. (*Jumps onto the sofa and rips down Lukas's portrait.*) There.

DORIS Gracious lady...?

MARIA (*struggling*) Do it, Doris...

STRANGER No, Doris, the bear stays here. Let him sit. That will be our boy's toy.

MARIA (*in joy*) And he shall be called Viktor!

STRANGER (*smiling*) Like me.

    Curtain

Part Eight:

Mama

"Mama" is undated but probably appeared in print around 1911.

Mama

A Scene
Tragicomedy in One Act

Characters:

Xaver Laitinger, Royal Ministerial Councillor
Toni, his wife
Franz, their son, Royal Ministerial Assistant
Marie, the maid

Time: Present – Place: Large City

Living room at the Laitingers'. In the center background, a door to the corridor; to the right, the door to the Laitingers' room; to the left in the foreground, a table, sofa, armchair, and recliner. When the curtain rises, Mrs. Toni Laitinger (45 years old, looks younger: full brown hair, somewhat portly figure) sits on a chair facing the audience, knitting a potholder. Xaver L. sits to the right of the table in an armchair, reading the newspaper and smoking a short pipe. He wears a light waistcoat, gray trousers, and a dark frock coat. He has a full gray beard, sparse hair on his head, and a stocky build.

Mrs. Toni L. casts a desperate glance at the regulator clock and, with a violent gesture, puts it down. Potholders and knitting on the table and goes to the door in the background, opens it

TONI Marie... Marie...

MARIE *(arrives)*

TONI Have you checked the young man's room? Isn't the young man back yet?

MARIE The young man isn't here.

TONI Go *(MARIE exits)* directsighing Where is he? This is the fourth time this week he's been late for dinner. But this late...

XAVER *(over his newspaper)* Hmm...

TONI Didn't you meet in front of the office today like usual?

XAVER I waited for him for a quarter of an hour, but he didn't come. By the way, he's been assigned to the Directorate of Operations for a few days now. We don't work in the same office anymore. His office is in a side wing...

TONI It doesn't matter. It's outrageous.

XAVER *(puts down the newspaper)* I heard he was late for work this morning too – by half an hour.

76

TONI Yes, but that's impossible... You both left on time together.

XAVER Yes – it is – but on the way, as he said, he had an errand at a stationery store, and we separated. Then he was late. The department head was really surprised – and I don't understand it either.

TONI What's gotten into that boy? He's been completely transformed for the last week. That's not normal. But that's the thing, we're not paying enough attention to him.

XAVER We??

TONI We're not paying enough attention to him. My God, despite his 22 years – he's still a boy, a kid who doesn't know a thing about life.

XAVER Dear Toni...

TONI Who knows what sorrow weighs on his heart. But — it's not my fault, not mine. I've always trusted him — I haven't been sparing with good advice — you, of course, with your weak character —

XAVER Dear Toni —

TONI You still have to be guided so you don't fall. You're both so dependent —

XAVER Dear Mama — if I may also say a word, I think you're holding Franz too tightly. He's 22 now —

TONI And clumsy and worldly-wise like a schoolboy. Good God, when I think of the dangers our big city surrounds him with every day, every hour – one can't protect one's child enough –

XAVER Dear Toni – he's your only child, you have no standards or comparisons, you too easily exaggerate your opinions and advice to the limit –

TONI It's not my fault that he's our only child –

XAVER Certainly not mine either - (*silence*)

XAVER I just think, for example, the other evening, that you didn't give him the house key when he wanted to go bowling with his friends – he rarely socializes with people his own age – that was hard, yes – unwise – forgive me.

TONI I know what I'm doing. My little Franz – the house key, that makes you anxious all night long, not knowing where it is. He's far too young and dependent for that; ...he wouldn't be able to make proper use of this freedom. And the temptations of the night – and his friends...who can guarantee me that they're decent people? Oh, one knows these friends! It doesn't stop at these so-called bowling nights — or over a glass of beer, oh... then comes the second, then the third, the young people lose control of themselves — I want Franz to be protected from such dangers — then they go to the cafe — and the ending — you can imagine it —

XAVER I'm telling you, you're immediately thinking beyond all bounds: Perhaps you have — forgive me — just as little idea about life as Franz. You don't have to see everything in black and black, you don't have to try to impose your own view — in the literal sense: on everyone...

TONI But Xaver...

XAVER Yes, you want to impose — I maintain that — that's what you want. And you're just playing mama with me, too...

TONI Dear Xaver, you should be glad that you have a wife who takes care of you, like I do; You alone are a poor guide through the world, as disorderly and disorganized as you are...

XAVER Disorganized – disorganized...

TONI That's why you're completely unsuited to raise Franz — unsuitable, because you yourself still need raising —

XAVER Excuse me, you might be going a bit too far – as a ministerial councilor –

TONI A ministerial councilor... certainly... that's something exquisite... insignificant – in uselessness. I'd like to know what all these ministerial councilors are for... to have breakfast and smoke a pipe –

XAVER It comforts me, dear Toni, that as a man I can still claim some value from you.

TONI If only you didn't smoke your horrible, breath-suffocating cigarette in the living room, the curtains are already so smoky and puffed on — smoke in your room as much as you like — do you think curtain washing doesn't cost money? Neither of you has a salary that's so high that you could buy new curtains every day.

XAVER Let's just read the newspaper in peace. When you come home from the store, worn out...

> *The doorbell rings. Doors slam. A voice sings in the corridor: "We're not from Pasig, we're not from Lain, We're from Obermenzing..." MARIE's voice screeches as if someone had pinched her arm or cheek.*

XAVER That's him.

TONI How changed the boy is! (*The door opens: Franz L. in a straw hat and blue suit. Tanned, boyish face. Very well-groomed. Hair parted neatly, almost pulled back on his neck. Walking stick: a Malacca cane. Franz's speech has a hint of Munich dialect.*)

FRANZ Hello, Papa, – Mama, how are you? You must excuse me for being so late; I can't do much about it (*TONI sits motionless in her chair. XAVER appears to be reading the newspaper, grumbling now and then*) I ran into George Ketterer, whom I hadn't seen in ages, right on cue, as I was walking across St. Stephen's Square, and in the joy of seeing him again, you know, Mama, he was abroad in three months, in Prussia, so we got to talking over drinks, I didn't even realize it was already 5 o'clock – thank God that it's Wednesday afternoon, at least there's no more work.

TONI You're still wearing your hat.

FRANZ Oh – excuse me...

TONI Singing and prancing around, flirting with Marie outside –

FRANZ But Mama!

TONI Be quiet, I heard it... While Papa and I are anxious about you and worried sick –

FRANZ Papa?... (*looks at both of them questioningly*)

XAVER Yes, dear boy, what's gotten into you?

TONI Your behavior over the last week has been so strange that all natural attempts at explanation fail. You're showing an unacceptable lack of respect for Papa and me. Dear Franz, I'm not used to that from you.

FRANZ Mama — if I've given you cause for complaint — forgive me.

TONI So that's all you can look at to excuse your behavior... You haven't changed for the better, Franz, come here — look me in the eye —

FRANZ (*approaches anxiously*) Yes — Mama —

TONI Are you worried... you won't hide anything from your mother. Can I help you?

FRANZ (*hesitantly*) Mama – it's... really... nothing further...

XAVER I'm going next door to smoke my pipe – because of the curtains – I think I'm superfluous here, dear Franz, here stands your Mama and all of ours... ease your heart, (*quietly, half to himself*) Then she'll only make it even more difficult for me... Revoir. (*exits, right into his room*)

FRANZ (*stands at a window on the left*) Mama... just look at the chestnut tree... no... God, spring is so beautiful, just look – and up there – truly – neighbor Sedlmeyer has already let his tame squirrel out... – There it is hopping on the branches, always amidst the bright flower buds, sniffing their scent... And now it even has a large blossom between its paws – yes, spring is merciless too – spring.

TONI Boy, the ideas you come up with! Who taught you that you should be on time for work in the morning? Why were you late for work today?

FRANZ (*embarrassed, hesitant*) Oh, you know, I can't write with the pen they have at the office, and so I had to get my number at my stationery store, and I was late. Late.

TONI (*watching him closely*) Is that true?

FRANZ Mom — you think that I —

TONI Why are you always late for dinner? As punishment, you won't get lunch today. You might as well go hungry.

FRANZ (*increasingly helpless*) The last few days have been so wonderful, and I just wanted to take advantage of the lovely lunchtime and took a little detour through the English Garden.

TONI Today too?

FRANZ But Mom – today, I met George Ketterer – (*looks at the clock*) already 10 to five –

TONI What's wrong – why are you looking at the clock?

FRANZ I only arranged to meet George Ketterer at 5:30. We want to go for a trip to Starnberg in this nice weather, and

XAVER (*sticks his head through the door to the right*)

XAVER I just wanted to say, don't get too worked up. If you're looking for me, I'll lie down on the bed over in the bedroom.

TONI Franz?

FRANZ Yes, Mom!

TONI You're lying!!!

FRANZ Mom!!!

TONI It's all lies: ...that thing with George Ketterer and everything.

FRANZ Mom –

TONI So things have sunk so low — in such a short time — that you can no longer be honest with your mother.

FRANZ I can, Mama.

TONI No, you can't — liar.

FRANZ Mama, understand...

TONI I understand nothing except that you're deceiving me, me...

FRANZ (*looks at his watch again*) Mama, you're mistaken, but I don't have time now. I have to go. I made an appointment. Otherwise I'll be late, I have to go.

TONI You're staying — that you're neglecting your duties and arriving late at the office doesn't bother you —

FRANZ Mama — let me go.

TONI Then tell me what you're hiding from me.

FRANZ Another time, Mama, — when I'm prepared for it — it's so unexpected — let me come today... look — how beautiful spring is.

TONI You will go to your room immediately. You will not leave the house today – as punishment for your stubbornness.

FRANZ (*still barely under control*) Mama – – I am no longer a child.

TONI You will remain my child all your life.

FRANZ (*looks at the clock*) It is the last time. I have to get ready for the train... tomorrow, yes, Mama tomorrow! I want to tell you everything... but today – now... let me pass, (*pleadingly*) Please...

TONI You do as I commanded. I don't usually repeat my wishes twice.

FRANZ I am not a child, Mama, for you to treat me like this.

TONI Franz, you dare to contradict me? To your room immediately.

FRANZ Mama... dear Mama, I have to go to the train, (*TONI stands in front of the door*) for the last time – give me leave...

TONI Out! (*points to the door on the right*)

FRANZ Please... please... (*groans*)

TONI No.

FRANZ That's how you'll find out – everything –... I have to go – (*bursting out*) You always held me down,... like a boy, so that I knew nothing, well... not at all, that I existed, and that there was life – and youth. -Youth... Yes... I lied... everything, everything... lied because you wouldn't have understood the truth... because you would have desecrated it - even spring, Mama, what do you know about spring? Yes... I have a girl, I have a girl, I have to go there - now - a sweet girl... I never knew, through your fault, that such girls existed. Because you showed her to me as stern and cold — and repulsive — and loathsome — That's it...that's it...and in the morning I accompany her to the store...and at noon I pick her up...and we go to the English Garden — and now she's waiting for me — she has this afternoon off. Let me go to her... Mother...

TONI You scoundrel...

FRANZ Mama!!!

TONI Where are my kind words and warnings about you falling into the trap of the first woman you see.

FRANZ Mama — you're cursing her...

TONI Woman...

FRANZ I...can't...I. (*grabs her by the arm*) Go on, let me go.

TONI (*fights back*) You dare touch your mother?

FRANZ Yes, your time is up... (*throws her aside; storms out. She falls onto the carpet*)

> XAVER *enters from the right*

XAVER - My pipe absolutely won't light, do you have any matches here? (*sees TONI lying on the floor; freezes*) .. Mama... (*screaming in fear*) Mama...

> *Curtain.*

Part Nine:

Temptation

"Mama" is undated but probably appeared in print around 1911.

Temptation

A Scene
Comedy in One Act

Characters:
Alfred Schluckebier
Trude Bräunlich
Mrs. Schabatsberger, Landlady
Erwin Arnim Knöckel
Student Teacher Julius H. Geppert
A Lady

Place: Berlin-North – Time: Present

A furnished room in Berlin-North, near Linienstrasse or Auguststrasse, furnished in shabby elegance. To the right and left of the viewer: To the left, in front, a desk, above it a regulator clock that doesn't work – the large hand is broken off. Next to the clock, a picture meant to cover a hole in the wallpaper: "The Kiss." Towards the center: a desk, a bed. Above the bed, a wooden sign with the words "Awake joyfully every morning" burned into it. Below this sign, another, made of paper, red, with a green wreath around it, and white lettering: "God bless the bride and groom" – (as is customary at all kinds of festivities).

Then, a washstand, concealed by the high bed back. In the background, to the left, a door; to the right of the door, a cupboard, a chaise lounge, and a stove. To the right, towards the foreground, a door, a table, a chair, and an armchair. At the very front right, a window.

The curtain rises. ALFRED SCHLUCKEBIER *is sitting at his desk, smoking a cigar and reading. He suddenly closes the book and makes a movement, as if he wanted to look for his pocket watch; suddenly realizes that he doesn't have one and goes to the window and looks out.*

ALFRED Hmm – (*He walks cautiously to the bed where* TRUDE *is still sleeping; breathing calmly, he struggles with himself whether to wake her or not. There's a knock on the door on the right.*)

ALFRED Yes? (*behind the door*)

FRAU SCHABATSBERGER Herr Schluckebier, the coffee.

ALFRED Yes, Frau Schabatsberger, – it's impossible. Just put it out in the kitchen. I'll get it myself in a minute... (*strolls over to the bed, bends down, sighs, finally lightly grabs* TRUDE *by the arm*) Oh my God – that girl is so sleepy! – Wake up, it's already half past ten.

TRUDE (*makes incomprehensible noises – half sits up and wipes her sleepy eyes with one clenched hand*) Fred.

ALFRED That's terrible, you late riser, you can't do anything.

TRUDE What are you up to? (*yawns*)

ALFRED You never consider that we have things to do, after all. After you slept on my chaise lounge all afternoon yesterday from 2 a.m. to 7 a.m. – alone – you were wearing a corset – and went to bed at 10 a.m. – I think you should finally have had enough.

TRUDE Did your landlady say anything?

ALFRED No – that's not even mentioned.

TRUDE Did you say I have dirty teeth?

ALFRED No – you're a girl – how did you figure that?

TRUDE Then I dreamed it. But I just brushed my teeth yesterday morning with slurry chalk.

ALFRED Don't you want to get up? (*Pacing angrily up and down the room*)

TRUDE Have you been up late?

ALFRED At least an hour.

TRUDE What have you been doing?

ALFRED Reading.

TRUDE And?

ALFRED Writing letters.

TRUDE To whom?

ALFRED To a friend.

TRUDE You're lying — give me a cigarette.

ALFRED (*gives her one and matches*) Will you get up then?

TRUDE (*smiling*) Sure — just one cigarette, (*puffs*)

ALFRED I'll get the coffee, (*walks to the door on the right and unlocks it*)

TRUDE (*looks at the cigarette*) Listen, last week it was 3/2, and now it's only 2? — (ALFRED *leaves, leaving the door ajar*)

TRUDE (*puffs*) Idiot.

> ALFRED *returns with a tray, a pair of boots with a parcel of letters in them; places the tray on a small square table in front of* TRUDE

ALFRED Drink!

TRUDE You too...

> ALFRED *gets a broken beer glass and pours himself some coffee, which he hurriedly downs*

TRUDE (*stirring her cup leisurely and looking at the roll*) Eat.

ALFRED No.

TRUDE Then don't, (*eats*) – What kind of package is that?

ALFRED Manuscripts.

TRUDE ...and I regret that I can't make use of it. Yours sincerely.

ALFRED From the satirical magazine "Kakerlaken." It seems to me, it seems to me, I have to correct my erotic views again. It's not enough yet, miss... Or too much? There's never too much!! –

TRUDE Slacker.

ALFRED (*putting on his shoes*) It's raining outside... you can't go out on the street again without taking a foot bath. My soles are already more than waterproof!

TRUDE Do you have any yellow shoe polish?

ALFRED How you can still describe your shoes as "yellow" is beyond me – even brownish doesn't quite fit anymore. The only correct epithet is dirty – really dirty. Why didn't you put them outside? She would have cleaned them by now.

TRUDE Your landlady – so she'd snap at me – no, we don't do that.

ALFRED So, get up now.

TRUDE Just one more cigarette.

ALFRED But you already have one.

TRUDE One more... the last one. Come sit here.

ALFRED (*Reluctantly sits down on the edge of the bed, gives her a cigarette and a match*)

TRUDE You know, when I lie in bed like this in the morning... I always have to think of home... it was lovely, wasn't it?

ALFRED Yes, do me a favor?

TRUDE Stay, direct takes him by the hand Now I'm home here – yes? – it's different. -Oh, it was nice... In the morning, Mother brought me coffee or milk in bed. - Hey, do you know buttermilk?

ALFRED Yes.

TRUDE And after coffee – I stretched and yawned – and then I slowly got up – slowly, oh how slowly – I had time. – And then I played the piano for an hour. If only we had a piano.

ALFRED Yes, you're right... Music, music, the good lady only cares for out-of-tune barrel organs.

TRUDE Before dinner – I rode my bike, with my brother or alone – into the woods – I'd gotten a hammock for my birthday – I strapped it to the back of my bike. And in the forest I tied them to two trees and then I slept — I slept — and after dinner I slept too... only you won't let me sleep. Sleep is the only thing you have left. (*starts laughing*)

ALFRED What is it...

TRUDE And once — when I think about it — it was for shooting, the first horse shop had just opened in Neisse. I was twelve years old and my brother was eleven — and when we heard about it, my God, a shudder ran through us — the horses that ran around in front of us, you could have eaten them. It seemed monstrous to us at first, as monstrous as if we were supposed to eat human flesh. But from that day on, the craving for horse meat wouldn't leave us alone — it was downright crazy — and when we had 20 Pfennigs together, we went to the horse butcher — you had to buy it — and I stood outside to make sure no one saw us — and we were afraid... of what, I don't know myself — do you remember?

ALFRED Certainly, little sister

TRUDE Oh, and then we went behind the woods and ate them... with devotion, it really tasted quite good; while I was eating, by the way, I kept thinking about the lame gray horse from the mineral water manufacturer Böhmer. Funny, isn't it?

ALFRED Why? (*quietly annoyed*) But now you're getting up. Yes?

TRUDE You haven't even given me a kiss today!

ALFRED (*kisses her*) But now. Yes!

TRUDE (*sighs*) All right, you can be a real pain in the ass. (*Throws back the comforter and sits on the edge of the bed.* ALFRED *gets up and walks around the room, his head slightly bent, his back slightly bent, his fingers to his mouth.*) Throw me a petticoat.

ALFRED (*Hands her petticoat, skirt, etc. from the chair*)

TRUDE (*Puts on her petticoat and goes to the sink*)

TRUDE (*While washing*) I was mean to you yesterday, wasn't I? Yes, you know, I sometimes have moods, then I'm disgusting... unbearable, I tell you, - but I can't do anything about it, I just can't help it.

ALFRED Yes, yes.

TRUDE What are you thinking about?

ALFRED About your horse butcher from Neisse – By the way – did you ever write to your father, the highly respected headmaster in Neisse, and ask for money? I find it very inappropriate that he disowned you like that.

TRUDE Since I ran off with that Black boxer a year ago, he's only sent me money once – 100 marks. But I worked hard and whined and cried until he sent it. But 100 marks, what are 100 marks?

ALFRED Yes, what's 100 marks? A trifle! 50 Pfennigs a day is better for me and is more than 100 Marks all at once.

TRUDE Well, of course – 50 marks are at Kempinski – and you used the other 50 marks... for... postage. I won't say anything about that! .. but – the fact that you gave the doorman at Kempinski a 5 mark tip, I still find that outrageous... that's a waste –

ALFRED Other people want to live too – besides, I was drunk. (*There's a knock*) Come in.

TRUDE But!!

ALFRED Oh, who could it be?

> *Armin Erwin Knöckel enters. He has a full blond beard, but is only 21 years old; headgear: a sports cap. This shouldn't be played with affected theatrical pathos; on the contrary, KNÖCKEL speaks quite quietly.*

KNÖCKEL Greetings to all. Is this Miss Cressida?

ALFRED It's her.

KNÖCKEL Greetings, beautiful young lady of the Greeks. The field captain greets you with a kiss. (*kisses her on the forehead*). I used to have a lovely occasion to kiss you.

ALFRED But there's no occasion for a kiss now.

KNÖCKEL Oh, bitter shame! I'm out of work.

ALFRED Man, my German Agamemnon... didn't Friedrich Wilhelmstadt liquidate it?

KNÖCKEL I was thrown out of my room too. Where do pilgrims find accommodation? Tell me!

ALFRED On this sofa, noble lord.

KNÖCKEL I don't see a sofa.

ALFRED Me neither.

TRUDE (*gurgles*) We can sleep together.

KNÖCKEL Yes – tell me, Schluckebier – can't you lend me a hand with 25 Pfennigs? I'll sue the management for damages... 5,000 marks... and I'm convinced the courts will agree with me —

ALFRED Please go to the cashier — there, (*gesturing to TRUDE*)

KNÖCKEL So, miss — come on — lend me some money.

TRUDE If you start whining again, you'll get nothing. I don't have anything left either. George Knöckel. (*quietly*) I didn't go for a walk yesterday — afternoon.

KNÖCKEL Yes, everyone here is gloomy. Our blood no longer obeys heaven.

ALFRED Crazy connoisseur and quoter of Shakespeare, unforgettable performer of the mute blind man in "The Picture at Sais," the waiter in "Charley's Aunt," "a peasant" in Antony and Cleopatra,... it's, as you say, sickening. (*There's a knock.*)

ALFRED Come in. (*Dr. jur. Julius H. Geppert, medium height, somewhat over-weight, handsome face, tastefully elegant clothing, round straw hat, cane with a round silver crutch, sometimes speaks a bit quickly, hastily, Jewish*)

JULIUS Morning, Alfred, – oh, you have – a lady's visitor?

ALFRED If you don't mind. You haven't been here in a long time.

JULIUS Oh, you know, the exam papers.

ALFRED May I congratulate you?

JULIUS Thank goodness, yes, but – it's turned out bittersweet – not the exam, but the work for it (*uneasy*), don't you want to introduce me?

TRUDE Nonsense, it's pointless (*sitting on the edge of the bed again, buttoning her shoe*). I couldn't care less what your name is, just help me tie my shoes.

JULIUS (*kneels down by the bed, puts down his hat and cane*) If you don't mind —

ALFRED (*looks at him half-ironically, half-enviously*) So you passed your exam?

KNÖCKEL Congratulations —

TRUDE So you're a trainee lawyer? My God — and so young... and so handsome.

JULIUS Of course, I won't stick with law — out of the question — I'm going to my uncle's in Trieste — into business — people with legal training are highly valued, and if I don't earn at least 10,000 marks a year in five years... (*stands up*) The shoes are tied...

TRUDE Ten thousand!!!

KNÖCKEL Ten thousand!!! (*shakes his head*)

JULIUS You'll admit, Miss, a decent person these days — let's say 500 marks a month, that's the least — and —

ALFRED Nonsense, it's pointless (*sitting on the edge of the bed again, buttoning her shoe*). I couldn't care less what your name is. Can you lend me 10 marks?

JULIUS With pleasure... 20... my old man, to celebrate passing his exams — (*more quietly*) By the way, I would have liked to speak to you alone (*pulls out his wallet and gives him 20 marks.*)

ALFRED Nonsense, it's pointless (*sitting on the edge of the bed again, buttoning her shoe*). I couldn't care less what your name is. Thank you — they'll go right away.

KNÖCKEL (*smiling*) Who's giving poor Thoms something? – whom the evil enemy led through fire and flames, through flood and whirlpool, over moor and swamp, who placed knives under his pillow and snares under his church pew, who placed rat poison next to his soup, who gave him the arrogance to ride a trotting brown horse over footbridges one inch wide and chase his own shadow like a trailblazer. God bless your five senses!

TRUDE You're right, Erwin.

KNÖCKEL Thoms is freezing – Give alms to poor Thoms, whom the evil enemy is afflicting –

ALFRED Nonsense, it's pointless (*sitting on the edge of the bed again, buttoning her shoe*). I couldn't care less what your name is. Edgar, this time you spoke from my heart. I want to cry, Edgar. Give him 5 marks, Julius.

KNÖCKEL Knöckel is my name

JULIUS Geppert – if I can do you a small favor (*gives him 10 marks*)
　　　　TRUDE is finished and puts on her hat

TRUDE I'd like to go for a stroll. The weather is nice now – into the tents. Erwin will accompany me. (*to ALFRED*) You – – I don't need to go for a walk this afternoon.

ALFRED Nonsense, it's pointless (*sitting on the edge of the bed again, buttoning her shoe*). I couldn't care less what your name is. No – you don't need to go for a walk this afternoon.

KNÖCKEL Thank you very much. When my position with Reinhardt is confirmed – and I have no doubt about it – you should get it back with 100% interest, with usurious interest, as if you were a Jew.
　　　　JULIUS, somewhat uncomfortable

TRUDE You have no sense of style, Erwin. The gentleman is a Jew after all – you are a Jew, aren't you?

JULIUS (*embarrassed*) Yes —

TRUDE It doesn't matter, I have nothing against Jews. I even find the little Jewish brats, around 4 or 5 years old, cute. Only the Jewish girls — too fat, too small figure when they get old — when I was a man —

ALFRED Nonsense, it's pointless (*sitting on the edge of the bed again, buttoning her shoe*). I couldn't care less what your name is. Shut up now, okay! Goodbye, enjoy your summer morning in the zoo —

TRUDE Goodbye... humm...

KNÖCKEL My apologies.

JULIUS Oh...

ALFRED Goodbye...
　　　　TRUDE and Erwin Knöckel exit.

JULIUS That was a bit much for me. The company you keep now — to be honest, I don't understand you. Doesn't your sense of cleanliness rebel against these people?

ALFRED Oh, sense of cleanliness — if you only knew how long it's been since I last bathed.

JULIUS What do you actually live on?

ALFRED As you can see —

JULIUS Do you always have this young lady with you?

ALFRED In the summer — two in bed — you sweat — but you do it anyway.

JULIUS I'd like to help you — but —

ALFRED Help? How do you know I need help? — (*Short pause*)

JULIUS My sister Mimi has terrible nervous tics now.

ALFRED Poor dear — I think I loved her once, back when I was in high school. I've never seen anyone so clean, so incredibly clean. She must be the ideal of a decent wife. Wives don't always tend to be clean. That's because they haven't yet learned the art of sleeping together and have to learn it first. Oh my God, even here there will be a compromise later!

JULIUS And yet, I believe you long for a decent environment, a decent life. I completely understand that you broke with bourgeois society back then, you were younger — but today — you are 25 years old and there —

ALFRED What are the other little girls from back then doing, playing tennis?

JULIUS (*pleased*) I spoke to Grete Wota the other day; she asked about you.

ALFRED She asked about me?

JULIUS She's become even more beautiful, more mature. And her eyes already have an almost impossible beauty. That's someone... I would marry her on the spot – not because she has money – something so soft, harsh, reserved, and impetuous –

ALFRED Go ahead and marry her, you have titles and honors now.

JULIUS You know perfectly well that she wouldn't take me. – You were the biggest fool back then, leaving her, childish, childish.

ALFRED Please – why are you getting so upset?

JULIUS It would have been your good fortune... She loved you... and she had money... you could have had adventures to your heart's content... but like this? I mean, people need to have a normal, practical foundation, including in their thinking. That seems to be where you're lacking.

ALFRED After going through all the hellish filth — and if there was ever anything of heaven in me, it hangs in tatters, like my worn-out frock coat — I have a tiny bit of faith in myself, a tiny bit — that's the only thing I have left. No one believes in me, not my parents, not you — and how is one supposed to gain faith? You don't see any success, no success. And anyone who has no success is simply worthless, that's the harsh, mocking morality of our society.

JULIUS That's what you're telling yourself: we like to believe so much — but you have to get out of here, otherwise it won't work. You can't stay stuck in these whorehouses forever. Grete Wota said that too — who still loves you, you understand — still loves you — you should hear how she talks about you...

ALFRED It's unbelievable what strength a loving woman has for foolish illusions.

JULIUS She believes in you unshakably — unshakably — and I know that she recently saw you with one of your prostitutes.

ALFRED I'm fed up with women — to this point — every beautiful face is repulsive to me because I know that afterward, once I've had her, it will be old, decayed, gray — I see old age, I see death, in the most beautiful, healthy female face. And yet a wild will whips me — is it within me, is it outside me, into this chaos.

JULIUS Character... character... it must at least be enough to earn money.

ALFRED (*walks to the desk, bangs his fist on the surface*) Here... here... it lies buried... more precious than your mother's earrings... richer than your Fraulein Grete Wota's millions...

JULIUS You deliberately conceal your better nature behind blasphemy; one never knows whether you're speaking seriously or madly.

ALFRED With whom you absolutely wanted to marry me off, here they rot, the fruits of my life, the works of immortality, my novellas. Apart from my other virtues, I'm also a poet — poet — poet! Maupassant gets 500 marks for a single, even the tiniest, novella — what do I get? Consumption. Damn it, I basically have so little talent for the bohemian, the bourgeois from the other side — and I'm no bohemian either... but it will come to that.

JULIUS You long for the other shore... that Charon would carry you back to life... why don't you listen to Grete Wota, who must still speak within you... Because... it's impossible, you can't have forgotten her.

ALFRED Damn it, why aren't women statues! Is there anything more worthy of veneration than the breasts of Nike of Samothrace? I would travel the world if I had the money... to see her... But she shouldn't live for me. Then she would be dead to me. Then I wouldn't have to bring her back to life. When she confronts you in life, you are seized by a frenzy, a daze, but then something rises up within you, sweet and sad, tearing and tugging at you and making you impure, impure —

JULIUS (*looks at the clock*) But I have to go now. I have an appointment at Under the Linden Trees at 12 o'clock. Shouldn't I at least send Grete Wota a greeting —?

ALFRED If it pleases you...

JULIUS Goodbye, Alfred, I feel sorry for you...

ALFRED (*quietly*) I'll tolerate this kindergarten tone.

JULIUS Why didn't you reply to my last two cards inviting you to dinner? You received them, didn't you?

ALFRED Because the whole thing no longer serves any purpose.

JULIUS No purpose?

ALFRED No, dear friend, no point. Do you think I'll ever find my way back into your circle? – Haven't we already become strangers? You're only coming from an old feeling of attachment, which I respect – but forgive me – find a little weak. It sounds ridiculous, the word "weak" in my mouth and as a reproach, doesn't it? That's the courage of the coward who throws the word "coward" around like an Australian black man with a boomerang. It flies back – and knocks the thrower over. (*already at the door*) Goodbye, Julius, say hello to little, pure, poor, nervous Mimi for me... and... Grete... Wota.

JULIUS Goodbye – Before I leave for Trieste, I'll visit you again.

ALFRED Better not – my address – who knows how long I'll stay here. But you can write to me, poste restante[12]; Dear God, then it's already happening to me. (*Closes the door behind JULIUS, goes to the window, looks out, comes back, reaches the middle of the room, stops*) Yes... Grete, Grete... yes... (*there's a knock on the right*) (ALFRED *resumes his walk through the room*) Just come in, Mrs. Schabatsberger

    FRAU SCHABATSBERGER *enters, gets the coffee set, then stops*

FRAU SCHABATSBERGER I just wanted to tell you, if things continue like this, I'm going to fire you.

ALFRED ...

FRAU SCHABATSBERGER You owe me a month and a half now, and you know perfectly well that I'm a woman who needs it, but of course, you try to make your way through the world decently, and then some scoundrel and streetwalker comes along, and you're always so good-natured. But that's not good-natured anymore, you're stupid, nothing more: stupid.

ALFRED (*reaches into his pocket*) Here are 10 marks, as a down payment; I honestly don't have any more.

FRAU SCHABATSBERGER God, yes, I believe it, but we want to live too, and you're such a – dear – handsome young man – yes – only: women, they're on your conscience, women and poetry.

ALFRED Poetry, Mrs. Schabatsberger, poetry – that's certainly like a whore in disguise.

FRAU SCHABATSBERGER I'm the last person who would wish you ill, Mr. Schlucke-

---

[12]to be held at the post office

bier. Just give up poetry, it doesn't achieve anything. I've already seen that with my Gustav, my eldest: he could write beautiful poetry for all occasions: silver wedding anniversaries, baptisms, funerals... a medal for service, but what did it achieve: 1 penny a line, just imagine, a penny! (*The doorbell rings outside. Alfred listens, becoming restless*) Good Lord, it's been ringing nonstop today (*puts the dishes back down*)

ALFRED Take a look, Mrs. Schabatsberger.

> FRAU SCHABATSBERGER *goes out. Alfred stands motionless, his head bowed slightly, as is his custom.* FRAU SCHABATSBERGER *comes back.*

FRAU SCHABATSBERGER It's a young lady.

ALFRED What?

FRAU SCHABATSBERGER Lady! Not the kind of girl you're imagining...

ALFRED A lady... lady.

FRAU SCHABATSBERGER Yes, she must have gotten the house number wrong too. And her face — oh God — is so pretty and decent —

ALFRED Let the lady in.

FRAU SCHABATSBERGER But, from the looks of things here, Mr. Schluckebier, it hasn't been tidied up yet – and the dishes – and the bed – my God – Miss Trude left a hairpin lying around here again, what will the lady think? I want the bed –

ALFRED Let the lady in... that's just right.

> FRAU SCHABATSBERGER *comes out and then lets the lady enter.* FRAU SCHABATSBERGER *walks into her room with the coffee set, turning several times to the right. The lady is slim, with a hint of fullness. Barely 18 years old, with blond hair, large blue eyes, and a broad face. She walks very gracefully, has a delicate, soft voice, is intelligent, and has a strong temperament hidden behind shy movements and a shy look. She is elegantly and inconspicuously dressed in a blue cloth suit. She wears a white silk blouse underneath, a black pot hat with a gold cord, and an umbrella with a round porcelain handle. She carries the umbrella in her left hand as she enters.*

GRETE (*walks towards him, shakes his hand*)

ALFRED Good day.

GRETE (*looks around the room a bit*)

ALFRED Please, don't you want to take your coat off?

GRETE (*looks at him*) Thank you – yes (*puts umbrella on the bed,* ALFRED *helps her out of her jacket, she fiddles with her hat*) Oh – no – I can keep it on, surely. (*looks around the room again, completely unconcerned*) How long have you been living here?

ALFRED For half a year...

GRETE And when did we last see each other? That is, we spoke, I saw you some-times, once or twice on the street (*pause*) – a year ago.

ALFRED Why have you come now? What do you want from me?

GRETE (*walks to the desk*) The desk! – Do you still write a lot of poetry? Not anymore, do you?

ALFRED directconcerned Why no poetry?

GRETE You can't write poetry in such an environment.

ALFRED I don't write poetry anymore.

GRETE (*grabs a picture from the desk*) Look – the picture – of your parents.

ALFRED (*snatches it from her*) Leave the picture.

GRETE Where – did you put my picture?

ALFRED (*quietly, persistently*) I never had it.

GRETE Yes – you just don't know that.

ALFRED Shall we sit down?

GRETE Yes. (*sits down in the armchair at the table, ALFRED sits down opposite her. – GRETE has the habit of occasionally tilting her head back slightly with her eyes closed and brushing her hair from her forehead with her left hand*)

ALFRED (*as if to initiate a conventional conversation*) I can imagine that it's been difficult for you to come here.

GRETE Difficult – oh no – I still love you.

ALFRED Grete –

GRETE By the way, why do you call me that stupid "They?"

ALFRED Grete, nearby – all things are gray and painful – those that shine in the distance – Julius Geppert was here earlier – is your visit perhaps connected to his confused speeches? Are you two perhaps in cahoots and have arranged everything?

GRETE Oh no – – I did meet him – and he told me he was coming from you and that you were very, very ill. Nothing else.

ALFRED Sick?

GRETE Aren't you ill? I would love to be your doctor.

ALFRED Grete – you – –

GRETE (*holding his hand*) I know you still love me too.

ALFRED (*fervently*) Perhaps – perhaps –

GRETE You still love me – Why aren't you honest with yourself?

ALFRED You think too highly of me, too well, Grete – I've never been honest –

least of all with me. Oh, I don't want to see the truth either – it must be terrible. You don't know what kind of life I lead, you'd be disgusted by all this filth –

GRETE You can still turn back – (*Changing voice*) What do you live on? What do you earn? – Your parents don't support you anymore?

ALFRED No – I live... partly... from a little journalism... partly... partly

GRETE Please...

ALFRED Do... you... know... what... that... is: a... a...?

GRETE (*looks at him silently after a while*) I love you – you must get out of this stifling, stuffy air – I will carry you out on my back –

ALFRED Oh – you have no idea how much I long for civility and decency – I cry out for decency... the most bourgeois, most stupid decency. You bring with you a breath of that world that I must – despise and – long for, a breath that numbs me. That world of civility in which I had citizenship, and yet which I gaze upon like a pariah with envious eyes through the bars of my despair –

GRETE Then come – you will find a home in it (*more quietly*) in me.

ALFRED I want her – but I would – like I do from women – also suffer from her – suffer – what a big word – when I have her, I'll be sick from the food.

GRETE I have often hated you – out of necessity – – out of love – reflect – come with me...

ALFRED Perhaps.

GRETE I — I'm being completely open with you — I'm proposing marriage — if we love each other, why shouldn't we get married?

ALFRED That's what you wanted? Me?

GRETE Yes, you — I want you, only you — I would force my parents to consent.

ALFRED I almost think you don't know what you're saying.

GRETE Yes — that's why I came.

ALFRED If I were to accept your proposal, which honors me so much — now (*bitterly*)?

GRETE (*joyfully*) You shall! It's the only way out for you. (*embarrassed.*) It would be only incidental, but in this respect I have wealth, you know that. It would be enough for both of us. You could write novellas and plays without hindrance — and you would also learn to write poetry again.

ALFRED Poems — that's probably over.

GRETE You do love me — why don't you want me just once? kiss?

ALFRED Grete – (*kisses her*).

GRETE The best thing is – you'll come with me right away. Leave everything as it is, there probably won't be anything valuable among it. Just your manuscripts

– we'll pack them up. Show me, where are they? (*Goes to the desk, opens a drawer, takes out a pack of written papers. Her gaze falls on the top one; reads, aloud:*) You're just one more among all the thousands of others. II took you here once, girl, now you have to wander again – wander again, (*remains silent, shocked*)

ALFRED It's a silly, foolish song, and bad to boot, but I can go on: (*speaks slowly to herself, head bowed*) There's the door, you can go now, If your feelings are lost, I have a rendezvous at nine-thirty at Bellevue station.

GRETE That's all nonsense, dear.

ALFRED It's nonsense, sure — but the truth is usually stupid and vile, too. Once you're on the slide — then it's down, down — even an angel can't stop — until you reach the swamp — splash — headfirst — splat — just a few bubbles — frogs croak — fish snap — whatever swims in this pond is a delicious, appetizing love corpse — and the carp — they appreciate it.

GRETE Alfred, you're talking like a madman — leave it all... don't think about it anymore... come —

> Excited voices outside, the FRAU SCHABATSBERGER's voice, TRUDE's voice: "Leave it, Mrs. Schabetzberger, so he's got a woman with him, so he's like that to me?" — The door is flung open and Trude Bräunlich storms in excitedly.

TRUDE A woman with you? So! A woman (*a small organ begins to quietly play a religious song from somewhere*) You want to seduce him, Miss, what, because you're so finely dressed, because you have that hat and such decent eyes, (*hangs on to* ALFRED) But you can't get him — no — what do I have then? I was once so finely dressed, don't get me wrong — my father is a senior teacher in Neisse, I also once attended the higher girls' school — (*shouts*) Do you want to go now, Miss —

ALFRED (*firmly*) Trude – be quiet –

TRUDE (*whimpers*)

GRETE What's that terrible music up there?

ALFRED (*stands motionless, tormented*) Whoever lets God rule... That's the Protestant youth group over there from St. John's Church, who have set up their Christian home above me... And hope in him forever...

GRETE And I know you – love me – what do you want with that – girl?

ALFRED (*strokes* TRUDE))Yes – did I say that – that I love you – yes – I must – yes... I love you...

GRETE Come with me – Come

TRUDE Fred... I want to – bite her throat off...

ALFRED Yes... no, I don't love you – ... don't believe that – no – maybe – but I can't –

GRETE You-

ALFRED Can't – whoever said Y must also say Z – There's the door, you can go now – if your feelings are lost –

TRUDE Miss –

ALFRED (*breaks away from* TRUDE) I'm falling apart... I'm fluttering away... I can't read a good, long book in one go anymore... That's how it is with you, I can't finish reading you – As simple as you are, you're too heavy for me...

GRETE (*walks quietly, jacket over her arm, toward the door.* ALFRED *opens the door for her, and they bump into each other with two young men from the youth club together*)

ALFRED Excuse me – (GRETE *goes out.*)

> the two young men approach

THE ONE Two girls at once.

ALFRED (*closes the door*)

ALFRED How can I be of service to you gentlemen?

THE OTHER We were sent by Pastor Lindemann – would you like to join

THE ONE our Protestant youth club...

THE OTHER and come sometime. He says your soul might need it – –

THE ONE – but no one has sunk so low that God the Lord will not save them (*upstairs, the organ plays again: "He who Lets Only God Rule"*)

THE OTHER We're just having our Wednesday midday devotion, if you would do us the pleasure...

ALFRED But of course – isn't that right, Trude – that's the only worthy conclusion – and the lady wants to join the young women's club.

THE ONE Yes?

ALFRED What are you staring at? Protestant youth Have you never seen a virgin?

TRUDE Idiot.

ALFRED What Bible passage are you currently holding onto? Perhaps one that talks about the possible practical use of window cords, bedposts, and washbasins...

THE YOUNG MEN (*don't understand*)

ALFRED (*grabs* TRUDE *by the arm, who has lit a cigarette*) By the way (*to the young men*), let each one be sanctified according to his merits — can you lend me a mark? (*all four exit*)

> *Curtain falls.*

Part Ten:

Hannibal's Bridal Journey

"Hannibal's Bridal Journey" – A farce in three acts and an epilogue.
Written in 1912 and published by Erich Reiss-Verlag Berlin.

Hannibal's Bridal Journey

A Scene

A farce in three acts and an epilogue.

Characters:

Old Eisermann.
Hannibal, his son.
Plüddecke, master tailor.
Miss.
Liddy, a mute factotum.
A. Schulz, commander of the volunteer fire department.
B. Schultz, major of the rifle club.
C. Schulze, president of the "Harmonie" bowling and skat club.
Miss Pompe.
Maxi Beerbaum, high school student.
Handsome Oskar.
Mädele, his daughter.
Lisa.
A waiter.
A mayor.
A young man with a camera.

Time: Before the War. Place: Small Town.

Act One

A comfortably furnished middle-class living room. HANNIBAL is sitting at the breakfast table, eating breakfast, the newspaper beside him. He is very well and tastefully dressed, with a strikingly bright green silk tie, very blond hair, a carefully parted left part, and a monocle.

HANNIBAL (*reading the newspaper*) The millionairess Miss Mary Eleonore Tunderstam, connected to our city by family ties — how is the construction here — dative? To whom? By what means? — there are still problems in the world... Her late mother, who was buried here, was the daughter of the local herring merchant Mr. Goegle — she is honoring our city with a visit dedicated to piety and is staying at the hotel "Three Crowns." We wish the young, delightful lady — Schmock has good taste — who, moreover, as our reporter F. F. personally confirmed through interview, speaks perfect German mixed with a soft English accent — a pleasant, enjoyable stay in our exceedingly charming little town in these mild autumn days, and would only like to conclude by pointing out that our gasworks, whose excellent officer in the magistrate, Mr. Eisermann, we by the way mean no disrespect toward, still lacks a second gasometer. — How finely expressed! How delicate! (*He rings the bell. The maid appears*)

LISA What would the young gentleman like?

HANNIBAL The eggs are hard again, as hard as bricks and cold, you can only eat them sliced.

LISA But Dad...

HANNIBAL Dad! Then just have extra-soft eggs cooked for me. Plum-soft. Three minutes. Tell that to the cook.

LISA I've told her many times, but the young gentleman knows, when I say something to Marie, she thinks I'm trying to harass her.

HANNIBAL I don't like those cold, sliced eggs topped with anchovies. I don't like a cold, sliced life topped with anchovies either.

LISA ...?

HANNIBAL (*pinches her breast*) Plum-soft, do you hear me?

LISA (*giggles embarrassed*).

HANNIBAL Is my room heated upstairs?

LISA Eleven briquettes. I put them in half an hour ago. As the young gentleman wished.

HANNIBAL That's right.

LISA It really wasn't necessary to use so much, it's thawing... and if Papa found out, he'd scold me again for being so wasteful with the briquettes.

HANNIBAL It's fine. You can go. Clear the coffee table. (*LISA clears and leaves. HANNIBAL lights a cigar. He watches LISA leave. He calls out to her*) Lisa...?

LISA (*turns around, embarrassed*).

HANNIBAL You haven't paid me your tribute yet today...?

LISA (*approaches slowly*).

HANNIBAL Well, will it be soon?

LISA (*takes his hand. Kisses it*).

HANNIBAL You'll come tonight. I'll leave the door open...

LISA (*nods shyly*).

HANNIBAL (*pats her on the neck*). (*LISA goes out, meets EISERMANN in the doorway, and leaves in alarm.*)

EISERMANN My bouillon... hurry up (*to HANNIBAL*) Ah... the lord still wanted breakfast (*looks at his watch*). It's half past eleven. The rest of us have been toiling in the shop since eight o'clock, scraping together the little daily bread, and you...

HANNIBAL Why are you shouting like that?

EISERMANN Have you been sleeping until now?

HANNIBAL (*remains silent*).

EISERMANN (*shouting*) I want to know if you've been sleeping until now.

HANNIBAL Of course.

EISERMANN Of course... so... of course...

HANNIBAL And in any case, I slept better than you.

EISERMANN Nothing but lazing around all day.

HANNIBAL I can't think of anything nicer.

EISERMANN You're cheeky, you're frivolous, you're immoral.

HANNIBAL Amoral... a... a... you could even call it animalistic.

      LISA brings the broth, then leaves.

EISERMANN (*drinks while standing*) Of course, it's undrinkable, it's so hot. (*Drinks the cup in three gulps.*)

HANNIBAL Why don't you pour the broth into the saucer to cool it, like you usually do.

EISERMANN What's that supposed to mean? Are you perhaps making fun of your old father's manners? It would be just like you. You have no respect for anything. Sometimes I want to slap you.

HANNIBAL Then why don't you do it?

EISERMANN (*approaches him*)) ... Because... because... because (*screaming*) because I hope you'll come to your senses again.

HANNIBAL Optimist... sensible... never... never... better to be put in a madhouse.

EISERMANN I'd like to throw you out.

HANNIBAL But you don't dare! You're afraid!

EISERMANN Afraid? Ridiculous! Of what? That you haven't been lying on the pavement for a long time is thanks to your mother, your good mother, who, God rest her soul, was crazy enough...

HANNIBAL Yes, she was very unreasonable. It's already evident from the fact that she married you...

EISERMANN I take offense at your impertinence. She was crazy enough to be completely infatuated with you. You were fifteen years old then... and I had to swear to her on her deathbed... that I would always take care of you... Since you would never find your way in the world... you were so gentle... so ideally suited, so good... And we had the means, and I wasn't to force you into any job you disliked. Yes, that was your mother.

HANNIBAL I can't understand how you two got along... but even more incomprehensible is how I got out of it.

EISERMANN And we have the means? Yeah, cake! We're in a tough spot, we small manufacturers in the small towns... compared to the big industrialists. We have x times as much operating overhead. And we can't properly recycle the waste. And then we have to feed a... guy like you around the world.

HANNIBAL You just can't properly recycle the... waste. — You just recently transferred ten thousand marks to the Workers' Foundation, three thousand marks to the hospital, and five thousand marks to the municipal orphanage. For what, please?

EISERMANN It's been hard enough for me...

HANNIBAL (*convinced*) I believe it!

EISERMANN How? Yes! But after all, you owe it to yourself.

HANNIBAL Yourself? i.e., to the title of Commercial Councilor!

EISERMANN Well, the world looks at appearances.

HANNIBAL And ever since cloth manufacturer John received the Order of the Crown, Fourth Class... I asked you a long time ago... not exactly begged you: why don't you give me five thousand marks for a trip to Italy?

EISERMANN (*bangs on the table*)) That's outrageous... The brat, who can be glad I'm not throwing him out... that's the most natural thing of all, isn't it? I must, I'm forced, I'm practically obligated, to throw five thousand marks your way for such trifles. No, my son, you have your usual pocket money, which is already plenty enough.

HANNIBAL You often enough, always, as a matter of principle, waste your money on phantoms, so why don't you want to sacrifice it to the living? I don't see how five thousand marks could be better used than for me.

EISERMANN Well, you're truly close to being stupid. No sane person talks like that.

HANNIBAL Again, that horrible word: reason, with which you pay like tokens that are supposed to replace money. You're usually for real money... you... counterfeiter.

EISERMANN Not so loud... the girls, one could hear it —... what would they think?

HANNIBAL Oh, you can shout the truth as loudly as you like, no one hears it. To make it understandable to people, you have to whisper it. Oh, if only you were a counterfeiter, but a real one.

EISERMANN Silly... nonsense... (*picks up the newspaper*). What does it say? So, so... the Miss and the gas works. We've arranged this very cleverly.

HANNIBAL It could be that you're rid of me forever, with those five thousand marks. It could be that I'll choose a burial site down there in Italy... (*looks at his fingernails*)...

EISERMANN You? Nonsense!

HANNIBAL A burial place for me and my unborn children. — It just occurred to me: Did you send the alimony money to Fanny in Leipzig? It's already the fourth one today.

EISERMANN Yes, yes... Thank God that here in the city, people are only aware of the smallest part of your misdeeds. I would like to ask you not to compromise me. Thank God, we've been able to maintain the appearance that you work in my office... in my private office... at least there, no one can check. But if you do the slightest thing, you'll have to leave the city. I always hope that one day you'll learn to work.

HANNIBAL Work! That's for bunglers.

EISERMANN Hannibal! My whole life has been filled with hard, arduous work. I have never

HANNIBAL rested or relaxed, nor allowed myself any rest.

EISERMANN I despise you!

HANNIBAL And I despise you no less. I don't love you: you give me money, that's all. I acknowledge that... nothing more. But you only give it under duress,forced by my dead mother... because you fear her demon...

EISERMANN You accuse me of cowardice, for daring to publicly call the former city council chairman an idiot? Ha ha... But you? Weren't you afraid of the dark at night almost until you were twenty?

HANNIBAL I also had reason to fear the dark. For my ghosts are real.

EISERMANN You're worth no more than handsome Oskar, the city scoundrel.

HANNIBAL Certainly not... since I'm convinced that this city scoundrel is the only honorable man in the entire city. He has passion, a sense of life, humor... humor... and that's what you all lack. You take yourselves seriously, deadly serious, which makes you so infinitely comical. By the way, handsome Oskar doesn't work either, on principle, to quote your dictionary.

EISERMANN Lack of stability, nothingness, uselessness, laziness: those are your ideals.

HANNIBAL Laziness, yes, because work was only invented by those who didn't know what else to do with life. To numb their inner emptiness and inability for a contemplative existence, the only existence worth living, and to bring rhythm into it, they became stone cutters and philologists. After all, art isn't worth much more than that. Art is just the rage that one has nothing solid, that everything is melting away in our hands. And so as not to despair, one must pretend to have some part of life, to grasp it in its quintessence. In reality, art is dilution.

EISERMANN Don't talk to me about art! That's the one thing I don't understand.

HANNIBAL Yes, it's your only virtue I could envy. (*Stands at the window.*) The houseboy is coming downstairs with the midday mail. You must be coming down.

EISERMANN I still have time. By the way, were you woken up by him this morning at nine o'clock, as I ordered?

HANNIBAL By whom?

EISERMANN By the houseboy.

HANNIBAL Of course not. He knows more about what's proper than you do.

EISERMANN Everything I said today, I was just talking into the wind.

HANNIBAL Yes, I am the wind. You don't know where it comes from or where it's going.

EISERMANN If it continues like this, to hell.

HANNIBAL (*after a short pause*) I'll give you some sweet consolation: I intend to better myself today, to improve, as they say.

EISERMANN God grant it. I can't believe it. Are you finally going to get to work on that doctoral dissertation you've been planning for three years?

HANNIBAL No, I seriously intend to work.

EISERMANN Work?

HANNIBAL Yes, work. By the way, everyone has a doctorate these days. It's downright rude. If I cared about using the doctorate title, I would simply use it.

EISERMANN ...without having taken the doctoral exam first?

HANNIBAL Of course.

EISERMANN : Then you'd be in prison the day after tomorrow.

HANNIBAL But, Dad! You don't know the penal code. I'd get a month in prison at most. And even that could probably be commuted to a fine.

EISERMANN And who would pay for that?

HANNIBAL You, Dad. However — that's beside the point now. You know, of course, that Miss Mary Eleonore Tunderstam arrived here yesterday and took up residence at the Hotel Three Kronen.

EISERMANN She is one of the richest women in the world. A fortune of nine hundred million dollars is said to be in the works.

HANNIBAL Seven hundred and thirty-seven, dear Papa, but that's enough.

EISERMANN How do you know that?

HANNIBAL I've gathered my information.

EISERMANN What's all this about?

HANNIBAL I told you I'd get serious about serious work.

EISERMANN Well?

HANNIBAL I'm getting married.

EISERMANN Oh! So?! Who, if I don't mind asking?

HANNIBAL Miss Mary Eleonore Tunderstam.

EISERMANN You... you... are crazy!

HANNIBAL Not at all! If I'm going to marry, it has to be the richest woman in the world, or at least close to the richest.

EISERMANN You're completely out of your mind.

HANNIBAL (*slowly emphasizing each word*) I'm begging you, Papa, I'm going to marry her!

EISERMANN A good-for-nothing like you, with no fortune...

HANNIBAL She has enough money for two.

EISERMANN Without a title...

HANNIBAL She holds a doctorate in philosophy and law. She earned it summa cum laude in Munich. On the statistics of illegitimate children. Munich seems like a perfectly suitable field here. Perhaps she has one herself.

EISERMANN What?

HANNIBAL An illegitimate child! My God, Dad, you're slow on the uptake.

EISERMANN Hannibal!!!!!

HANNIBAL I would like to ask you to maintain absolute silence about my plans.

EISERMANN You can count on it. They'd lock me up in a mental institution immediately... if I were to let them out... (*the doorbell rings*). What's all this constant ringing this morning? It's practically tearing your ears apart... (*there's a knock*).

HANNIBAL Come in!

LISA (*in the doorway*) Your Grace... the tailor.

EISERMANN The tailor?

HANNIBAL Just let him in.

> *Tailor PLÜDDECKE enters, carrying a suit wrapped in black cloth.*
> *LISA exits.*

PLÜDDECKE Most obedient servant, gentlemen, most obedient servant, Mr. Eisermann, it is my honor, Doctor.

HANNIBAL There you see, Papa... Mr. Plüddecke graciously awards me his honorary doctorate.

PLÜDDECKE Oh, my goodness, pardon me if I expressed myself awkwardly...

HANNIBAL Not at all, dear Plüddecke...

EISERMANN What do you actually want?

PLÜDDECKE The good Doctor... for heaven's sake...

HANNIBAL Feel free to call me Hannibal, dear Plüddecke, and if it makes you happy, you can even call me informally.

EISERMANN I don't appreciate these kinds of jokes... what's up with that, Plüddecke?

PLÜDDECKE I was given the honor and pleasure of ordering a... a... a... so to speak... a tailcoat from me...

EISERMANN Tailcoat?

PLÜDDECKE Tailcoat!!

EISERMANN Who?

PLÜDDECKE Oh, for heaven's sake... (*embarrassed gestures, nods at* HANNIBAL).

EISERMANN You?

HANNIBAL Yes, Papa...

EISERMANN Who gave you permission?

HANNIBAL But Papa... here in front of Mr. Plüddecke, who's a family man himself, isn't he, Mr. Plüddecke?

PLÜDDECKE God bless him... oh, for heaven's sake, pardon me, pardon me. Pardon me.

HANNIBAL to perform a family scene. I could say: the beautiful day outside or the butter lady or the umbrella stand... or you! That's not the point. I needed a tailcoat, I needed a tailcoat, and very logical, isn't it, Mr. Plüddecke...

PLÜDDECKE Oh, for heaven's sake, pardon me, indeed, pardon me, yes.

EISERMANN That's outrageous...

HANNIBAL Go ahead and unpack, dear Plüddecke.

> PLÜDDECKE *removes the handkerchief and a light green tailcoat appears.*

EISERMANN But it's green!

HANNIBAL Thank God!

PLÜDDECKE Indeed, pardon me, yes.

HANNIBAL Exactly as I intended!

PLÜDDECKE The gracious gentleman has, if I may say so, original taste. But, it is after all... a

HANNIBAL taste, as you would say, dear Plüddecke.

EISERMANN What's the meaning of this clowning around?

HANNIBAL The world must become greener again, Papa... Let's try it on, dear Plüddecke... (PLÜDDECKE *helps him try it on.*)

HANNIBAL Well, how does it fit?

PLÜDDECKE Oh, for heaven's sake... excellent... if I may put it that way.

EISERMANN I'm not paying him... for all I care, go ahead and declare bankruptcy.

HANNIBAL Oh, that wasn't difficult for me at all. But Master Plüddecke doesn't lose his wages. Someone else is paying him.

EISERMANN I'm curious who...

HANNIBAL (*slowly, emphasizing each word*) Miss Mary Eleonore Tunderstam.

PLÜDDECKE (*opens his mouth*).

EISERMANN You... You

HANNIBAL are crazy. I am, I know. Leave it, Dad. I had this tailcoat specially made to wear when I ask for her hand in marriage.

EISERMANN Whose hand?

HANNIBAL Miss Mary Eleonore Tunderstam's hand!

EISERMANN I don't have the money to pay the expensive costs of a cold-water sanatorium for you. (*He has sunk into a chair*).

HANNIBAL Oh, Miss Tunderstam will pay for everything. Provided you want to undergo the cold-water cure. I'll put in a good word for you with her. (*He rings the bell.*)

EISERMANN What do you want? (*LISA appears.*)

HANNIBAL Has the gardener already sent the orchid for the buttonhole?

LISA No, young sir.

HANNIBAL Send it over to him immediately. And pay right away, it costs twenty marks. Papa, perhaps you'd be so kind as to pay the small sum?

EISERMANN (*heaves a heavy sigh*) I don't want to embarrass you. You're not worth it. (*Hands the girl twenty marks. LISA exits.*)

HANNIBAL Where's the bill, Plüddecke?

PLÜDDECKE Please, pardon me, pardon me, most respectfully allow me to keep it here in my breast pocket.

HANNIBAL (*Takes the bill out of his pocket*) Three hundred and fifty marks? That's not too expensive. The bill will be paid the day after tomorrow at the latest. – You can go, Plüddecke. (*PLÜDDECKE exits.*) Today I'm asking for her hand.

EISERMANN For whose hand?

HANNIBAL For Miss Mary Eleonore Tunderstam's hand.

EISERMANN : If only Mama had lived to see this!!!!

HANNIBAL : She would have smiled and searched her memory — and found that perhaps... someone else could be my... father... and not... you!

EISERMANN Hannibal!

HANNIBAL Eisermann?!? (*Contemptuously.*)

Curtain.

Act Two

Miss's hotel room. Miss rings a bell on the table. Liddy appears from the next room.

Miss Tell the head waiter to have dinner served in my room. I don't feel like staring at fashion tourists and law clerks at the table d'hôte. Who else is outside?

Liddy *(tilts her head and goes out, returns momentarily, indicating with facial expressions and hand gestures that someone is waiting outside).*

Miss So, so... there's a lady here... did she give her name?

Liddy *(shakes her head).*

Miss Didn't she give you a card?

Liddy *(shakes her head).*

Miss Could she be related to me on my mother's side?

Liddy *(shrugs).*

Miss Please invite her in!

> Liddy leaves and immediately lets Miss Pompe enter. Miss Pompe is thirty-seven years old, thin, wears pince-nez with a black rim and band, and has sparse hair. She approaches with many curtsies.

Miss You can go, Liddy. *(Liddy leaves.)* How can I help you, Miss?

Miss Pompe My name is Pompe... Miss Pompe...

Miss Very pleased, please, will you not have a seat?

Miss Pompe Oh, thank you, you are so kind.

Miss What brings you to me?

Miss Pompe I am a needlework teacher at the local girls' middle school. This job... however rich my involvement in it... doesn't quite fill my spiritual life... so to speak. There's always a place left in it...

Miss Needlework teachers are very poorly paid, I imagine?

Miss Pompe Oh, if you only knew, Miss! Three hundred thalers!

Miss A month?

Miss Pompe You're making fun of me. You shouldn't. - A year, of course.

Miss That's not much, though. That's how much Papa's chauffeur gets a month. But we're getting off topic. You wanted to talk about the space that's still free in your soul, so to speak. Do you intend to get married? Do you need a dowry? How much? Liddy will pay it for you!

Miss Pompe My dear lady, you are too kind. My visit is connected with marriage, though I don't intend to get married. Men are so rude these days.

Miss Terribly rude.

Miss Pompe Don't take offense at my strong words, my lady... but: I know men.

You can't be forceful enough with them.

Miss I completely agree.

Miss Pompe I, too, loved once... let's not even mention it. I wanted to humbly invite you to become an honorary member of the General International Association of Virgins, whose chairwoman for Silesia and the Margraviate of Brandenburg stands before you. I've brought the certificate with me.

Miss How much does honorary membership cost?

Miss Pompe That's entirely up to you, my dear lady. Not less than ten thousand marks. You will then receive the title of honorary virgin.

Miss How do you know if I'm still a virgin?

Miss Pompe (*startled*) My dear lady... you must be joking... that goes without saying. If you're not married, then you're a virgin!

Miss Perhaps... but what are the tendencies of your society? Chastity?

Miss Pompe Also... by the way... It's essentially an economic organization intended to pioneer the social question of women.

Miss That's still not entirely clear to me. The members of your society pledge themselves to remain eternally virgins and never to marry?

Miss Pompe Absolutely not, my dear lady, absolutely not: anyone who marries may only marry a man who is capable of fully supporting a woman. The shameful dowry is completely eliminated. In recent times, men have increasingly disregarded and neglected their social duties. Anyone with a reasonably pretty face and not stupid married a rich girl and then indulged in a lazy and effeminate life of dissipation.

Miss There are a great many rich girls?

Miss Pompe I think so.

Miss Aren't girls to blame for this neglect of social duties by men?

Miss Pompe I beg your pardon, my dear lady! How can you confuse cause and effect like that? Someone like me, even someone trained in economics...

Miss I, too, studied economics, but I find I have too much money to fully understand poverty or despise stupidity. It's merely ridiculous and can be classified as a phenomenon and stimulus in our lives.

Miss Pompe Your life.

Miss Yes... my life. For me, there are only two kinds of people... those I like and those I dislike.

Miss Pompe That's a very simplistic view of life. Does that make you happy?

Miss I think so.

Miss Pompe And to which category of people do I belong?

Miss Of course, the former, my dear lady. So, of course, I'll gladly join your alliance and pay 20,000 marks. (*She rings the bell, LIDDY enters.*) Liddy, please be so kind as to give the lady 20,000 marks. I think there are a few dozen 1,000-mark notes left in the bedside table. Or do you have a few more in your apron pocket?

LIDDY (*takes a 10,000-mark note from her apron and gestures to indicate that she has no change*).

MISS Perhaps you could run over to the bakery; perhaps they can give you some change. Or let me... I'll look in my pocket; perhaps I still have some change. (*Opens her crocodile leather bag.*)

MISS POMPE Don't bother yourself, Miss.

MISS It's true... there are 20,000 marks here.

MISS POMPE (*rising*) In the name of the General International Association of Virgins for the Fight against Dowries, I hereby present to you, my dear lady, our certificate of honor. It is already signed (*kisses her hand*). My most heartfelt thanks in the name of all womanhood.

MISS Very well. Goodbye! Liddy, escort the lady out. (*MISS POMPE leaves with many bows. Exiting.*)

MISS POMPE Should I perhaps send you our brochures and leaflets... cash on delivery...?

MISS Please, as you wish. Goodbye.

> *MISS POMPE and LIDDY exit.*

MISS (*to herself*) ...These people... no, these people...

> *LIDDY returns, facial expressions.*

MISS So? A gentleman wishes to speak to me? Well, if you please, I'm in the mood to hold court today... show him in.

> *LIDDY opens the door. A. SCHULZ enters, saluting, wearing the uniform of a fire captain.*

MISS Sir?

A. SCHULZ Schulz is my name, Schulz, simply A. Schulz, not to be confused with B. Schultz and C. Schulze...

MISS Oh, please, no, you are not to be confused at all... wouldn't you like to sit down? Do you have a toothache?

A. SCHULZ Oh, please, no... it's just a habit of mine, twitching the left corner of my mouth. It's kind of hereditary in our family. Ever since my great-grandfather, Hyronimus Schulze. It's a very unpleasant thing. Especially on celebratory occasions, like funerals or the Kaiser's birthday celebrations. It looks like you're constantly laughing. But you're not actually laughing. I assure you, Miss, I'm a very serious person and a coal merchant by profession.

MISS How much do you need?

A. Schulz I... I don't know... I don't understand, what do you mean... to ask, humbly?

Miss How much money do you need?

A. Schulz Please... (*rises*) I am the court coal dealer to the Prince of Hohenzollern-Sigmaringen, who owns large hunting grounds in this area.

Miss And you supply him with coal for rabbit hunting?

A. Schulz I stand before you in my capacity as commander of the local volunteer fire department.

Miss Very pleased. But there's no fire here. So what is the purpose of your visit?

A. Schulz Please allow me to humbly point out that your mother was a native of this place, and I humbly wanted to ask you, on behalf of the volunteer fire department, not to take offense if you gave us a flag.

Miss For what?

A. Schulz For the volunteer fire department.

Miss Why does the fire department need a flag? You can't use it for firefighting, can you?

A. Schulz The volunteer fire departments of our neighboring towns, Schwiebus, Züllichau, Spremberg, Reppen, Drossen, even little Bobersberg, which has only nine hundred inhabitants but is home to a cloth factory, have long owned a flag. So it's painful for us to have to stand back during festive processions. Our cash register...

Miss Approved. (*Miss rings.*) (*Liddy comes.*) Liddy, please, give the gentleman from the bedside table a few hundred marks.

> *Liddy contemptuously slips a hundred-mark note into A. Schulz's hand.*

A. Schulz (*clears his throat*) My dear lady... the local volunteer fire department hereby humbly appoints you as its honorary member. You are kindly invited to the flag consecration ceremony. Good hose! (*Liddy lets him out, A. Schulz exits, Liddy returns, play of facial expressions.*)

Miss So...? Another gentleman is outside... Bring him in. (*Liddy opens the door: B. Schultz enters, saluting, in the uniform of a rifle major.*)

Miss Sir?

B. Schultz Schultz is my name, B. Schultz... simply B. Schultz... not to be confused with A. Schulz and C. Schulze. I come in my capacity as major of the local rifle guild. While the rifle guilds of our neighboring towns, Schwiebus, Züllichau, Spremberg, Reppen, Drossen, even little Bobersberg, which has only 900 inhabitants but does have a cloth factory, have long possessed a club flag, the Krossen a. O. rifle guild still has to do without one. Since your mother was born here — pardon me, I know — she is also buried here, and since you have honored us with your presence, my deepest condolences (*gets tangled up*).

MISS (*rings bell*). (*LIDDY enters*) Liddy, please give the gentleman a few hundred marks.

> *LIDDY contemptuously slips a few hundred-mark bills into B. SCHULTZ's hand.*

B. SCHULTZ (*clears his throat*) My sincere thanks. My dearest Miss... The Krossen Shooting Guild hereby appoints you, Miss, honorary markswoman for life. You are kindly invited to the flag consecration. Tally-ho.

> *Exits with LIDDY. LIDDY returns, speaking to another gentleman.*

MISS Sir?

C. SCHULZE (*in tails and top hat*) Schulze is my name... C. Schulze, simply C. Schulze... not to be confused with A. Schulz and B. Schultz. I take the liberty of standing before you in my capacity as president of the "Harmonie" bowling and skat club. While the bowling and skat clubs in our neighboring towns of Schwiebus, Züllichau, Spremberg, Reppen, Drossen, even little Bobersberg, which has only 900 inhabitants but is home to a cloth factory, have long since possessed a club flag, the "Harmonie" bowling and skat club still has to do without this ornament. Therefore, please humbly allow me... MISS (*signals LIDDY with her eyebrows*). (*LIDDY contemptuously slips a few hundred-mark bills from the bedside table into C. SCHULZE's hand.*)

C. SCHULZE (*clears his throat*) Most esteemed Miss! I hereby appoint you an honorary member of the "Harmonie" bowling and skat club. You are kindly invited to the flag consecration ceremony. There will be bratwurst with salad. I'll leave the certificate here. Good luck!

> *LIDDY exits with C. SCHULZE. LIDDY returns: contemptuously pushes MAXI BEERBAUM in front of her. LIDDY exits.*

MAXI BEERBAUM (*clicks his heels together — he's about 16, pince-nez, confirmation frock coat, angular movements, school cap*) Maxi Beerbaum.

MISS Very pleasant.

MAXI BEERBAUM My... my lady (*hands her a bouquet of roses*).

MISS Thank you very much, but thank you very much... is this for me? The beautiful roses? And they're red, too!

MAXI BEERBAUM Yes, they're red.

MISS So your name is Maxi, a lovely name. What grade are you in?

MAXI BEERBAUM If... even if you have a lot of money (*excitedly*) and are a millionaire, and that's why I'm coming to you, you can't address me informally. In the lower sixth form, we're already addressed formally!

MISS Oh, you're in the lower sixth form, I'm so sorry I forgot that. This school only goes up to the lower sixth form, I suppose.

MAXI BEERBAUM Yes, until the one-year anniversary. We're the first class here.

MISS So, of course, you play the leading role in this society...

MAXI BEERBAUM Indeed... we've mastered the dance lesson.

MISS Do the teachers allow these excesses?

MAXI BEERBAUM Oh, the teachers! If only you always followed what the school allowed you to do. You just don't ask them – and you don't get caught.

MISS So? So you indulge in forbidden pleasures?

MAXI BEERBAUM (*proudly*) Yes!!! We have a fraternity.

MISS What do you have?

MAXI BEERBAUM A fraternity. But you mustn't betray us.

MISS No, never!

MAXI BEERBAUM Marchia is your banner, and your first officer (*bows*) is Maxi Beerbaum.

MISS Congratulations!

MAXI BEERBAUM Thank you very much!

MISS What do you mainly do in the fraternity? Drink?

MAXI BEERBAUM Yes, mainly drink.

MISS Does that serve any purpose?

MAXI BEERBAUM Of course! The students do it too. The beer mug is the symbol of masculinity, and of freedom from school. Because it's forbidden. And that's what matters.

MISS So?

MAXI BEERBAUM You should only do what's forbidden, then you're already doing the right thing, says Hannibal.

MISS Who says that?

MAXI BEERBAUM Hannibal! Don't you know him?

MISS Not a bit.

MAXI BEERBAUM He's our honorary member. And he's the one who gave us the courage to send me here to you. And he also said I should give you his regards.

MISS Thank you very much. – But what do you actually want?

MAXI BEERBAUM We wanted to ask if you could transfer a small contribution to our fraternity's funds for the anniversary celebration. You can afford it, can't you?

MISS Oh?

MAXI BEERBAUM You know, our finances are in a pretty tight spot!

MISS It's like that all over the world — how much do you need?

MAXI BEERBAUM If we could perhaps ask you for a loan of five marks — for ninety-nine years.

MISS Ninety-nine years? Who told you that?

MAXI BEERBAUM Hannibal! He says it's Chinese law. A decent person could only abide by Chinese law.

MISS But Chinese law gives crooks and fools wooden collars — does Hannibal know that?

MAXI BEERBAUM I think so. Hannibal knows everything.

MISS He must be a genius.

MAXI BEERBAUM That's the right word: he's a genius, pardon me, as we say in our corps language.

MISS So, at his —...at Hannibal's intercession, I want, even though it's actually immoral —

MAXI BEERBAUM Immoral? Why? Hannibal says there's no such thing.

MISS So, I'd like to enrich your corps fund with a fifty-mark note. Here you go (*gives him the note*).

MAXI BEERBAUM Thank you very much. My mission is accomplished. We'll allow ourselves to rub an honorary salamander on you, my lady, at the next pub. Marchia vivat crescal floreat in aelernum[13] (*bows, exits*).

> *The doorbell rings, the MISS looks amused at the bouquet of roses. LIDDY goes out, back, beaming from ear to ear.*

MISS What's wrong, Liddy? What happened? Did he pinch your arm?

LIDDY (*still laughing, making all sorts of signs*).

MISS Good God, there's another gentleman outside... and a strange one? It's all in one. Let him in! (*LIDDY goes out, lets HANNIBAL enter. HANNIBAL casually presses a five-mark piece into her hand. LIDDY suddenly becomes serious and disappears. HANNIBAL is wearing a green tailcoat, knee breeches, and black silk stockings. Chapeau claque. An orchid in her buttonhole.*)

MISS (*looks at him, wants to smile, meets his gaze, holds back the smile, serious, a little uneasy*) Sir, how can I help you?

HANNIBAL My name is Hannibal.

MISS Hannibal?

HANNIBAL Hannibal! Hannibal! A name that suits me extraordinarily well.

MISS A name that suits you extraordinarily well.

HANNIBAL Please, I have said, it stands before me. The other name can be found

---

[13] May the March live, grow, and flourish forever.

nowadays in every farce. No one laughs about it anymore. This "it" means "pro," in Latin as in "to protect," "to shield," because this name stands before me like a guard, so that no one can get close to me.

Miss What is your last name?

Hannibal The last name doesn't matter. That's my father's name too. I have nothing else in common with him.

Miss So your name is just... Hannibal?

Hannibal At least for you. My mother gave me the name. She must have bore a great resemblance to you.

Miss (*smiling*) How do you know?

Hannibal If I hadn't known, I wouldn't have come here at all. – I saw you walking down the street yesterday. The way you walked charmed me, and I thought if I had ever seen my mother walk, her walk would have been like yours.

Miss Did you never see your mother walk? That's strange.

Hannibal Oh... not so much! She was paralyzed when she gave birth to me.

Miss (*silence – then*) Hannibal... isn't that the general of whom it is said: he came, he saw, he conquered?

Hannibal I don't know for sure, because I've never studied history. But it must be so.

Miss What are you actually looking for from me?

Hannibal What all the others who have already been with you, and those who are yet to come, will be looking for: money. And maybe a little more...

Miss Are you in financial difficulties? Do you owe me? If only you're not mistaken about me. I won't lend you anything.

Hannibal I don't want to borrow anything.

Miss But?

Hannibal A gift... Completely voluntary... Of course...

Miss So... that goes without saying?

Hannibal Yes!

Miss I've never met a person like you.

Hannibal I believe that. But it's a good thing. If there were more people like me, I wouldn't be so highly regarded. — And that would be a shame. I'm at least 529. Then I wouldn't be able to rate myself so highly compared to you.

Miss You are very... conceited, very... proud.

Hannibal I think I have the right to. At least as much right as the others have to their so-called humility. But won't you have a seat? (*Sits down. The Miss sits down. Hannibal pulls out his cigarette case*) Do you smoke?

Miss Please... (*takes a cigarette*).

Hannibal Do you have a light?

Miss (*Rings the bell.*) (*Liddy enters*) Liddy, a candle! (*Liddy exits, immediately returns with a candle, holds it out to Hannibal first; one senses the respect she suddenly feels for Hannibal. Liddy exits.*)

Hannibal I only smoke American cigarettes. That's the most honest way.

Miss Are you so enthusiastic about honesty?

Hannibal Oh! Not in the least! But in this case, yes.

Miss I don't understand. Is it supposed to be a compliment to me, because I'm American — at least by nationality — that you smoke American cigarettes?

Hannibal Certainly! It's also a compliment to the American spirit, which is so amiably embodied in you. I pay homage to it by openly smoking American cigarettes, cigarettes that sail under the American flag. While the good German generally smokes American cigarettes, which are under a good German company, and behind which lies only the American cigarette trust.

Miss You seem to be intensely concerned with national economic issues. Are you perhaps (*in view of Hannibal's tailcoat*) a disguised government assessor?

Hannibal My dear lady, you underestimate me when it comes to economic matters. Incidentally, I could be a government assessor. It seems quite decorative. At least in word.

Miss And what are you?

Hannibal Why so curious? I only allow myself curiosity, never others.

Miss So a kind of... moral philosopher?

Hannibal Unfortunately, I tend to moralize. But I fight this fatal tendency most vigorously.

Miss I don't even fight it; I indulge all my... inclinations. What is your profession?

Hannibal I'm a lyric poet...

Miss Ah, you write poetry?

Hannibal For God's sake! I've never written a lyrical poem and never will — that's my pride. I'm a poet because I live my whole life lyrically and emotionally. I've never expressed myself so thoughtfully — that's all your fault!

Miss But what do you actually want from me?

Hannibal Marry me!

Miss Marry?

Hannibal Marry me!

Miss And on top of that, first, I'm supposed to pay your debts and second, possibly your dowry.

HANNIBAL Something like that.

MISS Because the girl is surely very poor? Poets always love very poor women.

HANNIBAL I can't say the same about myself.

MISS Who do you actually want to marry?

HANNIBAL You!!!

MISS Who?

HANNIBAL You!!!!!

MISS (*jumping up*) Me???

HANNIBAL Yes! Of course!

MISS Of course?

HANNIBAL Does that seem so surprising to you?

MISS After all...

HANNIBAL I don't think so at all. I consider it the most natural thing in the world. If you love me, why shouldn't you marry me?

MISS I... love you???????

HANNIBAL I think so!

MISS You're a delightful person!

HANNIBAL You see!

MISS But love!

HANNIBAL Why not?

MISS And marriage?!!

HANNIBAL Yes, marriage will probably be unavoidable!!

MISS Why?

HANNIBAL Because I really don't just love your money.

MISS Oh?? How lovely!

HANNIBAL But also you as a person...

MISS Then why don't you try to seduce me and make me your lover?

HANNIBAL But I've been doing that ever since I stood here before you!

MISS Excuse me... Hannibal... I can't marry a man with such principles, let alone... love him. Do you even have a job where you work?

HANNIBAL No! Never! How could I?

MISS And then you want to marry me, the daughter of Tunderstam, who from early childhood was told: Work! Work! Man must work! Look at your father! In winter at six, in summer at five in the morning, he gets up and works with little interruption until the gray evening. He's become surly, bitter, nervous, and a misanthropist, so nervous that he can no longer sleep alone at night — but he's become rich, and in all the school textbooks you'll find his essay: "Work, Life's Ornament." He's amassed a fortune of eight hundred million dollars.

HANNIBAL Seven hundred and thirty-seven, please. I asked at the information office. But he only amassed this wealth so that a reasonable person — reasonable in my sense — would one day make proper use of it. That reasonable person is me!

MISS You know that for a fact?

HANNIBAL Yes, indeed.

MISS You may be mistaken! I followed in my father's footsteps. I learned to work... As a student at universities on both continents. I hold doctorates in law and philosophy.

HANNIBAL (*melancholy*) Not me...

MISS I've studied humanity in particular, and now I'm looking for someone to whom I could donate my fortune... a person, a poor devil... no, not some humanitarian organization for rescued suicides, or anti-vaxxers, or free universities. This humanity disgusts me. To one person, to one person, I want to give everything. That seems to me true humanity!

HANNIBAL Excellent, Miss! We agree perfectly.

MISS If I gave the seven hundred and thirty-seven million dollars to someone, someone who knew what to do with it, and kept only the bare minimum for myself... would you still want to marry me?

HANNIBAL But no! Never! Without money, never! I can't live without money.

MISS As we all know, other people can't either.

HANNIBAL But I can't live without a lot of money.

MISS Create the money you need, produce it, isn't productivity the highest thing?!

HANNIBAL Wrong! You're mistaken. The highest, or if you will, deepest life is led by what I would call passive genius, who gathers all life forces within himself for his own use, for private use, and doesn't altruistically scatter them to the winds, where they have indeed been given over to the wind, and like flower seeds, are only just by chance used by the right person. The fable about the sole value of productive genius was only invented by vain artists, poets, and men of letters. They live off it in the people's estimation. It's also a kind of priestly lie. The audience in the stalls claps when they see one of their gods, tenors, dancers, or poets hopping across the stage. I'm disgusted by playing the fool for others. At most, I play him for myself.

MISS (*looks at his clothes*) You look colorful enough to be a clown.

HANNIBAL Green is the color of my soul. If I were to appear in a farce in this green tailcoat, it would be a shocking joke for the frugal audience. It alone would be enough to fill three acts. Look, they would scream, and their bellies would rise and fall with laughter like the glass balls in the water features, look at the green boy. Isn't that splendid? Isn't that hilarious? Isn't that bursting?

MISS So what do you live on? You... passive genius?

HANNIBAL On myself! There's a saying that someone else brought out of me: A little intelligence is acquired by cultivating the imagination, and much nobility by looking at beautiful things.

MISS And that's how you live?

HANNIBAL Yes... even at this moment, as I look at you, I am increasing my capital of nobility again, speaking in the presumed language of your hopefully immortalized father.

MISS Why?

HANNIBAL You are beautiful!

MISS It's no use to you... I'm not marrying you... Apart from your mother, I don't even know your family.

HANNIBAL They're not worth looking at. With one exception.

MISS Who is that?

HANNIBAL My sister.

MISS Can't I meet her,... your sister?

HANNIBAL If you wish.

MISS Is she sweet... your sister?... She must be very sweet!

HANNIBAL Yes, very... But if you like her... then agree to the marriage...

MISS To what marriage?!

HANNIBAL To our marriage!!

MISS Oh, I hadn't thought of that anymore.

HANNIBAL That's unfortunate.

MISS I always just thought... that you had a sister.

HANNIBAL Whom you'd like to meet. So please be at Prangerstrasse eleven for coffee today at four o'clock.

MISS That's where you live? What neighborhood! The "Father Rhine" restaurant is there, too, isn't it?

HANNIBAL How do you know about this, the only worthwhile restaurant in this area?

MISS Someone was talking about it, not too quietly, at the table d'hôte yesterday... Man, that means some toothbrush and woolen goods travelers. – So that's where you live, in Prangergasse?

HANNIBAL Not me. But my sister does. We'll celebrate the engagement party at her place.

MISS I don't think so!

HANNIBAL I hope so!

MISS It's surprising that you don't live with your sister. Is she married?

HANNIBAL No. It's only natural for people like me and my sister not to live together.

MISS Is she employed?

HANNIBAL As a maid, you mean? Yes! She's a cook for the handsome Oskar.

MISS Who's that?

HANNIBAL My father! May I say goodbye now?

MISS Please... what are you putting on the table?

HANNIBAL Oh... a small thing... an unpaid bill... for the tailcoat I'm wearing... I
had it made especially for you. Just for you! Within 24 hours.

MISS It's fine. See you at four o'clock at your sister's.

HANNIBAL You're coming?

MISS Certainly!

HANNIBAL (*kisses her hand*) I could... kiss more, but I can wait. (*Bows, exits.*)

MISS (*watches him go, examines the bill, smiles, becomes serious, LIDDY appears*)
How do you like the gentleman who just left?

LIDDY (*play of facial expressions*) Excellent!

MISS You don't really have bad taste. But I don't know... (*The doorbell rings.*) Go
see, Liddy. (*LIDDY exits, returns with a card, which she hands to MISS.*)

MISS Eisermann? Eisermann? What's that? Hopefully the last one for this morning. Hannibal's visit really got to me. I've grown quite hungry. - Bring him
in.

LIDDY exits, returns with EISERMANN, LIDDY goes into the next room.

EISERMANN Eisermann is my name... Eisermann... Excuse me, Miss, for intruding
on my plans... But it's an important matter. I'm partly here to discuss the
new gasometer at our gasworks...

MISS Gasometer?

EISERMANN Yes, haven't you read the newspaper?

MISS I only read scandal sheets — you know the "truth," for example — but not a
newspaper.

EISERMANN Then, while you're here, you should take a look at our local paper
every now and then. It's excellently edited.

MISS I'll follow your advice.

EISERMANN But secondly, I came to prevent a stupid prank, hopefully soon enough.

MISS What stupid thing did I do?

EISERMANN (*laughing*) Oh, no! I mean a stupid prank someone wants to play on you... Has my son been here yet?

MISS Excuse me: What's your son's name? Schulze, perhaps, or Maxi?

EISERMANN My son's name is Hannibal... Hannibal Eisermann.

MISS A young man named Hannibal was just here with me.

EISERMANN (*drops into an armchair*) Then it's too late... oh, don't hold a grudge against me, an unfortunate father, for what he failed to do.

MISS Then you are... Excuse me, your son called you that, the handsome Oskar?

EISERMANN (*startled*) The handsome Oskar? The handsome Oskar? (*twitches his lips convulsively.*) The handsome Oskar... me? I? That city scoundrel, me, me? Miss... do you mean to insult me?

MISS Pardon me if I did you wrong. – By the way... your son didn't do anything wrong, nor did he play any mean tricks on me. He just wanted to marry me!

EISERMANN The fool! The impudent...

MISS Oh, I think that's very reasonable and, since he's a charming man, not at all impertinent. (*There's a knock.*) Come in! Come in!

    A WAITER *enters.*

WAITER I wanted to set the table for dinner. Miss Hall ordered it to be served in your room.

MISS Yes, please, set the table. And bring two place settings. Mr. Eisermann is my guest. You'll do me the pleasure, won't you? We'll talk about the gasometer later!

EISERMANN I've already eaten once... but if I can atone a little for my son's impudence, I'd be happy to... I would be delighted to bring home favorable news of the gasometer to the city council.

MISS We'll see... As an hors d'oeuvre: caviar on toast... You'll like it, won't you, Mr. Eisermann?

EISERMANN You've perfectly matched my taste. Caviar could get me out of bed at midnight.

    The WAITER *bows, exits.*

MISS What's that? My purse was just lying on the table? (*Pauses*) Oh, I see... Hannibal was with me...

EISERMANN (*dismayed*) Hannibal stole the purse... I dare not say the word, stole it?

MISS Oh, no... just took it. Without my permission. But I'll give it to him later...
    Curtain!

Act Three

Handsome Oskar's sparse and poor apartment in Prangerstrasse.
Maedele at the window, a shard of glass in her hand. Handsome
Oskar is busy repairing a clock.

Oskar I... can't stand the Nordhäuser... anymore... I can't stand it anymore, it always pinches my stomach like a cancer. I have to switch to Kottbuser... or cold grog...

Maedele Father, I've found another piece of glass...

Oskar Show me, what does it look like?

Maedele (*holds the glass out to him without turning away from the window*) It's from a wine bottle, I've never seen one that color before, Father.

Oskar Holy moly, the world looks like brown mush in it.

Maedele (*looks through it*) The sky looks completely rusted in it, Father. – If you press the glass up close to your eyes, you see nothing but this rust on everything, on the houses, on the trees, on the people – and the people have eyes as red as rabbits. Or have they been crying so much? I could spend my whole life looking through glass.

Oskar God has given us enough shards, you didn't need to collect them, Maedele.

Maedele Of course, not always with the same shard: sometimes blue, sometimes green, sometimes yellow, sometimes violet, but I prefer red. Then everything burns, the streets and the trees and the towers and the clouds and the forests, everything burns brightly. And everything that doesn't usually burn burns brightly. The clouds and the forests and the people, who don't usually burn, burn brightly. — Father, I love to watch when things burn.

Oskar Your mother, girl, was mistaken, God bless her. In the ninth month, there was a roof fire over there in the night, and mother saw the light through the curtain.

Maedele Father, I'd like to set something on fire sometime, a haystack in the field, when the moon is shining.

Oskar If the police come, Maedele, they'll throw you in jail.

Maedele But I don't want to light it with matches. With my eyes, Father, only with my eyes.

Oskar They'll tear your eyes out of your head, Maedele.

Maedele Then my heart will still be burning, Father. (*Pause.*)

Oskar Where did you find the shard, Maedele?

Maedele At the scrap heap by the gasworks.

Oskar Must be from old Eisermann, the wine bottle; he drinks such fine brands and leaves his son thirsty.

Maedele Hannibal...

OSKAR Hannibal, that's a proud name, it's Hebrew and means something with the devil, with Baal, you know.

MAEDELE I think Hannibal drinks the fine brands and father must be thirsty — can't he give anything to his father?

OSKAR No, Maedele. He doesn't even have a glass to drink from.

MAEDELE What if I gave him this shard?

OSKAR He'd laugh at you, Maedele.

MAEDELE Father, I had to dig this shard out of the earth first. All shards that glitter so beautifully in the sun have to be dug out of the ashes first. Don't you think, Father, that the shards lie unjustly in the ashes, where the sun can't even see them? And the sun loves to reflect itself in the shards; they both have so much in common, the sun and the shards. That's why I put all my broken pieces every noon, the red and the blue and the green and the yellow, on the windowsill in the sun, Father (*short pause*). (*MAEDELE steps in front of a framed photograph hanging to the left of the door.*) You — Father

OSKAR Yes?

MAEDELE The day after tomorrow is her birthday...

OSKAR (*sighing*) I know... I know...

MAEDELE I'll go to the meadow and look for forget-me-nots and weave a wreath for her...

OSKAR Do it, Maedele, she'll thank you in heaven.

MAEDELE Is she in heaven, Father?

OSKAR How can you ask, Maedele! She was so good.

MAEDELE And beautiful.

OSKAR And sad...

MAEDELE And sick...

OSKAR Yes; But only later, Maedele, not when she brought me this picture...

MAEDELE Tell me more about her... How did you get to know her... Father...

OSKAR Oh... I was still young then... and handsomer than now, you can believe me... I hadn't met your mother, the brown Marie, God rest her soul, yet... I was young... and cheerful... and in summer nights I loved to sleep outside in the open field, under a wild bush, with only the dark sky and God's starry eyes above me... Of course... I was already a city scoundrel back then... my father had also been a city scoundrel... and such things are inherited... this dignity is inherited like the dignity of emperor or king... One evening, it might have been around ten o'clock, I was lying in the grass by the swine pool — you know that pond, it's very deep, deeper than the Oder, and the creeping plants grow rampantly at its bottom, and they won't let go of anyone once they have them. — The crickets were chirping only sporadically — when suddenly the bushes next to me cracked, I heard soft footsteps... I thought it was a deer going to drink... it was a woman... and what she was planning... you can imagine... she wanted to jump into the water... I was on my two feet like lightning and pulled her back... "By what right do you drag me back to this hated life?" she said. "By the right I claim for myself!" I said. Then I suddenly recognized her... And she recognized me... I was the town tramp... and she... she... — But she wasn't afraid of me. We sat down in the grass. Then she said all sorts of things... stammered... cursed... cried... suddenly we kissed and were very happy. Then she went back to the city. I knew she would stay alive... want to live... (*Pause.*) I mean, Hannibal hasn't been here for a long time.

MAEDELE Not for at least two weeks.

OSKAR The next time Hannibal comes... we'll have very long conversations, philosophical ones. I don't even know if you'll be allowed to be there. Maybe you'll have to go to the closet.

MAEDELE Please, Father, let me be there, I want to be completely quiet too.

OSKAR Hannibal, with all due respect, Mädele, that's a man who really understands life and (*points to his heart*) has it here. (*There's a knock.*)

MAEDELE There was a knock, Father. (*MAEDELE goes to the door and opens it.*)

HANNIBAL enters, without his monocle.

MAEDELE (*pleased*) Hannibal! We were just talking about you.

HANNIBAL Greetings, my friends, good day, Mädele, let me kiss you on the forehead, my little sister! (*kisses her.*)

OSKAR (*he stands up, shakes his hand*) Well, Hannibal, how are you?

HANNIBAL Tolerable. I just had a nasty mishap.

MAEDELE I'm getting scared, Hannibal...

HANNIBAL Imagine, I'm just walking past the school building and thinking, God rest my soul, my school days — then...

MAEDELE Then...

OSKAR Then...

HANNIBAL Then the monocle pops out of my eye like an animal... like an independent being, falls to the pavement and shatters!

MAEDELE (*holds out the shard, laughing*) Here, take this, Hannibal.

HANNIBAL Thank you, Maedele, for your participation. By the way, the humanistic high school is solely to blame for the accident, like so many other misfortunes these days.

OSKAR You're absolutely right, I went up to sixth grade and can judge that. They kicked me out in sixth grade because I got sick one day.

HANNIBAL Yes, alcohol poisoning.

OSKAR Isn't that perhaps an illness?

HANNIBAL The monocle, so to speak, shied away from this repugnant institution, so inwardly hostile to it; it wanted to fight against it personally and on principle — but it was crushed under the force of fate. Do you have a good schnapps, Oskar?

OSKAR Right away... right away... Maedele, go into the kitchen.

MAEDELE Right away, Father (*exits*). (*Back right away with a bottle and two glasses.*)

HANNIBAL There, I brought you some imported liquors too.

OSKAR Ah! Your old man is quite useful sometimes.

HANNIBAL Yes, when he's buying cigars, not otherwise. Apart from that, I don't care about my God-given dependence on him, which I'll soon shed.

MAEDELE Here you go, Hannibal, help yourself.

HANNIBAL Thank you very much, Maedele.

OSKAR Why?

HANNIBAL You'll find out in a moment. — Cheers, Maedele!

MAEDELE Thank you, Hannibal.

OSKAR Cheers, Hannibal!

HANNIBAL You'll be receiving a visitor today (*looks at the clock*), in ten minutes...

OSKAR Visitor? – Us?

MAEDELE From whom then?

HANNIBAL From a lady!

MAEDELE A lady?

OSKAR Does she want me to repair her watch?

HANNIBAL Not so much, but her worldview, so to speak. I told her about you and what an important philosophical mind you were...

MAEDELE Did you tell her about me too, Hannibal?

HANNIBAL Of course; I called you my little sister and told her how pretty and good you were. Then she showed great longing to meet you.

MAEDELE Is she — young, the lady, Hannibal?

HANNIBAL Yes, Maedele.

MAEDELE And beautiful?

HANNIBAL Very beautiful.

MAEDELE And blonde?

HANNIBAL Extraordinarily blonde.

MAEDELE And good?

HANNIBAL So good.

OSKAR And rich?

HANNIBAL Very rich!

OSKAR Why don't you marry her?

HANNIBAL I will!

OSKAR But she doesn't want to?

MAEDELE Father, it's quite impossible that a lady who wants to marry Hannibal doesn't like him.

HANNIBAL I brought you something too, Maedele, here you go!

Takes the stolen wallet out of his pocket and throws it to the MAEDELE.

OSKAR What is that?

MAEDELE A wallet, and it's filled with paper! How strange!

HANNIBAL It's from the young, blond, beautiful, good, rich lady. She's sending it to you as a welcome in advance and as a contribution to your future dowry.

OSKAR Let me see that, Maedele!

MAEDELE (*hands the purse to OSKAR*) There.

OSKAR (*examining the wallet*) But those are... one... two... three... four... five... six... seven... eight... nine... ten... eleven thousand-mark bills.

HANNIBAL They're even real. – Not the fake ones we once tried to make – unfortunately, without success.

OSKAR (*delighted*) Eleven thousand-mark bills! Maedele! And that's yours? That'll make a great cold grog tonight!

HANNIBAL Yes, it's Maedele's. But perhaps she'll give you some.

MAEDELE (*embracing her father*) Anything, if you want it, anything. I don't know what to do with it. – You should have brought me the coral necklace, Hannibal, that you promised me a long time ago.

HANNIBAL You'll have that too, Maedele, and with the ten thousand mark dowry – I'm inclined to increase the dowry if necessary – a handsome man to go with it.

MAEDELE I don't want to get married at all, Hannibal, I'll enter your household as a maid.

HANNIBAL I think that can be arranged, maid, if you promise me to always boil the eggs until they're soft-boiled, do you hear, soft-boiled.

MAEDELE Of course.

HANNIBAL Or even better, eggs in a glass and lots of cognac!

MAEDELE I'll do whatever you want. But I want to stay with you, Hannibal.

HANNIBAL But then you might suddenly marry. For example, my servant, a blood-thirsty Black Moor or a vermillion-skinned Fuegian.

MAEDELE Ugh, Hannibal, ugh!

HANNIBAL Or my chauffeur, who looks like a grizzly bear in his fur coat.

MAEDELE Brrrrrrr.

HANNIBAL Or my hairdresser! On Sundays, you let him curl your hair and spray you with perfume.

MAEDELE You're disgusting, Hannibal. If I were to marry anyone, I'd marry you at the very most.

HANNIBAL I'm very sorry. Unfortunately, I'm already taken. I realize that it'll be difficult for you to find a match of my own. You see, I hold you in such high esteem that, apart from myself, I don't really begrudge you to anyone.

MAEDELE Now we're talking all sorts of nonsense here and have completely forgotten that we're having visitors. I'll just quickly go into the kitchen next door and make some coffee.

OSKAR You can get cake too, but not from old Sehmücke with his three-pack cakes, but from Hofmann's pastry shop, but not too much. – For 150 marks at the most. You can pay from the dowry.

MAEDELE Goodbye, Hannibal, goodbye, father, see you in five minutes. (*MAEDELE exit.*)

HANNIBAL She's delightful, Oskar. She's becoming more and more like my sister.

OSKAR Why don't you marry her? I would if I were you.

HANNIBAL She's still too young for me... sixteen. Besides, you shouldn't marry your sister; there's a bad breed; that's bad breeding. And I don't want my son ruined.

OSKAR You're right. And a man like you can't marry without money.

HANNIBAL (*laughing*) Not even live. – But it's very disastrous that I don't have my monocle. I'm starting to give my facial muscles too much freedom and laugh... a man like me should only smile... and even smile rarely.

OSKAR There's someone outside the door.

HANNIBAL (*goes to the door, opens it*) Come in, please... You're on time, Miss. (*The Miss has entered.*) – May I introduce my father, the handsome Oskar, so named from his youth, and the street urchin. – Miss Mary – I've forgotten your last name, what was your name again?

MISS Mary Eleonore Tunderstam, Dr. jur. et phil.

HANNIBAL Ah, Tunderstam! Right. Miss Mary Tunderstam, my bride!

OSKAR Very pleased, Miss, to welcome you to my humble home.

MISS I've also brought your second father, Hannibal. (*Calling out the door*) Mr. Eisermann... (*EISERMANN appears, with a jealous expression.*)

HANNIBAL Forgive me, Papa, for poorly concealing my disappointment at having to welcome you here as well.

EISERMANN That's outrageous!

MISS Hannibal!

HANNIBAL Mary? – By the way, allow me to introduce you two. The handsome Oskar, my father – Mr. Eisermann, my papa. Please, won't you gentlemen make yourselves comfortable? The tea will be served immediately by galloon-clad servants – in green livery, of course, green like my tailcoat. (*They sit down.*)

OSKAR But there's only coffee – and it won't be too strong. We harvested and dried it ourselves.

HANNIBAL The handsome Oskar is the owner of a coffee plantation in the Indies. There he grows the finest mocha in the world. And we'll be drinking mocha today, mocha made by himself, in a machine.

EISERMANN (*to the Miss*) That you brought me to this... house! Directly across from the "Father Rhine!"

OSKAR I think I've seen you in Prangergasse before, Mr. Eisermann. If I remember correctly, you paid a visit to the house across the street quite late at night, it was 1:00 a.m.?

EISERMANN That's slander... that... that... I'll take it from you.

HANNIBAL It's a shame, Papa, that you weren't really there. I had hoped to pay you a compliment for once.

EISERMANN (*to Miss*) If only no one had seen me! It seemed to me as if the Deputy Mayor had been standing at the entrance to the alley when I slipped into the house! I can only excuse it by saying that I wanted to do some research... in the poorhouses... I'm a councilman — and in addition to the department for the gas works, I also have the department for the poor.

MISS You can say that. I hope you're not lying.

HANNIBAL Hopefully not? Unfortunately not!

EISERMANN (*to the Miss*) What do you mean? No! Certainly not!

OSKAR Will you be staying in our town longer, Miss? Or have you only come here to get engaged to Hannibal?

MISS I don't know anything about the engagement yet, Mr....

HANNIBAL He doesn't have a real name, Mary. You must call him the handsome Oskar... or Father.

MISS Then I'd rather... Father.

EISERMANN How?? How????

MISS I traveled here to visit my mother's grave, which is buried in the Bergfried-hof, as she wished.

OSKAR Yes, next to Frederick the Great's general. Your mother and the general, those are the two sights of the cemetery.

HANNIBAL You even have a star in the tourist guide published by the Beautification Society; I even believe your mother has two stars.

OSKAR Still not as much as a good cognac. – If Hannibal were to be buried here, with you, in an oak double coffin, we'd have one more sight to see.

HANNIBAL Thank you for your kind suggestion. It will be explored in due course. This place isn't unsuitable for burial. But for now, we're still alive. Thank God. And very much so. Aren't we, Miss Mary?

MISS Thank God!

HANNIBAL Where are we going for our honeymoon? I think Japan. To see the geishas. What do you think?

MISS You're starting to get a little... curious.

HANNIBAL Please, I can't offer my bride

MISS Bride!?

HANNIBAL Bride, don't allow that tone of voice towards me. By the way, you're just jealous. Because of the geishas. They are indeed intoxicating creatures. This Japan in general: The hotel industry is at a unique level. It is far more developed than the European one. In Japan, you rent a room including light, breakfast, service day and night – service: female, of course, in the best sense of the word. Love is also included.

EISERMANN Hannibal! Stop these obscene indecencies.

HANNIBAL Well, I can't imagine anything more beautiful than such a... enchant-ing... little... oh so little Japanese woman. Japanese women are so small. (*The Miss turns away. HANNIBAL pauses, looks at her.*)

HANNIBAL Yes, I can think of something even more beautiful: you, Mary, you!!!

MISS Oh, I don't believe you.

EISERMANN Don't believe him, Miss.

OSKAR Believe him, Miss. There is no one in the world more honest than Hanni-bal. In his way.

MISS In his way! Do you even know loyalty to women?

HANNIBAL Not yet! But you're supposed to teach me that!

MISS Because of my... money?

HANNIBAL Yes...

EISERMANN Hannibal!

HANNIBAL And because of your... humanity...

MISS Your flattery fails!

HANNIBAL On the contrary. I can see it in your eyes!

MISS What are my eyes doing?

HANNIBAL They shine — like the sea sometimes on a summer night.

MISS Are you far-sighted?

HANNIBAL Oh, no! But I see into the future. Into our future, Mary.

MISS Do they belong together?

HANNIBAL Yes.

MISS How do you know that?

HANNIBAL Because your hands tremble towards her.

MISS You prophet!

HANNIBAL I'm a... fortune teller (*takes her hands, kisses them*).

MAEDELE comes from the left with the coffee.

HANNIBAL My sister, Maedele —

EISERMANN Sister? Sister? Am I stupid?

HANNIBAL (*to EISERMANN*) Yes! (*to MAEDELE*) My bride, Mary.

MAEDELE (*stands embarrassed with the tray in front of MISS*).

MISS How old are you then?

MAEDELE Sixteen years...

MISS Come, show me your eyes! Give me your hand, you shall be my sister too. And address me informally.

EISERMANN (*is dismayed*).

MISS My name is Mary, and you?

MAEDELE Maedele.

MISS Come, I'll help you set the coffee table.

MAEDELE But I don't have any cake yet! Just imagine, Father, when the baker saw the paper I gave him to pay with, and you said it was worth a thousand marks, he didn't want to give me anything for it, saying it was fake or stolen.

HANNIBAL Stolen? The boy is slandering me.

EISERMANN A thousand marks, where did you get the thousand marks, Maedele?

MAEDELE From Hannibal.

EISERMANN Hannibal?

MAEDELE He gave it to me as a greeting (*to Miss*) from... from... you!

MISS (*kisses MAEDELE*) He was right. Thank God we don't need to buy cake from that baker who annoyed you so much; I brought some myself. (*Goes out into the hall, returns with a large bag of cake, which she pours onto a plate.*) Now, pour the coffee, Maedele. (*MAEDELE does it.*)

EISERMANN Hannibal... You, I don't know whether to say it laughing or crying: scoundrel.

HANNIBAL Do you want a liqueur, Papa... to calm your nerves?

EISERMANN Thanks... after the coffee... By the way, you seem to be playing the host here too.

HANNIBAL Being the host! Isn't that right, Oskar?

OSKAR Yes! Everywhere Hannibal goes, he's the host!

MISS Are you finished pouring? Maedele?

MAEDELE Yes, almost.

MISS Then sit here next to me, like this... now I'm going to give a speech, the first speech of my life. Hannibal, my fiancé, give me your hand.

EISERMANN (*wiping the sweat from his brow*) Am I sane?

HANNIBAL Papa, pull yourself together, the esteemed speaker didn't interrupt.

MISS Like Diogenes, I wandered about with the lantern of my instincts — forgive the bold image — seeking a man who, to put it philosophically, would be my equal. Father will understand.

OSKAR Completely.

EISERMANN Not me.

MISS In you, Hannibal, I have found him, the man of my kind and my time. I already knew that when you paid me that strange visit this morning. I at least suspected it, but I hesitated because I wanted to see you working in an environment that was foreign to me.

HANNIBAL Oh, Doctor of Philosophy!

MISS That's why I came here. I met you once again in your siblings: in Maedele and in your father. I know you will be faithful to me; you must be, after all, we are children of a race that is spread across the earth in so few specimens and sometimes seems almost extinct: the race of primitive people. You are brave, cheerful, uncomplicated, impudent, genuine, a dreamer and adventurer, in love with every reality. Kiss me, Hannibal! (*HANNIBAL kisses her.*)

HANNIBAL I ask everyone to rise and toast the newlyweds (*everyone does*).

EISERMANN (*shaking his head*) So it is, unless I'm completely daft. God knows, that rascal is lucky.

HANNIBAL As much as he deserves. And more than you deserve.

EISERMANN What did you mean?

HANNIBAL Yes.

EISERMANN Will you now continue your lazy life — completely without occupation, without any intellectual pursuit whatsoever?

> *HANNIBAL and MISS stand embracing.*

HANNIBAL Oh, no, I hadn't thought of that. For example, I will always have a very good breakfast. Eating a good breakfast is a thoroughly intellectual pursuit. People just haven't realized it yet.

EISERMANN So?

HANNIBAL Yes!... You, for example.

MISS Come, Maedele... Come, Father.

> *OSKAR and MAEDELE approach HANNIBAL and the MISS, who, all four of them, are standing in a chain, facing EISERMANN.*

HANNIBAL Besides, I'm going to write the comedy of my bridal journey...

EISERMANN What, you're writing poetry?

MAEDELE Ah, so beautiful!

HANNIBAL The comedy of my bridal journey in three acts, you'll see, the continent is rolling with laughter, even though the only comic character in it is you, you, my extremely serious and wanting-to-be-taken-serious papa.

EISERMANN I think you're making fun of me.

HANNIBAL You mean because the audience is laughing? Oh! They laugh at much sillier jokes than you. Miss *(gentle reproach)* Hannibal!

MAEDELE Hannibal!

EISERMANN Hannibal!!! – We're finished with each other *(turns to leave, his gaze accidentally falls on a framed photograph hanging to the left of the door. He pauses. Turns back)* How... how did the picture get here?

HANNIBAL You mean my mother's picture?

OSKAR Yes... that's Mrs. Eisermann, so to speak... Mrs. Eisermann... there's no denying that...

EISERMANN How did the picture get into this dump? *(in anger.)*

OSKAR Well, now... dump...

EISERMANN Did you drag it here, Hannibal? You'd better honor the memory of your mother, who loved you more than anything...

HANNIBAL I had nothing to do with the picture. It came here by itself.

EISERMANN What nonsense is that? It has no feet...

HANNIBAL No... but the original had feet... very beautiful feet, in fact...

EISERMANN And...

HANNIBAL And with these feet it ran here... my mother fled to this dive from you and from the rich house on the market... when her heart ached and she still couldn't cry...

EISERMANN My... my... wife was in this... hole...

HANNIBAL This hole seemed like paradise to her... compared to your grocer's shop.

EISERMANN What... what... did my wife want here? (*Slowly understanding. Whimpering.*)

HANNIBAL She... loved my... father...

EISERMANN Whom? Whom? Whom?

HANNIBAL She loved the — handsome Oskar. — The handsome Oskar was her lover...

OSKAR Yes... yes... yes... that's probably so...

EISERMANN (*dully*) The town tramp?

HANNIBAL The town tramp... she cheated on you with him, not just out of love... she also spat on your bourgeoisie out of revenge. She knew what she was doing to you, even if she didn't confess it. The town tramp is my father. She swore it to me even on her deathbed... without sorrow, full of joy. For the handsome Oskar is a man... and you are... nothing.

MISS Hannibal! (*soothingly.*)

EISERMANN My wife... my wife... (*whimpering*) Oh, my honor! What am I left with? They'll throw me out of the magistrate's office (*rushes out*).

HANNIBAL Goodbye, please don't come back so soon — Oskar, now we're alone together. Have the girl fetch a few bottles of champagne. (*Throws him a hundred-mark bill.*) (*Steps arm in arm with MISS under the picture of his mother*) Look how sweetly she smiles down at us!...

    Curtain!

Act Four

Epilogue

Path along the swine pool at the city park. Hanging willows. Bench on the left. Open meadow in front. Trees. Old EISERMANN enters the stage from the right. He carries a rope in his hand and looks very disheveled in his clothing and posture.

EISERMANN ... when I bought the rope, master rope-maker Kilian said: Why do you need a rope, Mr. Mayor? I said I was very interested in the youth movement, as it has taken root in our city, and wanted to let the hiking group and the Young Germany League pull the rope next Sunday. Kilian bleated maliciously like a billy goat, as if he sensed that I was not going to see the consequences of my actions... (*thinks*) ... hmm... actions... my actions?... The kind of twisted language people use these days is something you only realize shortly before your death, when you've come to terms with yourself... come to terms with yourself? Am I a safe?... Once you're stuck in a sentence like "consequences of my actions," you simply can't get out, even if it was your own actions that got you caught in the rope... Can an id put something in your hand?... Oh God, why haven't I been to church for so many years?... I've applied for dismissal from the Association of Municipal Corporations and for a disciplinary investigation against me... I've been dead for a long time.... Sometimes the organ plays beautifully... in church... I know that from my confirmation... At our wedding, the organ played a very atmospheric chorale... What was it called again?... In the "Father Rhine" they brew a strange drink called Turkish blood. Sparkling wine, red wine, raw eggs and fresh beer on tap... Life really always goes on alongside... Clothes make the man... If I wore a green tailcoat, I'd be my son... Whose son?... They haven't even managed to have their own children... Trees stand so strangely here... like... it's very indecent that I think such a thing... I'm a scarecrow, but I don't scare birds anymore... I should dangle over the water. Can't one hang from the sky?... But the sky isn't a tree... (*He bends over the water.*) I haven't even shaved today. (*Retreats in horror.*) My wife... (*A swan swims to the shore. EISERMANN strokes it. He rummages in his pocket for bread.*) Are you hungry?...I have nothing... Absolutely nothing for you... Never had anything... I'm hungry myself... (*The handsome OSKAR, in an ill-fitting tuxedo, enters the stage from the right, swaying quietly. He's drunk. He's looking for something. He stops behind EISERMANN at the pond.*)

OSKAR (*singing*) Here is the place where I was happy...

EISERMANN (*shocked*) The District Administrator!

OSKAR (*concerned*) A scoundrel!

EISERMANN ... Mr.... Mr.... Oskar... (*recognizing each other*) Allow me... Mr.... Mr.... Chairman of the City Council...

EISERMANN Are you looking for me?

OSKAR No.

EISERMANN Who are you looking for?

OSKAR Your... wife... with permission...

EISERMANN She was just here...

OSKAR I had her summoned.

EISERMANN You're not just the town scoundrel, you're a scoundrel in chief...

OSKAR (*notices the swan, steps to the bank, rummages in his tuxedo, and throws pieces of cake into the pond*) If I may, Mr. Mayor: The citizens cannot praise you highly enough for what you have done for the city as chairman of the

Beautification and Tourism Association. The swans here in the city park are also, if one may say so, your work.

EISERMANN *(looks at his watch)* It's already five minutes to seven. A beautiful summer evening. At this moment the mayor is holding my resignation letter, along with the simultaneous notification of my death. He will immediately alert the entire city. Excuse me... Mr.... Mr. Oskar, if I ask you to take a few steps further. It's high time I hang myself... *(A horn sounds in the distance.)*

OSKAR Are you listening?... The fire department!... We have a metropolitan fire department... All your work, Mr. Speaker of the Council... Ingratitude is the world's reward... That's what your wife always said when she spoke of you, Mr. Speaker of the Council... A metropolitan fire department. In Berlin, the fire department is always alerted when a tomcat tries to drown itself in the gutter...

EISERMANN Quick... quick... *(He climbs onto the bench and ties the rope to a branch.)*

OSKAR *(watches him calmly)* Why do you want to hang yourself, Mr. Speaker of the Council?

EISERMANN Because you... you... scoundrel... made me impossible. A man of honor draws his conclusions.

OSKAR What does he draw?

EISERMANN His conclusions...

OSKAR I understand. It's not very noble to pull a handcart.

EISERMANN You're the kind of person you really should address informally... If only a gentleman had seduced my wife... I don't want to say anything... Lieutenant Knallwitzer, for example... You see... he loved her... I know it... He once confessed it to me when he was drunk... But *(raises finger)* he was an iron character. A truly warlike spirit.

OSKAR I only know iron stoves... and even they don't heat well... Oops, should I help you with the noose? Go ahead and hang yourself... I don't mind at all... I've seen this before... People who hang themselves are the best comedians.

EISERMANN You're drunk!

OSKAR And you're sober... too sober... A glass of good schnapps won't do any harm, even before death... Or should I earn the lifesaving medal?... I've saved more people's lives... your wife's, for example.

EISERMANN Get lost... I have to draw my own conclusions...

He sticks his head through the noose and hangs from the tree. Shouts. Ringing. From the right, the fire brigade, led by A. SCHULZ. From the left, the riflemen's guild, led by B. SCHULTZ. Lots of people. Below, a band, C. SCHULZE, MISS POMPE, MAXI BEERBAUM, and PLÜDDECKE.

SHOUTING Where is he?... Where is he hanging?...

OSKAR (*shouts*) Help! Help! (*is busy untying him.*)

> *Firefighters use axes to cut down the tree from which EISERMANN is hanging. Commands from A. SCHULZ and B. SCHULTZ. A pointless mess. Finally, EISERMANN falls down, perfectly healthy. Lying on the ground.*

VOICES Is he dead? Is he dead? Where's a doctor?

OSKAR Let me do it... (*Everyone steps back.*)

OSKAR Eisermann... (*louder*) Eisermann...

EISERMANN ... (*spits in his eyes and rubs the mucus in them*) ...that's an old, tried-and-true home remedy, ever since Jesus Christ... He always spat in everyone's eyes, too. (*With gesture*)... Eisermann, you dog, get up and walk... (*EISERMANN rubs his eyes, rises, stands there, shocked.*)

VOICES Long live the Chairman of the City Council!... Long live the Chairman of the City Council.

OTHER VOICES (*over the top*) Long live the handsome Oskar! Long live the handsome Oskar! Long live! (*Handsome OSKAR and EISERMANN bow arm in arm. A car honks up. First farther away, now closer. Hannibal, with the MISS and MAEDELE on his arm, make their way through the crowd. Behind them are the mayor and LIDDY.*)

HANNIBAL What's up? Is he dead?

A. SCHULZ The Chairman of the City Council is alive! Mr.... Mr.... Oskar cut him down from the tree and, in the absence of a doctor, raised him from the dead.

B. SCHULTZ Without the slightest mechanical instruments. Purely through the power of his will and his... his... mouth.

HANNIBAL Yes, he has a very strong will... to alcoholic beverages.

EISERMANN (*approaches HANNIBAL with poise*) I place my fate in your hands, Mr.... Eisermann.

HANNIBAL Tietmonick is my name. My mother was née Tietmonick. I am an illegitimate child. I just had these minor formalities revised at the civil registry. Isn't that right, Mr. Chairman of the City Council?

MAYOR Certainly, quite certainly, Mr. -

HANNIBAL Tietmonick.

MAYOR (*bows*) Tietmonick.

HANNIBAL I'm not at all pleased that you're alive, Eisermann. I've already telegraphed a first-class funeral for you at the crematorium in Gotha — to make sure that nothing of you remains. Incidentally, I wouldn't even consider burying you personally and playing the gravedigger. Dear Mayor, what do we do with Mr. Eisermann now?

MAYOR As your Highness pleases.

HANNIBAL You must know, Eisermann... I perhaps owe you this explanation... today, on the occasion of our engagement party, we hastily organized a public festival and, on this occasion, donated one million dollars to our beloved town of Crossen for charitable purposes. (*The Mayor bows emphatically several times.*)

MISS I deigned to throw a few thousand dollars in small change among the people. What do the people know about charitable purposes?

OSKAR Boot tacks...

MISS It doesn't even have charitable goals.

B. SCHULTZ If you don't aim, you don't hit the target.

> *Voices: Long live Hannibal! Long live Miss Tunderstam! The band plays a fanfare.*

HANNIBAL On the occasion of this folk festival, our dear, handsome Oskar got so drunk that he cut you, my Eisermann, down from the tree again. As a result of the aforementioned foundation, my dear bride was appointed honorary chairwoman of the local branch of the Patriotic Women's Association, as well as the women's groups of the Colonial, Military, and Naval Associations, and the local chapter of the International Virgins' League.

MISS POMPE Long live Miss Tunderstam!

HANNIBAL As for me, I've been offered honorary citizenship and, at the same time, dear Eisermann, the city council seat vacated by your retirement. I'll stay in this city for the time being until I've driven them completely crazy. (*The mayor bows emphatically. Shouts: Long live Hannibal! Our benefactor! Long live the noble donor!*)

HANNIBAL Dear Eisermann, what will they do with you now?

EISERMANN I'm selling my factory. I'm leaving the city.

MAYOR There's a position available for police secretary.

HANNIBAL I beg you, we can only fill this position with an intelligent and energetic man. Oskar...

OSKAR Hannibal?

HANNIBAL Please, come here for a moment. I'd like to introduce you to the mayor. The mayor... the handsome Oskar.

MAYOR (*bows*) Pleasant... Very pleased...

OSKAR I believe we already know each other. From the police station.

MAYOR Very pleasant... Pleased...

HANNIBAL You see, dear mayor, that would be a man perfect for the position of police secretary. Loyal, hardworking, sober, intelligent, reliable, and determined.

MAYOR I will not fail to strongly recommend Mr. Oskar.

OSKAR I will maintain a strict regime! Anyone who gets drunk will be written up and put in a hole, simply put in a hole.

MISS Dear Mr. Eisermann, among our foundations there is one for rescued suicides. Would you do us the pleasure of being the first to take advantage of it and benefit from it?

EISERMANN I'm selling the factory. I'm leaving town. (*A young man with a camera appears on the right of the screen, he speaks to* MAEDELE, *shakes her hand.*)

MAEDELE Hannibal — a young man wants to speak to you.

HANNIBAL I'm at your disposal.

THE YOUNG MAN Nice to meet you! (*Shakes his hand.*) You're doing a great job. Please don't let me disturb you, I just want to quickly take a group photo... (*He sets up his camera.*)

HANNIBAL It will be a pleasure. Couldn't we have a small private party later? In the smallest of circles: my bride, the handsome Oskar, Mädele, you, and me. Mädele is an excellent girl, distinguished by many physical and mental virtues, wouldn't you like to marry her? She'll get — what will she get, Mary?

MISS Twenty million!

HANNIBAL Twenty million! Just think! What do you earn now?

THE YOUNG MAN One hundred marks a month.

HANNIBAL Excuse me! And you wrote to me for such a paltry sum?

THE YOUNG MAN Excuse me, Hannibal, if I interrupt you... one moment quiet, please, one moment — quiet, gentlemen! (*Everyone crowds around the young man.*) – I just want to quickly take a group photo. Would you gentlemen please? Hannibal in the middle... Miss Tunderstam and girls, please, on the left and right...

MAEDELE I want to stay with you.

THE YOUNG MAN Later, girls, later, now go over there next to Hannibal... There, the fire department on the left... the rifle club on the right... Oskar, take Mr. Eisermann under your arm... Mr. Eisermann, do you have your rope too? The rope has to be in the picture... Please be very friendly... Don't look so unfriendly, Miss Tunderstam... I'm sorry you have so little to say in this fourth act, but I don't know what. May I put you off until a later play?... Mr. Mayor, more profile!... Your Greek nose needs to be seen better... Mr. Schulz, move that Tree of Knowledge a little further away if it bothers you... There... there, now please look at everything on the camera... There, very friendly, okay? (*Pulls the shutter.*) So. Done. Thank you very much. You can go. (*Firefighters, riflemen, and people exit to the left to music.*) Come on, girl! Hannibal! Oskar! We'll take your car, Miss Tunderstam!

> *The aforementioned people and the young man also exit to the right. The scene remains empty for a few moments. Dusk is falling. Stars are in the sky. The young man with the camera re-enters the scene from the right. He walks along the pond. He's looking for something.*

THE YOUNG MAN (*quietly*) I forgot the swan. (*He looks at the stars.*)

> *The curtain falls slowly.*

Part Eleven:

Terzett

"Terzett" was written in approximate 1912, and was first printed.
in *Klabund Reader* in 1926.

Terzett

Dramatis Personae:

Tatzel, a young vagabond
Anny, a young woman
Bess, a very old man

TATZEL (*knocks outside once, twice, three times, each time more forcefully, finally enters*) A hospitable house — open to all. Good day, Mr. Chair. Good day, Grandfather Wardrobe. I hope you slept well, Miss Bed. Is there no comrade here to join me? No little comrade to keep me company? You're silent, Cousin Desk? So closed-off, are you. Let's try to pry your mouth open a bit. Maybe you've got an answer. (*Pulls out a lockpick, opens the top drawer.*) Well, look at that: a thousand-mark note! My respects! My respects! It's been a long time, friendly mulatto. If I'm not mistaken, your friendship is — genuine. (*Holds it up to the light.*) Come to my heart. (*Puts it in his breast pocket.*) Ah, you warm me — more than any woman. (*Starts to leave.*)

ANNY (*from the left*) Stop — who are you? What do you want? (*Draws a revolver.*) Hands up!

TATZEL (*raises his hands*) Who am I? Your prisoner, charming goddess or trickster or thief — whoever you are! And what do I want? Since you speak so kindly to me — to serve and assist you in any way.

ANNY (*approaches him, checks his pockets, finds the thousand-mark note*) Well now! Our last bit of money! A proletarian steals from another. Shame on you. Why don't you steal from some rich profiteer?

TATZEL You're right! I'm truly ashamed. I just don't always get the chance.

ANNY They say opportunity makes the thief. But a true thief makes opportunity.

TATZEL You misjudge my profession. I only steal on the side. Mostly, I'm driven — by wind and storm.

ANNY There's a stiff breeze blowing everywhere today.

TATZEL Don't you want to give your stiff arms a break? Lower that revolver a bit. If you want to turn me in to the police — go ahead. I won't run away.

ANNY I like you.

TATZEL I like you even more. I want to —

ANNY What do you want?

TATZEL Put the revolver down. I want to embrace you. I want to love you. I want to enter you like a stallion mounts a mare.

ANNY Don't touch me. Or I'll shoot you down like a rabid dog.

TATZEL That's what I am — a rabid dog. Rabid — for you.

ANNY I'm not some bitch in heat. There are plenty out on the street. Pick one.

TATZEL Girl! Girl! I smell the scent of your blond hair! It smells like grain.

ANNY And you smell like booze.

TATZEL Let me kiss your feet. I'm yours — unconditionally.

ANNY Unconditionally?

TATZEL Unconditionally.

ANNY Here — take the revolver.

TATZEL (*taken aback*) What — what am I supposed to do with the revolver?

ANNY Why the hesitation? Now that you've got the revolver, you've got me completely in your power, haven't you?

TATZEL That's exactly what I want. To have you completely in my power.

ANNY Then go ahead —

TATZEL (*snatches the revolver she offers him*) Hands up!

ANNY (*raises her hands*)

TATZEL Now I've got you in my power, you silly goose — I love you. Will you love me?

ANNY Maybe.

TATZEL (*waves the revolver at her forehead*) Will you love me?

ANNY Maybe. You won't force me with that revolver. You can shoot me down if that's what you want.

TATZEL The revolver probably isn't even loaded. (*Checks.*) Good God — I wouldn't have thought it, but it's loaded. Fully loaded. You're an incomprehensible woman.

ANNY I will love you.

TATZEL You will love me!

ANNY If —

TATZEL No ifs — or I shoot.

ANNY Fool. If you grant me one wish.

TATZEL A wish? As far as it lies within my feeble power.

ANNY Just a tiny, insignificant wish. It won't cost you much.

TATZEL Then out with it!

ANNY I gave you that revolver for one very specific purpose. I don't do things without a purpose.

TATZEL What do you mean?

ANNY I mean this: I will love you — if with that revolver —

TATZEL Well?

ANNY (*calmly*) You shoot my husband.

TATZEL Shoot your — husband? What did your husband ever do to me?

ANNY Nothing yet. But he will — if you don't get to him first.

TATZEL Is he strong? Well, I'm stronger. Why kill? Stealing's a lark — but killing —

ANNY Killing is a lark too, just bloodier.

TATZEL Who'll wash the blood off me?

ANNY I'll kiss it from your lips. (*Noise.*) He's coming. Pull yourself together. (*The door opens. The old man limps in.*)

BESS Good day, my sweetheart, my darling, my little dove, my sugar - snookums — Give me a hello kiss.

ANNY (*kisses him*) Good day, my darling. Allow me to introduce you to Mr. Know-Not-Who, from Know-Not-Where. I've known him for know-not-how-long. He'll be our dear guest today.

BESS Delighted, sir, delighted to make your esteemed acquaintance. How is your esteemed health? Excellent, I hope. And your dear wife? And the little children?

TATZEL Thanks for asking.

BESS Bring us a glass of wine, my dove. We must toast our rare guest.

ANNY (*exits*) Gladly. Right away —

BESS My wife has many friends. My wife's friends are also my friends.

TATZEL I love your wife.

BESS Who doesn't? I'm happy that she deems me worthy of her affection. She is a rarely beautiful and rarely good person. I give her my full trust.

TATZEL I... wouldn't trust her.

BESS Sir — you insult me. What right do you have to your distrust?

TATZEL No right — only a duty.

BESS I'm not a man of duty. I love life. And thank God I'm still spry enough to love it — (*clears his throat*).

ANNY (*enters with wine*) So, my dears (*pours*).

BESS To the health of our guest! (*They drink.*) May I ask whether your visit to our town has any special purpose? You only wanted to see my wife again? Or —

TATZEL I wanted to see your wife — yes — I already told you I love her —

BESS (*kisses her hand*) She is most charming. One must love her.

TATZEL But — precisely because of that — I do have another purpose for my visit.

BESS Oh?

TATZEL I have an enemy here.

BESS Who doesn't have enemies? Many enemies, much honor, as our late king used to say.

TATZEL I came to destroy this enemy.

BESS Love your enemies!

TATZEL I can't.

BESS We are all sinners.

TATZEL Give me advice.

BESS Gladly, if I can be of service.

TATZEL I love a beautiful young woman.

BESS You lucky man! Then you are a brother in my happiness!

TATZEL This beautiful young woman is married to an old brute of a man.

BESS (*sympathetically*) Oh... the poor little woman! (*Strokes his wife's cheek.*)

TATZEL The beautiful young woman hates the old, repulsive man.

BESS Understandably!

TATZEL But he refuses to separate from her and jealously insists on his legal and religious rights.

BESS How wrong! How despicable. There are only inner laws.

TATZEL He doesn't observe those. As an ignorant young girl, the beautiful woman fell for him. Because she could no longer bear the tyranny of her parental home. Because she wanted to be free.

ANNY Yes — that's how — it was —

TATZEL She didn't know she was exchanging it for an even worse tyranny.

ANNY (*sobs*).

BESS But darling, I don't understand how someone else's fate can upset you so? You are so kind, my darling, full of compassion for every creature.

TATZEL What should she do?

BESS Deceive the old man —

TATZEL She already does: desperately, but with a clear conscience —

BESS A clear conscience is a soft pillow.

TATZEL But she wants to be free — completely free.

BESS (*thinks*) She could kill her jailer. Yes, she could, even if it went against external laws: God would acquit her —

ANNY God — would — acquit — her?

BESS He, who suffers with all who suffer: he would acquit her.

TATZEL (*draws a revolver*) You've pronounced your own sentence. You have judged yourself. You will die!

BESS (*groaning*) Murderer! Murderer! (*He collapses.*)

TATZEL (*throws away the revolver*) What's happening to him? — He's rolling his eyes —

ANNY (*joyfully*) He's dying — without you having to kill him — the shock killed him!

TATZEL God has judged, he said so himself —

ANNY We have a clear conscience — we can look the whole world in the eye — I'm free — I'm free — oh, dearest. You murderer, scoundrel, thief, you living life, kiss me, kiss me! (*They embrace.*)

TATZEL I want to close his eyes —

ANNY No, leave his dead eyes open — they shall see my happiness, as vengeance for the torment I endured under his living eyes. (*Another embrace in the fore-ground; in the background, BESS has picked up the revolver TATZEL dropped and jumps up.*)

BESS On your knees, you dogs, I want to bless your union with death.

ANNY AND TATZEL (*scream*) He lives!

BESS I live — and I will live forever, at least as long as you, my darling, my little wife, my little dove, my sugar-lips. You thought I was finished. You thought you could begin. God has judged — but you! Come here, my darling, kiss your beloved's feet. Come, come now — will you hurry — or I'll shoot. (*She crawls to him on her knees and kisses his feet.*)

TATZEL You monster!

BESS I am a dragon of ancient times. I am Ahasuerus. I am Baal. I am the dragon guarding his treasure, his darling. Will you stay with me, my little dove? Never leave me? Always love me? Yes? You must do me a favor. There's the telephone — go to the telephone — not such tiny steps — not so hesitantly — now pick up the receiver — good — and now call the police station —

TATZEL (*makes a move*).

BESS Don't come any closer — (*to Anny*) Do you know the number? 33113! Well then?!

ANNY (*at the phone*) Please call 33113 — yes — is that the police station — (*she lowers the receiver*) what should I say?

BESS Say — that you caught a burglar in the act — in your apartment —

TATZEL (*moves*).

BESS Quiet, you.

ANNY This is Mrs.... I've caught a burglar — in my apartment — in the act —

BESS — and in self-defense —

ANNY — and in self-defense —

BESS (*Raises the revolver, shoots* TATZEL) shot him! (*TATZEL falls dead.*)

ANNY — shot him (*collapses sobbing at the phone*).

BESS Don't cry, darling, it ruins your beautiful eyes. As you know, we're invited to tea this afternoon at the Privy Councilor's. We won't lack for conversation topics!

(Curtain.)

Part Twelve:

The Fat Capon

Taken from the stage manuscript for the Munich Intimate Theater, probably published in 1914.

The Fat Capon

A Scene
A Scene - based on English, French, Dutch, and Italian newspaper reports.

Characters:
The Minister of War
The Minister of the Navy
General of the General Staff
First Colonel of the General Staff
Second Colonel of the General Staff
Mimi
Gabys
A Lieutenant
Jean
Christophe
Alois Huber, Drum Major in the Royal Bavarian 2nd Infantry Regiment
The Correspondent for the "Daily Telegraph"
First Courier
Second Courier
Two soldiers with fixed bayonets.

Place: Bordeaux – Time: Mid-September 1914.

To the left and right of the audience.

"The Fat Capon." Elegant wine bar in red and gold. Stucco columns. Round and oval tables. Plush armchairs. Large floor-to-ceiling mirrors on the sides. At the back left, the main entrance is draped with curtains. In the background, center and right, windows facing the street. To the left and right, separated from the hall by curtains, are separate boxes. As the curtain rises, the Sambre et Meuse can be heard, played on a gramophone. Laughter. Clinking of glasses. The two waiters, JEAN and CHRISTOPHE, stand bored in the background, leaning against two pillars. Suddenly, a curtain slides back on the left. Mimi, all in white, flutters lightly like a bird, chirping across the stage with two flaps of her wings, and disappears into a private room opposite on the right. Laughter. Clinking of glasses.

CHRISTOPHE Who's that?

JEAN Mimi.

CHRISTOPHE And what else?

JEAN Nothing more. Mimi. La belle Mimi.

CHRISTOPHE La belle Mimi? I don't think she's pretty...

JEAN Fool. Pretty! She weighs eighty-nine pounds, wears intoxicating gowns, is courted at soirées, and costs a fortune. That's why she's beautiful. That's why she's la belle Mimi.

CHRISTOPHE (*silent; then points to the left*) Who's sitting in there?

JEAN The Minister of War...

CHRISTOPHE (*Pointing to the right*) And there?

JEAN The Minister of the Navy...

CHRISTOPHE And Mimi?

JEAN Loves both. So to speak. Or they both love her. Since the war broke out, Mimi has been financed by the entire government. One person alone can no longer afford her. Ministerial salaries have been cut in half. But the heart — can this heart be cut in half?

CHRISTOPHE (*sighs*)

JEAN (*looks at him*) You love Mimi?

CHRISTOPHE (*turns away*)

JEAN But, my boy... why are you torturing yourself? You're a peasant. Tell her you're an Alsatian — and she'll throw her arms around your neck. That will save you all the compliments. Since the war, people no longer say, "Mademoiselle, I love you!" but, "Dear child, I am an Alsatian." The further formalities can be omitted.

CHRISTOPHE Perhaps it would be even better to say, "I am a Turk!' (*dreamily*) But my complexion is too light... (*Calls from the left box: Jean, Jean...*)

JEAN (*stops in front of the portiere*) Your Excellency?

VOICE Are there any new special editions posted?

JEAN Yes, Your Excellency.

VOICE Well?

JEAN The French Mediterranean Fleet is preparing to...

VOICE But, dear Jean, tell that to the Minister of the Navy. He'll be pleased to hear any news. As far as I know, the Minister of the Navy hasn't received a direct telegram from the Mediterranean Fleet since the beginning of the war. Don't bore me with your Mediterranean Fleet. (*exits*).

JEAN Very well, Your Excellency. (*bows*)

Calls from the right box: Jean, Jean...

JEAN (*to the right*) Your Excellency?

VOICE Dear Jean, tell the Minister of War about the Mediterranean Fleet; he'll be interested. Has Matin already announced the Minister of the Interior's uniform regulation of the price of caviar?

JEAN I don't know, Your Excellency...

MIMI's VOICE Christophe...

CHRISTOPHE (*hurries over*)

MIMI Christophe, another bottle of champagne. -

VOICE The Minister of the Interior will also have to uniformly regulate the price of champagne if this continues, listen, Jean...

JEAN Very well, Your Excellency.

CHRISTOPHE (*has fetched a new bottle of champagne) Mademoiselle...*)

MIMI Come in...

CHRISTOPHE enters the box

VOICE Fine, my son.

MIMI A cute boy...

VOICE A peasant lout... Why aren't you drafted?

CHRISTOPHE I have lung disease, Your Excellency.

MIMI If I ever had a child, it would have to look a bit like that one, tall, with hair bleached by the sea wind, almost blond... and... and... with lung disease...

VOICE Well, please... (*CHRISTOPHE returns. Movement behind the porter at the main entrance. Clash of sabers. Enter, greeted by the waiters: GENERAL, FIRST COLONEL, and SECOND COLONEL. Looking for a table.*)

GENERAL That one. Yes. That's right. It's been a damn hot day today. I was sweating like a miner in the office.

FIRST COLONEL Strategy is the mother of life and the father of the fine arts.

SECOND COLONEL By teaching how to cover wounds with... makeup.

GENERAL Strategy is a very grueling craft, insofar as, unfortunately, you have to practice it with your head.

SECOND COLONEL Well, the soldier in the field also practices it with his hands...

GENERAL My dear fellow, the soldier in the field is a lump of bloodthirsty flesh... a tiger... an animal that stabs, shoots, runs, roars... the spirit, the spirit... that's what we of the General Staff are. And the further we are from the front, the more unbiased we are. The more we preserve our freedom of action. We, we are winning the war... here at this table. At the so-called green table. – Jean, two Chablis, but well chilled.

FIRST COLONEL Today I traced the diameter of a German 42 cm shell with a compass. It was painstaking work. But the result was well worth the effort. I carry the drawing with me at all times now. It's very instructive. You see... (*he has taken a folded piece of paper from his breast pocket and unfolds it*)

GENERAL Very nice, really very nice... When you nail it to the wall and think, 'That's a hole...' Really very nice.

SECOND COLONEL The news from Paris is favorable.

GENERAL So!

SECOND COLONEL The immediate danger to Paris has been eliminated. The Germans have recaptured the right wing of Meaux.

FIRST COLONEL That means they've lost a battle.

SECOND COLONEL Not that. But they need troops in Russia. To relieve pressure on Galicia. Or for... England.

GENERAL For... England?

SECOND COLONEL Yes, for England. The first German sailor division is already in Belgium. It participated in a Belgian sortie from Antwerp. The first Bavarian army corps is also supposed to be in Belgium...

GENERAL But the Germans have enough troops in Belgium. What's the point of the first Bavarian corps? It fought in Alsace and Lorraine...

SECOND COLONEL It's intended for... England.

FIRST COLONEL AND GENERAL For England?

FIRST COLONEL You're fantasizing... on a set... for England?

GENERAL You show a lot of ingenuity in your combinations... (*laughs heartily*) but so much ingenuity that there's no reality left... (*The waiters bring the wine*)

GENERAL So... my dear Colonel... let's drink to the German invasion of England... When is it supposed to take place?

SECOND COLONEL In November... from Calais... during the November storms, when the English fleet is held back in its ports by the adverse weather... it will simultaneously be preoccupied by an attack from the German fleet...

GENERAL Long live the German invasion of England!

ALL THREE Long live the German invasion!

GENERAL That will make things all the easier for us... (*laughing*)

FIRST COLONEL (*shaking head*) I think you must return to the front, Soulier.

GENERAL I think so too...

SECOND COLONEL With great pleasure... (*enthusiastically*)

> *Pause... The curtain on the right of the separate room on the right is thrown back; and MIMI, all in white, flutters lightly like a bird, chirping with two flaps of her wings, across the stage and disappears to the left. The three officers watch her sympathetically.*

GENERAL Sweet girl...

FIRST COLONEL Pretty woman...

SECOND COLONEL She looked like France... delicate... seductively depraved, very expensive... all in white... only the tricolor flag was missing.

> *Laughter on the left, clinking of glasses. The Sambre et Meuse sounds again.*

SECOND COLONEL Damn, marching is tough on the legs... one wants to march... across the Rhine... across the Rhine...

FIRST COLONEL Be glad you're sitting here. In this rainy weather outside, lying in the soggy rifle lines on the Marne — thank you. An entire German battery is said to have sunk in the mud. You'll get rheumatism.

SECOND COLONEL (*jumps up*) Jean, my dressing room! – Gentlemen, excuse me,... excuse me, General... I can't stay here any longer... I'm not feeling well... (*JEAN with coat, saber, and shako*)... I've been so... dizzy all day. I should have declined your kind invitation from the start... There... (*JEAN bows*) – Once again, pardon me! Goodbye, gentlemen. (*CHRISTOPHE opens the curtain at the entrance. SECOND COLONEL exits*)

FIRST COLONEL A strange temperament.

GENERAL A gifted officer.

FIRST COLONEL Too gifted.

GENERAL Too emotionally gifted. A fiery mind.

FIRST COLONEL France needs officers, especially general staff officers, of sober disposition, of dry minds like you, General. May I take the liberty of drinking to your health?

GENERAL Oh, thank you very much, my dear.

> *A LIEUTENANT wounded in the foot enters, laughing. Arm in arm with GABYS, leans on a stick. Stands at attention. General winks. The LIEUTENANT looks around, searching for a table...*

GENERAL Young friend... just sit here... if you don't mind... (*looks at GABYS...*)

LIEUTENANT Your Excellency, you are very kind... allow me to respectfully remark... I am... accompanied...

GENERAL Oh, that doesn't matter... in war and before love... all men are... brothers. Aren't you, Mademoiselle?

GABYS Oh... Certainly...

GENERAL Just sit down with your girl...

FIRST COLONEL Waiter... a new bottle

> *JEAN exists. CHRISTOPHE takes the gentlemen's coats*

GENERAL I see you've already shed your blood for the fatherland. Where was that?

LIEUTENANT At St. Quentin, Your Excellency. I was shot by an Englishman because I didn't know the English password. The English speak a language even more terrible than their rump steaks, which I was forced to eat for a few days... if eating is the right word for it.

GABYS (*Laughs amusedly. The* GENERAL *and* FIRST COLONEL *laugh along*)

LIEUTENANT The English wouldn't even need to shoot. They could murder the enemy with their language. I'll never forget how I offered my canteen to an English captain at St. Quentin, and he thanked me: Baukanly remerssei. (*Everyone laughs*)

GENERAL (*Laughs tearfully*) Baukanly remerssei... Je vous remercie beaueoup... baukanly...

FIRST COLONEL Cheers, Mademoiselle...

GABYS Merci.

GENERAL Your feet are as small as a hummingbird's.

FIRST COLONEL Surely your gloves always have to be specially made?

GABYS Certainly, Colonel, thank you very much for the compliment. But I also like to have my lovers custom tailored too...

GENERAL Official order, Lieutenant: You must go home. If you drink more, you will damage your precious health. With excessive alcohol consumption, freshly healed wounds easily reopen...

LIEUTENANT I drink so little, Excellency... (*Rises, exchanges a sad glance with* GABYS)

GENERAL That's okay. Do you already have the Cross for Valor?

LIEUTENANT No, Excellency.

GENERAL It will be delivered to you.

LIEUTENANT Excellency...

GENERAL You needn't worry about your girlfriend. I'll take the lady home. Good-bye, my friend.

LIEUTENANT (*clicks his heels together as best he can, limps off*)

GABYS What kind of wine is that?

FIRST COLONEL Chablis.

GABYS Oh...

GENERAL Waiter... Champagne...

A COURIER *rushes in*

COURIER His Excellency, the Minister of the Navy...

CHRISTOPHE (*shows him to the box on the right*)

VOICE (*right*) Come in...

COURIER (*enters*)

GABYS What is it?

FIRST COLONEL A naval victory in the Adriatic Sea. The telegram has been hanging on every street corner for two hours.

MINISTER OF THE NAVY (*with the* COURIER, *excitedly from the box to the right*) That is... that is... magnificent... significant... sublime... (*The officers have risen*) Listen, gentlemen, listen: "The French fleet, which had remained outside the Adriatic since the effective cannonade of Punta d'Ostro on September 1st, appeared again off Bocche di Cattaro at 6:00 a.m. on September 19th and, for an hour, again shelled the forts and the entrance with the heaviest calibers. It scored three hits and wounded one gunner. Then, with approximately 40 units, it headed for Lissa and shelled the semaphore station and the lighthouse at 10:00 a.m. It wounded two men and caused damage. The bulk of the fleet operated in the waters off Lissa until about 5:00 p.m., then left the scene of its operations, steering southwest. Occasionally During this voyage, parts of the fleet appeared before Pelagosa. Here, too, the lighthouse was shelled. After destroying the flag station and contaminating the drinking water by sailors who had landed, and taking with them the lighthouse keeper's meager provisions and some laundry, this squadron also left the Adriatic."

GENERAL My most humble and sincere congratulations, Your Excellency...

FIRST COLONEL Please humbly allow me to join in the congratulations.

GABYS (*approaches the* MINISTER OF THE NAVY *and shakes his hand*) Congratulations, my dear man.

MINISTER OF THE NAVY Thank you very much... thank you very much... I must rush to the President to inform him personally of the successful operations of our fleet. Goodbye, gentlemen, goodbye, my child. (*hurriedly, leaves with the courier*)

GABYS When he sails on a pleasure boat on the Seine, he gets seasick. He's never seen a torpedo boat, and he's the Minister of the Navy.

GENERAL YOU are his torpedo hunter, my little one, cheers, drink...

GABYS My dear, I think I'm more his submarine... (*laughter*)

> SECOND COURIER *rushes in*

SECOND COURIER His Excellency the Minister of War...

CHRISTOPHE (*points him to the left*)

VOICE Come in.

> COURIER *enters*

VOICE That... that... yes, that's a magnificent catch.

MIMI Herrings?

VOICE My saber... (*CHRISTOPHE enters the box*) my coat... where's the cap...

MIMI Shouldn't I come too? Am I not your heart?

VOICE So...

> *The MINISTER OF WAR steps out of the box, behind him MIMI, the COURIER, CHRISTOPHE. The officers have risen*

MINISTER OF WAR Gentlemen, gentlemen, gentlemen, gentlemen... the very latest. Our brave troops have captured a Bavarian commanding general in Lorraine while fighting against superior numbers. The gentleman has already arrived in Bordeaux under special escort, and we will soon have the opportunity. (*The Sambre et Meuse military band plays beneath the window. Crowds shout. Vive la France.*)

GENERAL What is it...?

FIRST COLONEL Military music at this hour?

MIMI No, this noise.

GABYS And always the Sambre et Meuse...

MIMI My ears are about to burst... (*Everyone goes to the window*)

SECOND COURIER It's the Bavarian general. They picked him up from the train station.

MINISTER OF WAR (*Arm in arm with MIMI to the COURIER*) Hurry, run! Official order from the Minister of War: The Bavarian general is to be brought here. Immediately, and even if we don't give away Munich beer here, he should see that we, too, know how to live...

> *COURIER leaves. Everyone returns to the room. Only MIMI is still standing at the window, staring into the night.*

GENERAL It's a pity Colonel Soulier is no longer here. He could be talking to the Bavarian general about the Bavarian invasion of England...

GABYS I'm very curious about this Bavarian lion...

MIMI (*still at the window*) He's very fat, a plump capon...

GABYS Is he bald like all our generals? (*COURIER returns*)

COURIER He's coming, Your Excellency.

MINISTER OF WAR Let him enter... (*takes position*)

> *The porters part ways, and Alois HUBER, Drum Major in the Imperial and Royal 2nd Infantry Regiment, enters, escorted by two soldiers. The MINISTER OF WAR waves. The escort leaves. Meanwhile, the correspondent for the "Daily Telegraph" has sneaked in. He participates in the scene, barely noticed at first. The MINISTER OF WAR and the officers salute. Alois HUBER also salutes. Then he leans his right hand on his drumstick and observes the scene with wonder and amusement.*

MINISTER OF WAR Your Excellency, we greet you as the brave leader of the First Bavarian Corps...

HUBER What do you mean?

MINISTER OF WAR Rest assured that we will do everything to make your stay in France as pleasant as possible.

HUBER That's quite right...

MINISTER OF WAR We'll leave the baton (*pointing to the drumstick*) and the sword. Happy to be in your brave hands.

HUBER That's fine. I'm thirsty...

FIRST COLONEL Excuse me, Excellency?

HUBER (*makes a drinking gesture*)

GENERAL Ah! I see. Excellency is thirsty. From the long train ride. Excellency would like something to drink.

> *MIMI and GABYS have now filled two glasses with champagne and hand them to HUBER*

HUBER (*looks at both of them kindly, drinks first one, then the other in one gulp*) That hits the spot! You're a pair of fine girls... thank you kindly... (*The CORRESPONDENT for the "Daily Telegraph" suddenly stands next to the MINISTER OF WAR*)

CORRESPONDENT Will you allow me, Excellency, to interview the General? I speak fluent Bavarian.

MINISTER OF WAR (*obligingly*) Please...

CORRESPONDENT God that is a no... by God! (*approaches HUBER*)

HUBER Greetings...

CORRESPONDENT Ah... yes, greetings...

HUBER Servus... you can print again...

CORRESPONDENT Yes... I'll have it printed... in the *Daily Telegraph*... May I then... (*pulls out the notebook and pencil*)

HUBER I always say, he's an artist... a rascal... he's wearing me down. -

CORRESPONDENT (*writes diligently*)

HUBER But those two girls... a A few clean girls... and that wine wasn't bad either...

CORRESPONDENT (*writes busily*)

HUBER Oh my... the officers are like a carnival masquerade...

CORRESPONDENT (*steps back*) Thank you very much. Thank you very much. (*to the MINISTER OF WAR and the others gathering around him*) Here's my information: The German losses are unheard of. There's not a single horse left in the X. Army Corps...

MIMI Why a horse?

CORRESPONDENT In individual companies, 250 officers have fallen... The Prussian Guard no longer has any officers at all. It's commanded by one-year-olds.

FIRST COLONEL AND GENERAL AND WAR MINISTER The old French god is still alive...

MIMI There is no French god... only a French goddess...

HUBER Now I'll show those maleficent snakes that a real Bavarian can speak French... (*He grabs a champagne glass and throws it to the ground, clinking*) Bive Limperor Guillama!

GABYS He's got guts...

MIMI He's as strong as a bull...

OFFICERS Vive la France! Vive la France!

ALL Vive la France!

> *The gramophone starts playing the Marseillaise. The curtain falls.*

Part Thirteen:

The Debaucher

On March 25, 1914, Klabund wrote to Walther Heinrich that he had written a pastoral play in alexandrines. "The Debaucher" was performed in Munich in 1918 at the Marionette Theater of the 2nd Bavarian Infantry Regiment.

The Debaucher

A Scene
A pastoral play in alexandrines.

Characters:

Lysander
Chrysoleth
Amint
Dorothee
Phyllis

Setting: Park

CHRYSOLETH totters through the garden with stiff but dainty steps. He stops at a birch tree, pulls an exaggeratedly large pink letter from his pocket, wraps his right arm around the birch, crosses his right leg over his left, raises the letter with his left hand, and begins:

CHRYSOLETH : O sweet maiden, incline yourself to me in a kiss.
(*Kisses the letter.*)
Thus heart joins to heart in tender delight.
How good you are! How faithful! How gentle! And how fair!
As if Helios had bathed you in his own rays.
As if he had born you in splendor and midday,
As if he had lost himself completely in your body.
You sparkle from within. From the gate of your eyes
The sky itself bursts forth, mighty, blue, and deep.
— Ah, I forget myself and gallantry
Before your presence: therefore: how did you sleep?
How did you spend the smiling, balmy summer night,
Dorinde, how did you dream without me?
You lower your head! Oh, do not be ashamed,
That your grace weaves me the wreath of love!
I press it delightedly and proudly to my forehead;
Thus, bathed in light, an alpine snowfield rises into the light,
Into the dawn, Dorinde, my Eos — alas,
I slept very poorly last night and am still quite weak...
And whenever a dream tried to sweetly enfold me,
It was your gaze that sought to strike me like lightning and thunder.
Am I certain of your love, Dorinde?
And weeping, I tossed and turned in the darkness.

LYSANDER enters.

LYSANDER What are you holding there so pointedly and carefully in your hand?

CHRYSOLETH It's a letter!

LYSANDER A letter?

CHRYSOLETH A letter sent by her!

LYSANDER The size seems, well, a bit excessive?

CHRYSOLETH (*kissing the letter*) Dorinde's love can only come in such dimensions expressive!

LYSANDER (*pensively*) Dorinde? Sweet vision that called me into life...

CHRYSOLETH (*digs into his pocket and pulls out ten letters in all colors — yellow, red, blue, violet, etc.*) Behold...

LYSANDER Pardon?

CHRYSOLETH This is already the tenth letter today.

LYSANDER From her?

CHRYSOLETH What are you thinking! There are other women, by the way!

LYSANDER You've got them in every color, so it seems...

CHRYSOLETH The blue one's from Chloe (*kisses the letter*), whose tears bedewed my dreams. The yellow one: from Dorothee, figure: slim, hair: brown. (*Kisses the letter.*)

LYSANDER The green?

CHRYSOLETH Was penned by Amalie, brunette of great renown...

LYSANDER The red?

CHRYSOLETH Last night Phyllis joined me in my bed... And in memory of that night, it burns in fiery red...

LYSANDER Your brazenness defies belief! You loved Phyllis?

CHRYSOLETH Yes!?! Why shout so loud?

LYSANDER I demand the truth right now...

CHRYSOLETH Yes, I held her — am I not allowed?

LYSANDER Impossible! If you'll stand for that with your sword — draw now!

> He snatches the letter from him.

CHRYSOLETH Oh no, my letter! Give me the letter first!

LYSANDER No! Now I hold a document proving that false woman's game. God! Her handwriting!

CHRYSOLETH (*aside*) Does he really know her? (*aloud*) If you are a gentleman, then spare the girl's honor!

LYSANDER After you boldly tasted the berry of her lips, and now go around boasting like a dog in every low tavern that Phyllis let herself be embraced by you?!! What if I told you she slept in my arms last night?

CHRYSOLETH The letter says something quite different!

LYSANDER If only I could silence your impudent mouth with my sword! Draw!

CHRYSOLETH She loves me, not you. I'm leaving – away I go... (*exits*)

LYSANDER The cowardly fool flees with his squabbles, leaving me and my anger alone with this letter – How kindly the moon shone in our love tent last sweet night. The wedding was arranged for spring – and now it turns out that I was betrayed, that right after me she flew to this scoundrel's heart! Writing him letters! Telling him her mad love He stammers! Now the gates of paradise are barred for me... (*opens the letter*) Beloved! – This head, as hollow as a drum! How sweetly the bittern sang of our bliss last night, and the moon draped golden nets around the arbor. Damn it, if I put myself in her place! It was the same arbor, it seems – the same arbor where she welcomed him! Oh you snake! Oh dove! How could you fall for Chrysoleth, that musk-scented, dolled-up monkey! – What else is written? – You, for whom the world exists, around whom everything turns! – Everything revolves around Chrysoleth! When will you return? You – I can't wait. Meet me tomorrow morning at eleven o'clock in the garden. The garden? Here! Eleven o'clock? Ten minutes left, If he wants to meet her, Chrysoleth must hurry. He won't dare! The dog fears my sword! – Who comes? It's Amint! And not at a bad time.

> AMINT *enters, holding a yellow letter. He is sad.*

LYSANDER Amint...

AMINT Lysander... friend... I've grown weary of the world, I've reached the point where one envies a stone. I wish I were as unfeeling as one.

LYSANDER Look at me: I'm the same!

AMINT Then let us, moved, shake hands! (*They do so.*) – Look at this yellow letter. She wrote it –

LYSANDER Well?

AMINT Dorothee! The one I once loved...

LYSANDER As recently as...

AMINT ...last evening. Do I not see this letter today in the hands of some fool? She's unfaithful to me!

LYSANDER Unfaithful like all women. Phyllis deceived me –

AMINT Dorothee deceived me –

LYSANDER And with whom?

AMINT With that fool in the jester's diadem. That ridiculous love-braggart Chrysoleth.

LYSANDER I ran into the same man in my flower bed. – And if need be, I'll drive him off with a stick!

AMINT Oh, since we're so moved, let us shake hands once more! (*They do so.*) Just last night she lay lovingly at my side, and an hour later she leads him into the land of Amor!

LYSANDER That wastrel Chrysoleth again! He also enclosed Phyllis in his prayer last night.

AMINT The very same night! – And now this letter calls him here, like a dandy, at precisely eleven.

LYSANDER Where Phyllis also – summoned him...

> PHYLLIS *and* DOROTHEE *appear simultaneously, one behind a bush on the left, the other on the right.* LYSANDER *and* AMINT *don't notice them.*

PHYLLIS AND DOROTHEE It's striking eleven, yet why is he not alone?

DOROTHEE Lysander is with him! How cruel!

PHYLLIS AND DOROTHEE Amint is with him! How cruel!

AMINT Believe me, no lover has ever been so duped like us!

LYSANDER Let us take revenge together, by betraying love ourselves!!

PHYLLIS AND DOROTHEE He doesn't love me anymore! –

AMINT Bah! Let's play va banque now!

LYSANDER And this very day we'll —

AMINT Ha!

LYSANDER On the prowl for women.

AMINT Try touching her where Dorothee holds her heart!

LYSANDER I'm giving Phyllis to you, feel free to seduce her!

PHYLLIS AND DOROTHEE The scoundrels! Men!

PHYLLIS I can't bear it any longer...

DOROTHEE Then I'll tell this monster the truth!

> *She jumps out from behind the bushes, to* AMINT

DOROTHEE Sir...

PHYLLIS (*following her*) Sir, forgive me if I intrude — just this: that I no longer belong to you... (*Sobbing, to* LYSANDER.)

DOROTHEE (*to* AMINT) You're no longer a man, but a beast!

PHYLLIS (*to* LYSANDER) And you, sir, the same!

LYSANDER AND AMINT Oh, let us at least shake hands with some emotion!

> *They do so.*

DOROTHEE They're mocking us again!

AMINT Yes, yes, that's how it goes — the tables have turned.

LYSANDER How is Chrysoleth, the favorite?

AMINT Did you sleep well last night?

LYSANDER It was so cold — alone. The blood flows so hot...

AMINT I'll forgive you only if you freely admit your heart burns with love for the whole world!

LYSANDER Perhaps Chrysoleth even paid you in full. He's rich, after all!

PHYLLIS (*weeping*) Do you understand, Dorothee —

DOROTHEE Gods, protect me from madness! How they trample us underfoot — those we once loved.

LYSANDER To sweeten your bitter life, behold, the charming Chrysoleth comes to flirt.

AMINT With both of you.

LYSANDER We'll leave you alone.

>   *They begin to go.*

DOROTHEE Stay!

PHYLLIS Stay...

DOROTHEE Chrysoleth, you said —

LYSANDER Yes, your lord, whom you asked for a rendezvous...

PHYLLIS Monster! So you took my letter —

DOROTHEE You didn't get mine?

LYSANDER AND AMINT (*displays the letters*)

AMINT Here's a letter — I took it from Chrysoleth!

>   *CHRYSOLETH has approached, dreamily.*

DOROTHEE (*grabbing both letters, to CHRYSOLETH*) This mad farce must be put to rest — Did you have these letters?

CHRYSOLETH Yes...

DOROTHEE How?

CHRYSOLETH Did I steal them, or, if that sounds better, purloined them...

LYSANDER (*horrified*) You have desecrated your shield of honor with theft?!

AMINT You stole them, Chrysoleth??

CHRYSOLETH O, what an age, that never cries out for the poet, but immediately for the judge! I took the letters to adorn my heart with fragrance, with premonitions of distant women, to gladden my longing! Ah, not only these: a thousand brides pay homage to me, by virtue of whom I scattered happiness and incense for myself. I love myself so much... Should I not confess it to myself and see myself fantastically transformed into a woman? Often a faithful kiss tastes very maliciously of... snuff. I love only the daring vices of the imagination. You, Dorothee, I never desired... only your image!!! I abducted Phyllis into the wilderness of my dreams... If I stole the letters — who will steal you from me? I place you as golden stars in the distant blue firmament. You are constellations to me, like Venus, Pisces, and Ursa Major. Ah, if only my heart were not so rich in invention! It would wither away in the real world, which is only concerned with action and deed, with strength and strength. Like butterflies, the honeymoon flutters colorfully... Tender love is as easily broken as a reed... Phyllis knits stockings, and good Dorothee brews her brave husband chamomile tea for the night. The swords that gentlemen so bravely brandish today rust and gather dust in the linen closets... You, Phyllis, have grown so fat that you appear as a dumpling. Then my Phyllis is still as gentle and slender as ever. And if horror haunts Dorothee — my Dorothee remains the ornament of all women...

DOROTHEE He's a fool.

PHYLLIS Insane.

LYSANDER Let the rascal rave! A fool must be allowed his foolishness.

CHRYSOLETH Oh — I'm a fool? And you are good, proud, and wise?! Hear me, Venus! The world is coming off its tracks... I'm too tender, too soft for reality. Amint means Reality. Truth means Chrysoleth. You'll never understand me, and I'll never understand you. Farewell, mesdames, messieurs, never to be seen again! (*He exits, dignified and coquettish.*)

AMINT What now?

LYSANDER What now?

PHYLLIS AND DOROTHEE (*mocking*) What now? What now? What now? Can't you do anything better than make silly faces?

> AMINT *and* LYSANDER *fall at their feet.*

PHYLLIS AND DOROTHEE The fool is gone. Two new ones lie at our feet, to atone together for the folly of all men. And take Chrysoleth as your example. He stole the letters — and unmasked himself as a false suitor. So, dearest Amint? What now, my Lysander?? (*They run off laughing.*) He only stole the letters! So now you — steal the rest...

> LYSANDER *and* AMINT *follow after.*

Part Fourteen:

Tommy Atkins

This is the stage script for the Munich Intimate Theater production of 1914.

Tommy Atkins

A Scene
An English Comedy

Characters:
Nutall,
Allnutt,
An Orderly,
Miss Basingstoke,
Tommy Atkins

Place: London – Time: August 1914.

To the left and right of the audience.

Recruiting office. Spartan simplicity. On the left, two doors. On the middle left, a lectern, a wastebasket. Telephone. On the right, a window. In front, a table with writing utensils. Two chairs. In the background, five comfortable and elegant leather club chairs are lined up in a row against the wall. No decorations. Only above the club chairs on the wall is a garishly colorful poster: Led by a band, beautifully painted women, variety singers, and dancers ride through the city. Across the image is an inscription: You proud heroes, stream to the glorious banners of Britannia. One notices that this inscription is pasted on and covers another original one: Votes for Women, votes for women! – When the curtain rises, there is a moment of silence, and one sees Lieutenant Jack ALLNUTT and Staff Surgeon Davis NUTALL lounging in the background in two club chairs; they are smoking cigars or cigarettes.

NUTALL Actually, the club chairs are only for the gentlemen recruits; we are wearing them out unfairly.

ALLNUTT Actually, WE are there to live a decent life; we are being worn out unfairly. Through this so-called English military service, which is nothing but an English sermon transposed to the days of the week: stupid, sleazy, and boring.

NUTALL How is Elga?

ALLNUTT Thanks for asking. Not particularly well. She's bedridden.

NUTALL What's wrong with her?

ALLNUTT She's caught a cold.

NUTALL Are there any complications?

ALLNUTT The doctor says it's tonsillitis; but there's no need to give up hope for recovery.

NUTALL I think you leave her out on the street too late in the evenings. The damp autumn weather isn't good for her.

ALLNUTT You can imagine how much I suffer from her bad moods. Sometimes I don't even want to go home.

NUTALL You've spoiled her very much; but after all, she deserves it: she's well worth her two hundred pounds.

ALLNUTT Yesterday I wanted to give her a treat, and to cheer her up, I showed her the golden cup she won at the great dog show in Liverpool last year. How do you think she rewarded my goodwill?

NUTALL Well?

ALLNUTT She lifted one hind leg and... into the cup.

NUTALL Into the golden cup? (*a little horrified*)

ALLNUTT Into the golden cup of honor.

NUTALL It's strange how little sense of shame is developed in dogs, especially bitches. This negative sense of shame is the only thing that distinguishes them from humans.

ALLNUTT Incidentally, the Germans don't have this... sense of shame either.

NUTALL So they're not human.

ALLNUTT There's only one kind of human, and that's the English.

NUTALL Bravo, my boy, I must shake your hand (*does so*).

ALLNUTT Did you read in the newspaper how the Germans at Maubeuge refused to shake hands with our brave Tommies, who had fought bravely and were taken prisoner?

NUTALL I read it. The Germans are a rude people; they should rather be called Teutons. They have no culture in their bodies. They can't even pronounce the word gentlemanly correctly.

ALLNUTT I admit that there are many gentlemen among the Germans, but what good is that if, as you very rightly point out, they pronounce their own generic term incorrectly. Whether one IS virtuous seems to me very irrelevant; The main thing is to speak virtuously, since life consists largely of conversations, which would bore you considerably if you always told the truth.

NUTALL Dear Jack, why don't you join the press? It would suit you very well. Its points of view are entirely yours, which, incidentally, interest me greatly.

ALLNUTT Dear boy, you're mistaken; I don't like the press at all. They lie. Certainly. But they don't comment on their lies, and I comment on mine. There's a big difference. When I lie, I come pretty close to the truth; but the press lies when it tells the truth.

NUTALL The only beautiful thing in life is a football match in which you personally participate, followed by a footbath.

ALLNUTT You can only live with the most intense reactions possible. They alone make life worth living. That's why you don't live in England... (*The telephone rings*)

NUTALL Did you hear that?

ALLNUTT Yes.

NUTALL The telephone rang.

ALLNUTT It certainly did.

NUTALL Wouldn't you like to hear what's going on?

ALLNUTT Dear Davis, why don't you satisfy your own curiosity?

NUTALL I'm the senior of the two of us. It's your duty to answer the telephone and tell me what's going on.

ALLNUTT I'll be damned if I do, my dear boy. It's your turn today. I'm here more for fun, because I don't know what else to do in London, and the clubrooms are still not heated. (*The telephone rings*)

NUTALL Did you hear it?

ALLNUTT Yes.

NUTALL The telephone rang.

ALLNUTT Certainly.

> *The telephone rings again*

NUTALL It's ringing again. (*sighing*) This telephone is an unpleasant device. I think it was invented by the Germans. (*The telephone rings*)

ALLNUTT The telephone is ringing for the fourth time. It seems we're being mistaken for a fire station.

NUTALL I have no choice but to call the orderly. (*He rises, goes to the door on the left and opens it, calls out.*) Orderly! (*One appears.*)

ORDERLY What would you like?

NUTALL I'm sorry to bother you. May I ask you to answer the telephone and see what it's about. It's already rung three times. (*Sinks back into his club chair.*)

ORDERLY (*On the telephone*) Hello! This is Recruiting Office Z 1.17 on Lammer Street. What? ... How? (*Entering the room, delighted*) Lieutenant! Lieutenant! A volunteer is coming forward! (*The two officers jump up*)

BOTH What? A volunteer?

ALLNUTT That hasn't happened to us in two weeks. Hold him tight.

ORDERLY Here he is. (*Hands the receiver to NUTALL*)

NUTALL Most respectful good morning, sir! May I take the liberty of inviting you to join us for lunch today? How? What? At Johnson's. Gallantry? What kind of gallantry? Ah, gallantry goods! You want to volunteer... What?... But only as... What?... as a general?... You must be mad, for God's sake!... A thousand pounds, well, a general isn't that cheap around here... Ask again at the end of the war. That's it! (*Hangs up*) What do you say, Jack? (*to the* ORDERLY) After listening to the entire conversation and enriching your knowledge, you can go again, Billey.

ORDERLY (*bows, exits*)

ALLNUTT Kitchener and Asquith want to set up 25 army corps.

NUTALL What charming naiveté!

ALLNUTT You'd be better off calling it idiocy.

NUTALL Of our three thousand officers on the mainland, twelve hundred have already been killed, captured, or wounded. Who will train the twenty-five army corps?

ALLNUTT Calm down, we'll train and establish another army corps... for the sake of formalities... It will consist mostly of convicts, Black men, and Bengalis. War is nonsense. No Englishman is stupid enough to let himself be shot because Mr. Grey is weak at mental arithmetic and made a damned mistake in his additions.

NUTALL But Parliament!

ALLNUTT Parliament. Parliament. Parliament! What does Parliament want? War, perhaps? In a pinch, a second army corps could be assembled by sending over the German prisoners in France and dressing them as Highlanders. Over on the mainland, they'd all run away, but the honor of having formed a second army corps would have been saved, and the newspapers could report: After a gallant resistance, in nine days of incredibly fierce fighting, part of our left wing was forced into a successful retreat.

    The telephone rings

NUTALL The telephone is starting to ring again.

ALLNUTT It's ringing like a cowbell. I'm surprised they haven't invented a telephone bell with choral accompaniment in London yet.

NUTALL (*at the door*) Orderly! Orderly!

ORDERLY (*enters*) What can I do for you?

NUTALL The telephone has rung. Please talk to whoever is bothering us.

ORDERLY (*accusingly*) This is the second time you've disturbed me in my morning nap. You shouldn't do that; you should answer the telephone yourself. People like us need to get a good night's sleep before going off to war. In war, the unpleasant sounds of grenades and shrapnel often deprive us of sleep, and we're woken up for duty more violently than necessary. Before 7 a.m., no less, which is unparalleled human abuse.

NUTALL Don't chatter, there's the telephone.

ORDERLY Hello! This is Recruiting Office Z 1 17 on Lammer Street... Who is it? ... So the office of the Navy Ministry. Who is it? Please hurry... We don't have time, we're very busy. ... Could we lend the Navy Ministry some young officers for the fleet review and the naval parade on Saturday? How? Uniforms will be provided... Of course... With pleasure.

ALLNUTT But we're requesting a promotion for Saturday...

ORDERLY But we're requesting a promotion for our officers... No. You understand correctly, only for Saturday, only for the uniform. It doesn't hurt if there are a few too many captains... Yes, thank you, that's it.

NUTALL You're a gem. It's a shame you became a soldier.

ORDERLY Thank you for your well-intentioned compliment, sir, but I only became a soldier out of necessity, out of cowardice, so to speak.

ALLNUTT Like a soldier and cowardly?

ORDERLY Sir, I used to be a policeman, fought in the fiercest suffragette battles. "Votes for Women," that poster over there, I spat on it more than once. This medal on this chest shows the names of the battles I survived, I don't even understand how. Here, October 17: Battle of the Ministry of Justice, here, May 13: Battle of Wall Street, June 15: Battle of Hyde Park.

ALLNUTT Poor, unfortunate man! You are a hero! The Germans won't be able to harm you. Go!

ORDERLY (*exits*)

NUTALL Times are changing. The military has now entered into an official alliance with the suffragettes. They are our only reliable allies. (*sighing*) What will we have to pay them later for this? Even conviction isn't free in England and must always yield a certain percentage.

ALLNUTT The suffragettes lend us their posters, their marching bands, their furious women, their entire fighting method for recruiting. It would only be logical to depose Sir French and appoint a suffragette as Chief of the British General Staff.

NUTALL The mere news of this would cause panic in Germany.

ALLNUTT We can at least console ourselves: the Germans have their zeppelins and we have our suffragettes... They, too, drop bombs, unfortunately mostly into their own country. (*There's a knock*)

NUTALL (*hesitantly*) Come in! (*There's a louder knock*) Come in!

ORDERLY Sir, do you have a revolver? I left mine at home in the nightstand. Oh God, why am I always so forgetful? I'll go into battle and forget my whiskey.

ALLNUTT Yes, for crying out loud, what is it?

ORDERLY Outside there is a, a...

NUTALL Now, be quick about it!

ORDERLY A — a suffragette! (*The officers blanch*)

ALLNUTT Is... she... alone?

NUTALL Does she have an umbrella with her?

ORDERLY I don't know, but a gentleman from Whitechapel is with her.

NUTALL A robber, perhaps.

ORDERLY Certainly he is something like that.

ALLNUTT Perhaps she has a recruit. (*all three stand up*)

ORDERLY That's possible. I didn't think of that in my initial shock.

NUTALL That's it.

ALLNUTT I thought so.

NUTALL I'm relieved. (*To the* ORDERLY) Let the lady in.

ORDERLY (*Exits, lets in Miss Flora Basingstoke, an elderly, disgruntled lady, and* TOMMY. *The latter looks very ill and bedraggled.* ALLNUTT *and* NUTALL *push two club chairs toward the gentlemen.*)

NUTALL Please, won't you gentlemen sit down? Miss: (*Sits down*) Thank you. We had to wait outside in the drafty corridor for almost three hours before that stubborn orderly understood what I wanted.

ALLNUTT Billey is a little nervous and gets easily shy around ladies of your station — one might almost say timid, if that word hadn't been struck from the soldier's code.

MISS BASINGSTOKE (*To* TOMMY) Sit down!

TOMMY (*Sits down obediently and awkwardly*)

NUTALL Please, sir!

TOMMY (*snarky*) I'm not a sir!

NUTALL Forgive me if I went too far in my politeness, mister!

MISS BASINGSTOKE (*introducing*) Tommy Atkins!

ALLNUTT A lovely name!

TOMMY (*snarky*) Yes, a lovely name! Especially now in wartime, a lovely name is worth a lot. You can sell it, so to speak, if you're hungry, aren't you?

NUTALL Mr. Atkins, I don't know.

MISS BASINGSTOKE The gentleman is hungry. He has a wife, three children, they're all hungry.

ALLNUTT (*embarrassed*) Why?

TOMMY Because they threw me out.

ALLNUTT Where were you thrown out from?

NUTALL Perhaps you've had a little too much to drink after all?

TOMMY If gentleman were an insult, I'd call you: Gentleman.

ALLNUTT (*soothingly*) We're very glad you've decided to fight under the glorious banners of His Royal English and Imperial Majesty of India.

TOMMY I've decided. Very good! I've decided... I'm hungry. ... My wife is hungry... My three children are hungry... They threw me out of the factory. You don't get a job if you become a soldier; you get food and a few shillings a day to save for your wife. I met this woman when I was ready to do anything. She told me all sorts of things and took me with her right away. Here I am: I want to volunteer for the army.

MISS BASINGSTOKE A strong fellow. Just a little underweight.

NUTALL Oh, never mind. Malnutrition is precisely what makes you an excellent volunteer. Are you otherwise healthy? What kind of factory were you employed in?

TOMMY In an agricultural machinery factory.

NUTALL Good God, is there such a thing in England? Surely a factory like that would go bankrupt here even in peacetime?

ALLNUTT (*has gone to the lectern and is writing*) In any case, the word "agricultural" alone conjures up the healthiest images of villages and fields, of earth and the smell of barnyards. It is certainly healthier to work in an agricultural machinery factory than, for example, in a factory for industrial machinery.

TOMMY Why?

ALLNUTT Well, I already said agricultural, the word agricultural alone... but let's break off the philosophical discourse now and move on to the actual purpose of our pleasant gathering. I consider myself very fortunate to meet you. So, your name is:

TOMMY (*stands up*) Tommy Atkins.

ALLNUTT Thank you very much. Please don't bother. Just sit quietly. We are concerned with the comfort of our soldiers in every way.

TOMMY sits down, feeling very unhappy

ALLNUTT How old?

TOMMY 32 years old.

ALLNUTT Married?

TOMMY Yes.

ALLNUTT Your wife, I should note, is entitled to a widow's pension.

TOMMY (*horrified*) Am I going to die?

ALLNUTT (*benignly*) It's very unlikely that you'll die, except perhaps from boredom. Sir French is waging a very boring war: I know that from the Boer campaign. But you won't die. Most of our men are captured and then, according to treaty agreements, have just as good a life in Germany as they do here. The only difference is that at meals, instead of rump steak, there's boiled beef, and instead of curry, there's sauerkraut, which isn't much of a difference.

TOMMY Rump steak! I dream of dry rolls at night, (*dreamily*) And I have to hear the word rump steak.

ALLNUTT Just a minute. We're going to lunch right away and will consider it an honor to welcome you as our guest. Will you please sign this? It's the contract between the Royal English Government and you. You stand before the Royal English Government as an equal.

TOMMY (*signs*)

ALLNUTT Thank you very much.

NUTALL (*shakes MISS BASINGSTOKE's hand*) Thank you, Miss Basingstoke. You have fully fulfilled your duty as an English woman.

TOMMY (*enraptured*) Rump steak!

ALLNUTT My dear Davis! Would you mind quickly reading the poetically valuable call to enlist so that our friend Mr. Atkins knows what awaits him?

NUTALL (*reads*) You young heroes, flock to the proud banners of Britain. You will be paid five shillings a day and guaranteed hot lunch and dinner.

TOMMY Rump steak!

NUTALL As well as free time for church, sports, and reading.

TOMMY Reading, what's that?

ALLNUTT For example, reading the newspaper. We have our own reading room, where reading material — i.e., newspapers, detective stories, robber stories, and romance novels — is adequately provided.

MISS BASINGSTOKE (*indignantly*) Love stories too?

ALLNUTT Did I say love stories? Oh, not love stories, but anything else you want.

NUTALL (*continues reading*) If there's no battle, soccer, baseball, and football games are also arranged in the field. There's plenty of time for shaving every morning. To entertain the crews, sack races and egg and spoon races are planned during breaks in the battle. Fishing can be indulged in on the Aisne and Marne rivers, and the fishing license doesn't cost a penny. The risk of losing one's life is very small, as each soldier is equipped with a bulletproof wool shirt, in the mesh of which the German bullets, which, as we know, are very small in caliber and the size of peas, get caught, etc., etc. Are you satisfied now?

TOMMY I'm hungry... rump steak.

ALLNUTT Certainly, rump steak... and whiskey.

TOMMY Rump steak... and whiskey.

MISS BASINGSTOKE What... whiskey?

ALLNUTT Did I say whiskey? Of course not whiskey. That was a mistake. Excuse me, Miss Basingstoke. Come, Mr. Atkins, let's have lunch.

MISS BASINGSTOKE Lemonade. Just lemonade!

ORDERLY (*Entering, trembling, a newspaper in hand*) Sir, a blimp... a blimp.

ALL A blimp?... a blimp?

MISS BASINGSTOKE (*Exiting shrieking*)

TOMMY (*Trying to crawl under a club chair*)

ALLNUTT (*Creeping cautiously to the window, revolver in hand*) A blimp!

NUTALL (*Stands under the telephone*) I've heard it's best to stand under the telephone when a zeppelin approaches... the bombs are cut cleanly in half by the telephone wires and are then as harmless as eggshells.

ORDERLY (*Speaks trembling*) Sir, a zeppelin has appeared over Antwerp... oh God, just wait until we get one in London.

ALLNUTT AND NUTALL (*at the same time*) Antwerp! Fool! Why didn't you say so?

TOMMY (*From under a lounge chair*) Off to war!

   Curtain

Part Fifteen:

The Speed-Painter

"The Speed Painter" was published in the magazine "The Program,"
the journal of the Munich Intimate Theater - 2nd volume, 1915/1916.

The Speed-Painter

A Scene
Also a Character Farce in 4 Scenes

Scene One

Attic room. Casement window. (Northern light.) A young man, wearing a black velvet blouse and with flowing black hair, is working on a painting. Due to general exhaustion, the work progresses only very slowly.

Scene Two

The patron enters: bald head. Tuxedo. Entrance song:

Heavens above!
You haven't a clue:
Art – damn it – craves bread,
Bread craves art.

Esteemed Master – jokes aside, Rembrandt aside – you paint too slowly, much too slowly. That's the whole problem. You must throw your arms around art: always be quick, always hurry, hurry! Art is about leaving things out. Leave everything out: what remains is the real thing! Extract, my little dove, extract! (*He places a ten-mark note on the non-existent table. The painter begins to paint noticeably faster.*)

Scene Three

Cupid appears, disguised as a red cyclist; he has with him, in a hatbox, a young lady from the highest circles of society. He hands the painter a red-sealed letter. The painter opens it hastily and reads:

Today, a bill of exchange is due for 1,000 marks.
Venus and Company
Banking Business

The painter turns pale, glances at the hatbox, from which sounds like nightingales chirping, grabs the brush, and begins to paint furiously. Cupid smiles and thinks: Brush! – for he alone knows what "mark" means. It doesn't mean mark, but... girl's kisses...

Scene Four

Apotheosis of the art trade: the speedy painter sits panting at the easel and paints and paints: each painting is snatched from his hands while still warm. The thousand-mark notes fly like roasted pigeons through the sumptuously furnished ground-floor studio. Between each picture, a woman appears, young, beautiful, old, ugly, slender, fat. Intermezzo music. Transformation. Time appears, bowed down with grief, no longer able to keep up with the speedy painter. As it slowly passes away, showing signs of decay, the curtain falls.

Photographs and Illustrations

Klabund's Mother Emilie Antonie
Buckenau (1867-1945)

Kalbund's Father, Dr. Alfred Heneschke
(1858-1936)

Dr. Alfred Henschke's Pharmacy
in Crossen, Poland

Klabund, 1922

Klabund Lithograph by Orlik, 1915

Klabund with Fran Bruno at Walchensee,
1915

Brunhilde Heberle in 1917
(1896-1918)

Klabund and his first wife Brunhilde Heberle
on a trip to Mergosscia, Switzerland

Klabund with Brother Hans and Two
Cousins

Brunhilde Heberle, 1916

Carola Neher in 1925, (1900-1942)

Klabund in Davos

Klabund, Date Unknown

Klabund Portrait by Eric Buttner, 1919

Klabund, Date Unknown

Klabund, Date Unknown

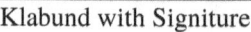

Klabund with Signiture

Klabund with the Actor
Alexander Granach, 1926

Klabund, 1925

Klabund, 1928

Carola Neher in 1925

Klabund's New Years Greeting
to Irene and Max Heberle, 1923

Klabund and Carola Neher, 1924

Klabund and Carola Neher, 1925

Klabund and Carola Neher on the Beach,
Date Unknown

Klabund and Carola Neher in 1928

Klabund, Last Photograph, Brioni,
Summer 1928

I thank you from the bottom of my heart for
your loving condolences at the passing
of my beloved husband.

Newspaper Clipping: Klabund and Neher in Vienna, 1927

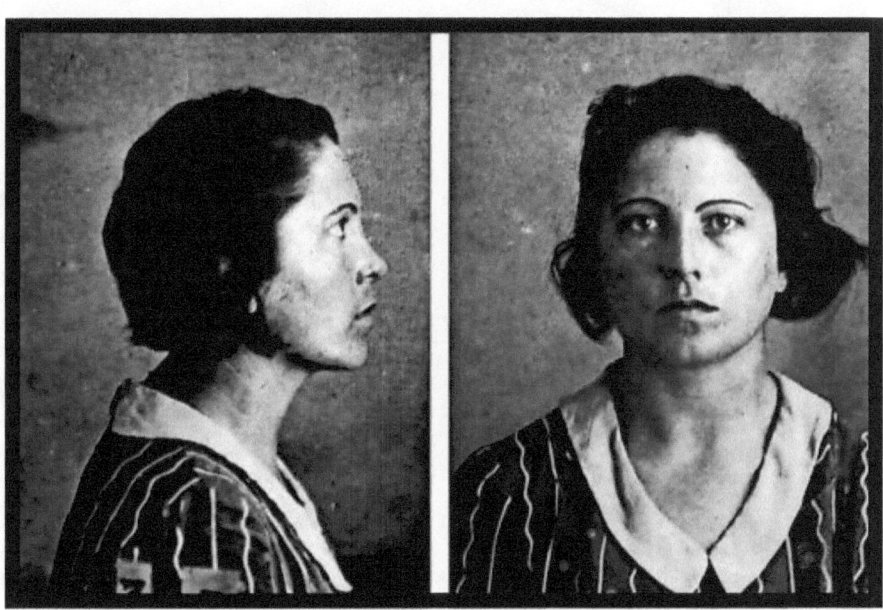

Carola Neher Prison Photo from KGB Archive, 1936

Klabund's play *The Chalk Circle*, 1925

Klabund's play *The Cherry Blossom Festival*, 1928

December 1919 program for the Sound and Smoke Cabaret

Script for Klabund's XYZ play

Klabund's Works Published by Eric Reiss Verlag

Klabund Statue with the Mayor of Crossen, Poland

Part Sixteen:

The Sleepwalkers

"The Sleepwalkers" published in 1917 by Erich Reiß Verlag, Berlin,
Some might call it a play of premonitions about Klabund's own life.

The Sleepwalkers

Characters:
Apollo,
First — (Nymph and Dryad)
Second — (Nymph and Dryad)
Third — (Nymph and Dryad)
Fourth — (Nymph and Dryad)
Cornelia – a girl
Silvius – a young man
The Man in Yellow
Organ Grinder
Boys and girls
Policeman
Waiter
Sailor
The Privy Councilor, Cornelia's father
The Privy Councilor's wife, Cornelia's mother
Maid
Passerby
Elegant and semi-elegant audience
Typewriter girl
Gentleman
First stockbroker
Second stockbroker
Art critic
Art connoisseur
Brother – In the interlude
Sister – In the interlude
Someone – In the interlude
A gentleman and a lady on their way home.
The Corps Student, Cornelia's Brother
Death as a Child
Midwife
Invalid
Doctor
First Officer
Second Officer
Railway Official
Conductor
Gentleman in Gray
Apparition of a Lady
Gentleman in a Cape

Basel, Christmas 1917.

Scene One

Forest Meadow.

APOLLO (*enters*) Ha, I ran through the storm... Clouds clung on my sides... I shook them off with laughter... I tore stars from the sky... I hurled them through the night... The sky bled... The moon's heart shattered... As the stars fell, people wished for their loved ones... The rain poured... Like strands of Cornelia's hair, it flowed down... hanging gently around my forehead... Women!

The gods often yearn for your death so they can hold you more tightly: The dead more tightly than the living... The living slip away even from a god... A god cannot hold the mountain stream that rushes over rocks: It rushes: it rushes over them too, shattering even those who seem immortal in the abyss. But the dead: remain. In the arms of the gods they lie, eternal children with the waxen faces of the dead. We rock them on our bosom; they hang there like fruit: grapes on the vine: eternally ripening under the dark wings of perfection.

My cloak slaps against my bare body. Zeus softened me with envy. Rain even dripped into my flute. (*He plays a few notes on his flute.*) Even in the thunder of the storm, Apollo's flute still sounds. Zeus hears it singing when he cries out...

I take off my cloak. Hang it on this bush. The wind may dry it when it comes along. I stride naked into sleep... (*He falls asleep*)

Nymphs and dryads come rushing up

FIRST NYMPH A man... completely naked... come closer to look at him... he is asleep...

Her companions scurry forward, bending over him in a circle

SECOND NYMPH How sweet his breath... Like laurel blossoms in autumn...

THIRD NYMPH His breast rises and falls like the waves of the ocean...

FOURTH NYMPH His hand caresses Brother Dream.

FIRST NYMPH He is slender... untrained in arduous and difficult tasks... delicate...

SECOND NYMPH His feet are only accustomed to walking lightly... to dance or march in the choir... perhaps skipping while he hunts...

THIRD NYMPH If I could see his eyes: I would know what mother bore him, what father begot him...

FOURTH NYMPH (*wrapping herself in APOLLO's cloak*) Brr, how wet... I'm freezing...

FIRST NYMPH Look at this flute... what purpose can it serve? (*She blows on it*) Ah... what a lovely sound... from my own breast... my heart is torn in two... it throws my breasts apart... they roll... like balls... ringing to the moon...

APOLLO (*awakening*) Who plays my game? Who sings my song? And disturb the god's sleep... which is as sacred as human sleep... (*snatches the flute from the dryad and strikes her with it. She freezes into a tree.*) Golden rabble. I will teach you, like parrots, to imitate the voices of the gods on frivolous moonlit nights.

THE NYMPHS *are amazed.*

SECOND NYMPH A god... Who is it?

THIRD NYMPH Mercy...

FOURTH NYMPH Apollo...

SECOND NYMPH Grace...

THIRD NYMPH Wait...

FOURTH NYMPH (*Putting her ear to the ground*) I hear human footsteps...

SECOND NYMPH I hear women's footsteps...

THIRD NYMPH Pain shuffles her gait...

FOURTH NYMPH Sorrow crawls like snails...

SECOND NYMPH Tear after tear drops, hard as stone, to the ground...

THIRD NYMPH She lays her hands before her face: Like the defeated warrior laying down his shield after battle...

FOURTH NYMPH She seeks solitude...

SECOND NYMPH Seeks a god...

APOLLO Seeks me! (*She plays her flute*) Tree and flower maidens vanish! Water children! I want to be alone with someone...

THE NYMPHS (*Laughter of THE NYMPHS fading away*) With a woman... with a woman...

Scene Two

Churchyard. Dusk.

CORNELIA (*At a grave, arranging flowers*) My beloved, I bring these wildflowers: poppies, buttercups, catchfly, and corn cockle. I picked them myself. There are a few ears of corn among them. I uprooted them and want to plant them in your grave. Perhaps they will bear grain, and I will eat bread from your life.

She weeps

SILVIUS (*Has moved closer, removes his hat*) You are crying, my lady. Let me cry with you. I have no one to honor my tears. Do not push me away.

He weeps

CORNELIA My lord —

SILVIUS Call me Silvius, for that is my name.

CORNELIA I will call for the cemetery caretaker.

SILVIUS Do so, at least. The bushes are muffling your cries. There are no bell pulls on the gravestones and crosses.

CORNELIA You're an animal. Help!

SILVIUS I'm a human being just like you. Yes: just like you, and like the one lying here under the moss.

CORNELIA Oh! He was good!

SILVIUS You loved him — and that's why he was good.

CORNELIA You're desecrating his memory by only speaking of him.

SILVIUS I knew him well. We went to university together and often went to neighboring villages together on summer evenings. There we drank brown beer and danced with the peasant girls. And then we sang our way back to the gabled town under the full moon.

CORNELIA He danced with peasant girls? That's not true.

SILVIUS Cry, little one, cry! It will make you, me, all of us feel better if you cry!

CORNELIA You're lying. He was never unfaithful to me!

SILVIUS (*stroking her hair*) No, certainly not. He remained faithful to you. But such a harmless little dance — what did you do? Did you want to deny him that? With you, the daughter of the secret councilor, he was not allowed to dance in taverns on summer evenings, drink brown beer, and caress your sweet, soft breasts.

CORNELIA You're horrible! I'm afraid of you!

SILVIUS I'm so horrible to look at because I haven't been able to shave today. I'm short of money at the moment. Do you happen to have 5 marks with you? That you could lend me until the day after tomorrow?

CORNELIA But you're a robber! Oh, ugh! There, take my entire purse. Because that's why you only spoke to me: to steal my wallet at the right moment. (*sobs*)

SILVIUS (*embraces her*) Girl! Dear girl! As you know deep down, your beautiful lips lie, out of love — lie...

CORNELIA What — out of love? What does that mean? Do you think I love you?

SILVIUS That's precisely what I think. And as for me, I know: that I love you

He kisses her.

CORNELIA I don't even know you —

SILVIUS You'll get to know me.

CORNELIA Won't you at least introduce yourself? I think you owe that to a young lady of society:

SILVIUS (*bows*) Silvius, a young man.

CORNELIA (*grinning*) Cornelia, a girl.

SILVIUS My girl!

> *Kisses her.*

CORNELIA Are you of legal age? Are you in a fraternity?

SILVIUS No.

CORNELIA For God's sake! We have to be very careful. My brother mustn't find out about our relationship. He'd slap you.

SILVIUS And I'd beat him to death like a mad dog.

CORNELIA You have guts! Show me (*checks his arm*) Do you have muscles?

SILVIUS No — I have nothing at all. Not even myself. And not even you.

CORNELIA (*kisses him*) And you're not shaved either: your mustache is tearing my whole face apart. I don't want to kiss a forest, but moon-kissed cheeks or sunny lips. The next time I meet you, you must be shaved. You must promise me that!

SILVIUS I promise you – with the love I feel for this dead man, since you once loved him.

CORNELIA Let's not speak of him. He had it easy. He no longer needs to think about where I could meet him. The thinking is now yours. When will we meet next?

SILVIUS Next time? Tomorrow!

CORNELIA So tomorrow, but where?

SILVIUS In the suburbs, out behind the last houses – there –

CORNELIA Good.

SILVIUS My sweet girl!

CORNELIA My Silvius.

> *CORNELIA breaks free from the embrace and easily slips away. SILVIUS remains sitting pensively on the dead lover's burial mound. Night falls. A few fireflies glow. A shooting star falls.*

Scene Three

SILVIUS's garret. Open window. Full moon

SILVIUS I have no more kerosene. But the moon shines so brightly, I will write my poems by heavenly light.

> *He sits down on the windowsill. Writes:*

> When I think of the sweet bliss
> That the sight of you brings me, Cornelia,
> I am completely swept away

As if by an drunken drink.

That seems excellent to me – except for the "drunken drink!" It should, of course, be "intoxicating." But then that's one foot too many. Let's leave it as it is: The drunken drink: It conjures thoughts like the sea, the torrent, the storm wind – and so it is good.

> *A GENTLEMAN in a yellow coat, yellow trousers, yellow boots, yellow gloves, a yellow top hat, and a yellow walking stick has entered the door on the left. The room is suddenly bright. The moon outside is eclipsed.*

GENTLEMAN You are reading a poetic colloquium — to whom? Your imagination? Do you believe you are a poet?

SILVIUS Why is it any of your business? And who are you, anyway? And how did you get into my room?

GENTLEMAN Excuse me, Moon is my name.

SILVIUS Mine can be of no concern to you; since you are determined to deny me the abilities and talent of a poet, you intend, even if I tell you my name, to forget it as quickly as possible.

GENTLEMAN Why so bitter? Why interpret my words so maliciously? Why offend someone who wants to lay his head at your feet, so to speak? Who has come to help you?

SILVIUS Forgive me, I've been a little irritable these last few days. A fierce passion – fueled solely by weak tea – is beyond my strength.

GENTLEMAN You're in love?

SILVIUS Forever, for ages, and I will love forever –

GENTLEMAN Whom?

SILVIUS Cornelia, my girl!

GENTLEMAN Ah! The daughter of the Privy Councilor! You have good taste! A pretty child!

SILVIUS And young as a child! 17 years old!

GENTLEMAN That means: Exactly your age!

SILVIUS Please, I'm 17 and three-quarters!

GENTLEMAN There are certainly 9 months... leeway between you! Just enough to bring a child into the world.

SILVIUS (*horrified*) How?

GENTLEMAN Don't you understand me? I said: What if Cornelia has a child?

SILVIUS But is that even possible?

GENTLEMAN Of course it's possible! You love Cornelia, don't you?

SILVIUS Certainly... certainly...

GENTLEMAN Wouldn't you like to have a child?... a boy, a son who looks like you, with blue eyes, blond hair — or another girl — just like Cornelia?

SILVIUS (*spreads his arms*) A child! A child!

GENTLEMAN Of course, you shouldn't make Cornelia an illegitimate mother. She comes from a very distinguished family, where that's not customary. You'd have to marry her.

SILVIUS Marry? But I'm not yet of age and don't have a penny.

GENTLEMAN I'll advance you as much as you need to travel to England with Cornelia. There, you don't need to be 21 to marry, and besides, no one there attaches any particular importance to valid identification papers. You'll get married in London and then return as husband and wife. The family is faced with a fait accompli.[14] They'll have to accept it. You can love Cornelia forever and have a hundred children with impunity.

SILVIUS (*Excited*) Sir — where do you come from?

GENTLEMAN From heaven — as my name already suggested. Here's a thousand marks, and goodbye!

SILVIUS How can I thank you?

GENTLEMAN Through action! Always do what you think! Listen! Don't poison your brain with undone deeds! Good evening, my boy! (*Through the door, turns left*)

> *The room grows dim again. Outside, the moon emerges from the clouds.*

SILVIUS (*On the windowsill*)
When I think of the sweet bliss
That the sight of Cornelia creates for me,
How I am completely and totally swept away As if by an intoxicating drink.

The moon is our kindest companion:
It wishes to be our servant and prophet
And on her golden magic steed
Leads us into the paradise of sighs.

Scene Four

Before the last houses of the suburbs. Large white back walls on the left. Forest in the background on the right.

As the curtain rises, the organ grinder, a rickety frame with a skull and a wooden leg, plays a military march. Invalid. Many commemorative coins. Children: Boys and girls dance around him. The

---

[14] A done deal.

organ grinder stops playing. He takes off his hat. Copper pieces fly into his hat from the kitchen balconies of the rear houses. He bows.

A CHILD Play on, man...

ORGAN GRINDER I've played enough... With me... with you...

A CHILD Please, man.

ORGAN GRINDER My craft disgusts me, you don't know it, you're too small.

A CHILD Even small people... are people...

ORGAN GRINDER Always playing... so that children dance... always turning the grinder so that maids sing... It would be something if I could conjure up magic with my music. Make the sun appear. Or make it stand still. That night would not come. Look, I have been playing, and twilight already hangs like dirty laundry between the houses.

A CHILD When our eyes shine because you are playing: isn't that magic? Aren't you happy?

ORGAN GRINDER No, it embitters me...

A CHILD It angers you? Are you a bad man?

ORGAN GRINDER It... pains me...

A CHILD Pains you?

ORGAN GRINDER It hurts me that you follow me... and don't know where... I am leading and seducing you.

A CHILD What for? Where?

ORGAN GRINDER To dark death, who lives there in the woods, calls himself a hermit, and shines with bearded kindness.

A CHILD Mother told me about him: Called him holy and pious.

ORGAN GRINDER Mothers lie... It is their handiwork and soul's work. Why do they give birth to you in childish pain? They buzz: For light, for pleasure, for life. I tell you: Don't believe your mother. She has a pact with the hermit in the forest there. All mothers have a pact with him. He gives them gold and vanity and a bestial lust of their double-breasted bodies. In return, they bear him children. He tears your heart from your belly and drinks your blood. He tells you it's great to die a heroic death; and you offer your breasts, jubilant, to his knife, denying the prospect of reaping immortality if he sows golden greed into your wounds...

A CHILD I understand you, man... I, too, must go to war when I grow up... then I'll march under the flag and kill the enemy...

ORGAN GRINDER You'll kill yourself... and your foolish mother... Oh, who bids you follow me when I play the wild marches on the barrel organ? Guard your spirit, so that it does not ignite at an impure flame! To earn my life...

and my death, I am forced to turn this black box... Beware! I know war! It resounds with destruction, it resounds with whimpering. It resounds of deafness, sluggishness, gloom, betrayal, cowardice, treachery, murder, robbery, incest, and every vice. Behold my medals here: each one the boastfully gleaming image of a battle. A lost battle... of spirits. A won battle... of idols. Beware... and your mothers too!

He begins to play the Radetzky March on the barrel organ

CORNELIA and SILVIUS come along the path, hand in hand

SILVIUS (*tosses him a coin*) Play us a wedding song, organ grinder.

ORGAN GRINDER At your service, gracious sir... (*Plays: Youth is beautiful in joyful times, youth is beautiful, it will never return.*)

The children dance in a ring around SILVIUS and CORNELIA. SILVIUS and CORNELIA stand completely still, CORNELIA resting her head on his shoulder. The ring dance dissolves. The organ grinder drones away, followed in a colorful line by the children.

CORNELIA Here we stand; alone and completely abandoned.

SILVIUS Are we not enough for each other?

CORNELIA (*shuddering*) Yes, dearest.

SILVIUS Do you see the forest beyond the horizon?

CORNELIA Yes; it looms as dark as our future.

SILVIUS We must pass through it.

CORNELIA I only have low shoes... and a silk dress... The thorns will tear it... the shoes will get stuck in the swamp...

SILVIUS I will carry you. I feel as strong as Christopher when he carried Christ across the river...

CORNELIA Am I your Christ?

SILVIUS My Christine! My Cornelia!

CORNELIA What will Mama say when I don't come home tonight? She'll cry, and Papa will go to the police station even in the middle of the night. They'll search the ponds to see if I drowned myself, the woods to see if I got lost...

SILVIUS They can't search the hearts of people. Otherwise, they would find you — with me.

CORNELIA We'll send Papa and Mama a telegram — from England — don't you think? Something simple like: Cornelia and Silvius, newlyweds, send their regards. Warm greetings until we meet again! (*both laugh*)

SILVIUS My angel! I'll lift you into heaven, where you belong!

CORNELIA Do you still have the money that the stranger gave you? Check!

SILVIUS (*rummages in his pocket. Pulls out a crumpled thousand-mark note.*)

Here...

CORNELIA You... Tonight we'll sleep in a first-class hotel, with canopy beds, a private bath, running hot and cold water, signal lights, double doors, a music band in red tailcoats, and a little Black boy as a lift attendant. We'll have supper served in our room! Salmon, turkey, ice cream with fruits. And we'll drink so much champagne that we fall asleep. We'll even have champagne brought to the bed and keep drinking until we just can't anymore.

SILVIUS Exorbitant! Limitless!

CORNELIA We'll play husband and wife and sleep in one bed and sign the guest-book: Silvius and wife. Darling (*kisses him*)

SILVIUS Are you excited about the ship, girl? We'll see the sea! The sea that touches no shores.

CORNELIA The sun that never sets.

SILVIUS The wind that never dies.

CORNELIA The lighthouse that stands... and shines forever.

> *A POLICEMAN approaches.*

POLICEMAN It's already late at night. What are you doing wandering around the fields? Are you homeless?

CORNELIA What does the blue devil want?

SILVIUS Stay calm, my love... We are neither homeless, officer, nor are we loitering. We are being driven around on this mathematical construct called Earth, in this movement of air which is called called Life. Do you understand?

POLICEMAN Stop babbling and get yourselves into town, or I'll take you to the station.

SILVIUS You have no authority to do that.

POLICEMAN Well, look at that: no authority. The police have authority over every-thing.

SILVIUS They seize authority. But they don't have the right, only the power, and that's a disgrace. To degrade people: nothing is lower than that.

POLICEMAN I sense resistance to state authority. Sadly, I don't understand you.

CORNELIA Good night, blue man. I hope you'll bring us as much luck as a chimney sweep or a white horse that crosses your path from the left. White horses crossing from the left are very rare. But even rarer is a friendly policeman. Guard us well, as we will sleep well in the bed of our heaven, our canopy bed.

> *Both exit laughing.*

Scene Five
A comfortably furnished room in a first-class hotel.

ROOM SERVICE *(holding the police registration forms)* Would you please register —

CORNELIA *(clinging to SILVIUS, who writes: Silvius and Wife. She claps her hands.)*

ROOM SERVICE Do the gentlemen and lady have any luggage?

SILVIUS The luggage will arrive tomorrow. It didn't make it onto the train.

ROOM SERVICE *(furrowing his brow)* Very well... very well... Do the gentlemen and lady have any other requests?

SILVIUS *(lighting a cigarette)*

CORNELIA *(dancing up and down)* We're living in a castle! We are counts! Royal highnesses! What a distance from the graveyard where we first met! There, ivy over damp moss! Here, silk covers over white down! There, the eternally unchanging moon. Here, electric light that you can switch on and off at will *(she flicks the lights on and off several times)*.

SILVIUS *(standing still)* Don't blame the moon! Child of the moon!

CORNELIA Once we had to sit on gravestones. Here, leather armchairs willingly receive our limbs. A marble boy, the image of death, extinguishing his torch in the sand, once seemed to be the embodiment, the beginning and end of art. Look here on the walls at these cheerful pictures: Venus floats atop the sphere of fortune, pursued by armored lovers on snorting chargers... Here: Brown harem women, made sluggish and dazed by opium, sweets, and love... and here: Nothing but color and line: violet, red, green, silver triangles glued one over another from paper scraps, circles, intersecting ellipses... parallels meeting in infinity...

SILVIUS In our hearts...

CORNELIA *(stepping to a door on the left, switching on the light)* Silvius! A bathroom — all in white and blue! Sea and sun combined.

SILVIUS *(kissing her)* Dear girl — let's bathe together — let's wash away the dust still clinging to us from that other world... of graveyards, family magazine novels, and department stores. *(He goes into the bathroom and starts running the water.)*

CORNELIA Silvius... you have never seen me naked... Do you think I am beautiful?

SILVIUS Beautiful as the statue of Artemis in her temple at Corinth... beautiful as the Nike of Samothrace... beautiful as a woodcut by a Chinese master... More beautiful, girl, more beautiful... for you are alive!

CORNELIA Silvius... I am not ashamed before you...

SILVIUS True love knows no shame anymore; it has risen beyond all virtues and vices; beyond the earth, into the thin ether where ordinary mortals can no longer breathe.

CORNELIA (*kneeling before him*) Let me loosen your shoelaces and take off your shoes — please.

SILVIUS I am not worthy —

CORNELIA Let me be Mary Magdalene! (*She begins to untie his laces.*)

> *The curtain falls.*

Scene Six

> *On the ship. SILVIUS and CORNELIA at the bow.*

SILVIUS I feel like I'm Columbus, discovering America... It cried out in my dream last night: Home... Someone cried out, Home... He should see home... from the stern... He pulls him up the mast...

CORNELIA Silvius... you're feverish...

SILVIUS My blood thunders behind my forehead. A palm tree is sprouting from the crown of my head... A pair of monkeys swings on it.

CORNELIA Silvius, you're dwelling in strange lands I do not know. Where are you? Fetch me! Take me with you!

> *SILVIUS pacing back and forth, then stopping, hand shading his eyes*

SILVIUS I see a black streak on the horizon...

SAILOR (*has come closer*) You suffer from nearsightedness. You need glasses. It's a dolphin.

SILVIUS I see a green island and I'm swimming towards it —

SAILOR Seaweed and algae.

SILVIUS A bird, flown from a nearby shore, is fluttering over the deck.

SAILOR It's a flying fish.

SILVIUS (*stamping his foot*) What do you want? Have you discovered perpetual motion? Are you preoccupied with squaring the circle? Did I ask you to correct my eyesight? I want to see with my own eyes — not with yours.

SAILOR Forgive me for telling the truth... (*disappears*)

CORNELIA What did the man want?

SILVIUS He wanted to steal you from me... you, the lord in the yellow cloak, my faith, my splendor, my golden happiness!

CORNELIA Listen — the ship's music is playing. Shall we go dance?

SILVIUS Dance in broad daylight?

CORNELIA At night we float with the stars, by day with the seagulls. Come, the ship is rocking.

SILVIUS The ship — our sacred bed — come, Cornelia, let us love...

Scene Seven

A bourgeois living room at the secret Councilor's *house.*

Councilor I've tried everything to track down Cornelia. Like a hunting dog, I dashed through the city. I have no reason to reproach myself. The police, both public and secret, have been alerted. Town criers rang their bells in the streets. Cyclists scattered in all directions. Posters on the advertising pillars scream in spinach-green and garish letters: Return, Cornelia, all is forgiven. — I did everything that could be done. (*rubs his hands*) It's so cold in this room. You haven't turned the heat up enough. Embarrassing, this thriftiness. I'll end up catching influenza, and the doctor will have to come. A doctor costs more than coal. Keep that in mind! Turn on the heat!

Councilor's Wife I beg you, Paul, don't get upset. Thank God you have me. You can't exactly do kangaroo jumps on a salary of six thousand marks. It's just enough for modest elegance, for Sunday veal roast, for an evening of skat with punch and mulled wine made from chemical cubes — barely enough for that. Coal has risen to unaffordable levels...

Councilor Spare me your household management. I'm freezing. Let that be stated, nothing more. That's it.

Councilor's Wife My little man!

Councilor Well, yes. —

Councilor's Wife Think of Cornelia!

Councilor Do you think I'm not always thinking of her? Am I not a father?

Councilor's Wife White slavers must have kidnapped her — taken her to a brothel... to South America... that's common nowadays. You read about it in the papers every day. Oh, my poor child...

Councilor Women wail. A man values action. One can do no more than one can do. I acted.

Councilor's Wife Send a telegram to Hamburg — have them close the harbor...

Councilor White slavery routes go through Marseilles.

Councilor's Wife Oh God... oh God...

Councilor Go pray in church. Sometimes there is a God. One can be a confident atheist, but one must believe in Him at the right moment... that works... miracles.

Councilor's Wife You are magnificent! Forgive me if I sometimes don't understand you. I'm foolish. Be patient with me.

Councilor All right — but what now?

Councilor's Wife In eight days we'll be married 25 years. A silver wedding without our child? Our golden one?

Councilor The celebration is canceled. We will wear mourning clothes.

COUNCILOR'S WIFE (*crying out*) You believe that —?

COUNCILOR Certainly not, calm yourself, Mathilde.

COUNCILOR'S WIFE You know something? You have some clues?

COUNCILOR One must be prepared for anything: nothing else. Black is most fitting for the dignity of our situation. Have a black silk dress made for yourself.

COUNCILOR'S WIFE Where are you wandering off to? The dressmaker no longer gives credit. The last bill isn't paid yet.

COUNCILOR Then find a new seamstress! I am a royal official! Who dares to question my creditworthiness?

COUNCILOR'S WIFE (*purring*) A black dress needs a black hat.

COUNCILOR It shall become reality, scarcely dreamt!

COUNCILOR'S WIFE Darling!

> *The doorbell rings*

COUNCILOR Visitors at this hour? Who could it be?

COUNCILOR'S WIFE Aunt Linchen?

COUNCILOR (*straightening up*) A report from the police?

> *The MAID enters*

MAID (*Embarrassed, playing with her apron*) Mr. Government Councilor...

COUNCILOR Well... Out with it...

MAID Mr. Government Councilor...

COUNCILOR Well... Is it going to take long?

COUNCILOR'S WIFE What's the matter with you, Emma?

> *The door opens: SILVIUS and CORNELIA appear.*

COUNCILOR'S WIFE Little Nelly!

> *runs towards her. Hug – SILVIUS stands, somewhat embarrassed, in the background.*

COUNCILOR What do you wish, young man?

SILVIUS I accompanied your daughter.

COUNCILOR Miss Daughter!

SILVIUS Mrs. Daughter!

COUNCILOR Don't contradict me!

SILVIUS Yes, I do!

COUNCILOR Modern youth!

SILVIUS Yes!

COUNCILOR (*stamps his foot*) Unbelievable.

SILVIUS True...

COUNCILOR Did you find my Miss Daughter? Do you want a finder's fee?

SILVIUS Fee? No. I've already given my reward. Found her? Yes, I found her! Among the dead! And I brought her back to life.

COUNCILOR Speak clearly and distinctly, precisely and firmly. Who are you?

SILVIUS Your daughter's husband!

CORNELIA Papa!

COUNCILOR What does that mean? Stop it with your inappropriate jokes and clowning around, trying to wound and mock a parent's heart!

SILVIUS I have no intention of hurting or insulting you, nor mocking you. I pity you, old man...

COUNCILOR I will not tolerate this rude disrespect!

CORNELIA Mama... Papa... Silvius is telling the truth... he is my husband, legally married to me... in London...

COUNCILOR'S WIFE Come to your senses, litle Nelly, you're confused...

SILVIUS Cornelia speaks the truth...

COUNCILOR'S WIFE My God... the shame! It can't be! –

COUNCILOR How old are you?

SILVIUS Seventeen and three-quarters.

COUNCILOR Wealth?

SILVIUS None.

COUNCILOR Income?

SILVIUS Likewise, none.

COUNCILOR How do you intend to live?

SILVIUS Off you, you are rich.

COUNCILOR Rich? Me? Extortion! I know it. I've already considered it. You'll get not a penny. Leave the house.

SILVIUS Not without my wife —

COUNCILOR Boy! Criminal! Murderer! Undermining the solid ground of the family, like a mole...

SILVIUS Solid ground trodden down by oxen and donkeys. Yes.

COUNCILOR You dare?

SILVIUS To be truthful!

COUNCILOR'S WIFE Little Nelly!

COUNCILOR Get out!

SILVIUS Come, Cornelia.

CORNELIA breaks free from her mother's embrace

CORNELIA I'll stay with you, Silvius.

COUNCILOR'S WIFE Little Nelly, don't leave me...

CORNELIA I can't do otherwise, Mama. I love Silvius, just like you love Papa. If they told you: Leave Papa – would you do it? Would you leave Papa?

COUNCILOR'S WIFE What will Arved, your brother, say? He's a fraternity member —

COUNCILOR I was a fraternity member too. I'm an alumnus of Saxo-Thuringia. Degenerate! Out of the house!

COUNCILOR'S WIFE Man! Be merciful.

COUNCILOR I am. Often, being merciful means being harsh.

COUNCILOR'S WIFE God be with you, Cornelia...

sobbing

Scene Eight

Street corner.

SILVIUS (*exclaiming*) National Newspaper – Evening edition. Big mining disaster in Silesia – three hundred buried – National Newspaper – Evening edition –

CORNELIA Buy matches – buy matches –

PASSERBY A nice little one. There (*Buys a box from her*). I would like to light my match on you – when and where can I meet you?

CORNELIA At this corner – nowhere else... I'm married...

PASSERBY Married? That doesn't matter. Is your husband also jealous if someone treats him to a grog and a warm dinner? How?

CORNELIA Just go on...

SILVIUS National Newspaper – Evening edition – big mining disaster in Silesia – three hundred buried – robbery-murder at Schlachtensee – the perpetrator arrested –

PASSERBY Who is that handsome young man hawking newspapers here next to you?

CORNELIA My... husband...

PASSERBY But that's not possible... You are both children... he's just a boy...

CORNELIA This boy – is my husband...

PASSERBY Keep the twenty marks – and the matches as well – Good evening (*exits*).

CORNELIA Silvius...

SILVIUS Did you sell well? You still have almost all the matches... Cornelia... we won't have anything to eat again tonight...

CORNELIA Yes, Silvius, look here... twenty marks.

SILVIUS How did you come by this wealth?

CORNELIA A distinguished gentleman gave them to me as a gift... At first he was thinking of selling me... then I moved him... he became kind — and gave them to me like this.

SILVIUS (*angrily*) Give it here (CORNELIA *hands him the twenty-mark note. He tears it into pieces*). There... there... This money smells like sewage... it feels slimy like jelly... There... how the pieces slap on the damp asphalt... little cockroaches everywhere... others run off like bedbugs...

CORNELIA (*on the verge of crying*) What are you doing, Silvius... we could have bought wood and coal... and bread and meat... and had a week to live...

SILVIUS I won't live off the filth of others... I'm not a coprophage. I want to eat fruits I grew myself on the trellis, and harvest where I sowed. I want to live in my room, sleep in my bed, with my wife – (*Shouting*) National Newspaper – big mining disaster in Silesia – three hundred buried – robbery-murder at Schlachtensee – the perpetrator arrested – in Treptow, a moon-struck man fell from the observatory –

>A GENTLEMAN *in a yellow coat, yellow top hat, yellow boots, yellow gloves, and a yellow cane stops*

GENTLEMAN The National Newspaper, please!

SILVIUS Here you go, sir... Thank you, sir.

GENTLEMAN Come here under the lamppost! Don't I know you? Don't you know me?

SILVIUS (*recognizing him*) My benefactor!

GENTLEMAN Is this how I find you again? I am saddened to see you in these circumstances. You told me about your girl when we first met. How is she?

SILVIUS This girl is my wife. She's over there at the curb, selling matches.

GENTLEMAN Selling matches? The daughter of the wealthy government councilor? Selling matches?

SILVIUS The government councilor closed the door on us when we arrived from England and stood before him married. We are too proud and too certain of our just cause to beg for his approval or goodwill.

GENTLEMAN And poetry, my young friend, how is that? Do you still write poems?

SILVIUS (*lowering his head*) Since our return from the island land, I haven't written a single poem. I only think about getting the necessities of clothing and sustenance. There's no time for poetry. And even – for love, time is so brief –

GENTLEMAN Do you play any musical instruments? Violin? Flute?

SILVIUS I play the piano.

GENTLEMAN Excellent. Does Cornelia sing? Is she capable of acting? Dancing!

SILVIUS Like a star. Like a dragonfly. Like a seagull.

GENTLEMAN Excellent. I currently run a small cabaret in my eccentric wine house. Follow me. I'll hire you as a pianist! Cornelia as a singer... actress... dancer... as the bouncing, sobbing, singing, living trinity.

CORNELIA *(calling)* Matches... matches... buy some matches...

SILVIUS Cornelia...

CORNELIA My Silvius!

SILVIUS May I introduce our benefactor? Forgive me, I've forgotten your name, but it sounded like Heaven or Light...

GENTLEMAN Names don't matter. Nothing to do with the idea. I'm delighted, madam, to make your acquaintance. Your husband, whom I had the pleasure of meeting before your wedding, spoke to me much about you on a lonely moonlit night. Yes: he spoke like a moth that keeps buzzing around the same flame. You have enchanting legs, madam, a lively gait, melancholic eyes! An extremely tasty blend of red wine, sparkling wine, and candied fruits. The audience will go wild. We can perform a one-act play for you, Silvius. An expressionist folk song – almost as a sketch. We will receive thunderous applause. We will succeed. Come, my children.

Scene Nine

Eccentric cabaret. Small stage on the far right with a curtain. Left, the audience area; many elegant and semi-elegant guests seated at tables and in boxes.

CORNELIA *(on stage, in a glittery skirt, singing, SILVIUS at the piano)*
Good moon, you stand so still
Between clouds, on watch.
Your creator's wise will
Placed you in our night.
Shine kindly on every weary
Heart that's tormented inside.
And let your glow pour peace
Over field, forest, and hill.

Good moon, you wander quietly
Under the blue sky's tent,
Where God has placed you
as a lamp to praise him.
Look down trustingly upon us
Through the night onto the round Earth:

As a new guardian of mankind,
You proclaim God's love.

Good moon, so gentle and mild,
You shine in the sea of stars.
You glide through the light,
Noble and solemn.
Comforter of mankind, messenger of God,
Enthroned on clouds of peace,
Lead us to the most beautiful dawn,
You good moon.

> *Bravo and applause from the audience. Even the gentleman in yellow is visibly moved. He wipes his flushed forehead with a yellow handkerchief. As an encore, Cornelia dances a Chopin waltz. More applause. As it dies down, the*

GENTLEMAN IN YELLOW (*jumps onto the stage and speaks*) My esteemed ladies and gentlemen! – After Miss Cornelia, the star of our ensemble, has delighted you with her singing and dancing talents, we now present a dramatic one-act play of the latest style – we always bring only the latest – titled "The Three," written by Silvius Lang, an up-and-coming talent. Stand up, Silvius! (*to the audience*) He's the young man at the piano. (*Applause*) The role of the sister will be played by Cornelia, the star of our troupe, that of the brother by yours truly, and the role of the stranger by the author himself. I ask for the utmost silence and attention. The distinguished gentlemen from the press are kindly asked for their special participation. There will be a five-minute break to prepare the stylistic set piece. The introductory music is by Mozart.

> *He jumps off the stage*

> *Conversations throughout the audience, from which the following snippets of conversation can be heard*

TYPIST All his poems come from me... I believe I typed them, and he slept one night at my place...

GENTLEMAN You'd better tap yourself on the forehead, Miss!

FIRST STOCKBROKER Throw yourself into grenade manufacturing. It's a knockout! A roaring trade! I'm giving you good advice...

SECOND STOCKBROKER I beg your pardon, who wants anything to do with war anymore? The goods of peace must be delivered!

FIRST STOCKBROKER You're good: The goods of peace! Where do you get them from, if not by stealing?

SECOND STOCKBROKER So steal them...

ART CRITIC Painting is getting crazier and crazier. Now they just nail boards on top of each other and photograph them. That's now a painting.

ART CONNOISSEUR I ask you, why shouldn't that be art – where many people have boards in front of their heads that they don't even photograph – and still call themselves artists...

CORNELIA (*offering postcards in the audience*) Would you like to buy a postcard from me? With my autograph, one mark...

PASSERBY I know you, beautiful child.

CORNELIA Not that I know of.

PASSERBY Do you remember the street corner where you sold matches? Have you changed your mind now? Fifty marks?

CORNELIA You are mistaken: I won't cheat my pain with such cheap means, for such cheap money...

PASSERBY So pain is the name of your worshipper? Your husband?

CORNELIA ...Tears my sister, sighs my brother... (*disappears into the dressing room*).

> *The orchestra plays a few bars of Mozart's Titus Overture. Then a bell rings.*

Scene Ten
The BROTHER with the fishnet is walking up the garden path.

BROTHER I caught nothing. Too much sky lay in the water. Clouds hung over the carp and pike. A lonely star shone in the eye of the stickleback. Flying water beetles appeared as eagles. My forehead flies from the depths like a sunken moon.

SOMEONE (*has leaned over the border fence*) Are you fishing?

BROTHER One can see it.

SOMEONE Luring them to death?

BROTHER Action wants death.

SOMEONE The spirit wants happiness.

BROTHER The fist grasps the distance.

SOMEONE Love wants life.

BROTHER You speak of love?

SOMEONE I create love.

BROTHER Are you an idol?

SOMEONE God's creation.

BROTHER Step closer.

SOMEONE Closeness transforms.

BROTHER Closeness enchants.

SOMEONE Brotherhood.

BROTHER You remind me of...

SOMEONE Of whom?

BROTHER You don't say: what. Smile when...

SOMEONE Knowledge brings happiness.

BROTHER Being recognized: Hurts...

SOMEONE Open your heart! Break into the barn! Bloom, bushes!

BROTHER Do you see it there on the lake? -

SOMEONE The white one?

BROTHER The gleam?

SOMEONE A swan?

BROTHER A dragonfly?

SOMEONE You mock me!

BROTHER Radiant dress in the boat!

SOMEONE A being! A woman!

BROTHER The oars sing.

SOMEONE In the rhythm of the sun.

BROTHER The bay lies in the shadow.

SOMEONE Your hair still remembers: light.

BROTHER Now a cloud is approaching.

SOMEONE It shivers in hostility.

BROTHER The dreadful vulture –

SOMEONE Devours sparks. Pecks at the day.

BROTHER The servant lights, in the cozy house the golden fireplace.

SOMEONE I wait in gloom. The whiteness becomes wisdom. The day has drained away, the night not yet begun, so between times I await the homeland and will surely find... home.

The boat has docked. From it emerges the...

SISTER My brother! Here I am! Embrace the little one you great one! You good one! I float, I live, I laugh, I wake, I dream, I am.

BROTHER Venus is already shining – are you hungry?

SISTER For love – for a lamp in the evening, for mother in a dream. You went fishing? –

BROTHER In vain.

SISTER May she forgive you – The fish also rejoice – In the rolling tide.

BROTHER Allow me – A stranger –

SOMEONE However strange I may seem – my beard hinders me from smiling, masks me like a little monk. I saw her from afar – and wished her near!

SISTER A man – like my brother, but served more gently. You are welcome here. Sebastian, the old one will prepare the chamber. We'll set the table for three.

BROTHER Too close, sweet swallow flying above the ground – pointing to a storm –

SISTER Leave it, brother – the stranger is friendly. You invited him.

BROTHER He invited himself –

SOMEONE I came. Because I had to. The house stood along the way. The lilacs stood burning and fragrant – far – beyond the woods there its scent drifted into the garden – this Japanese floral prayer merged with mine in the light, and the cat cried by the fence. And the pears rang like bells, and the crickets fiddled on the steel. That boat there offered itself to me. This being – is mine to possess –

SISTER Brother – I called to him – that I confess – through the nights I called to him. Vultures perish, veils blow away, gaze into his eye, and my heart is his heart.

BROTHER Jugglers and thieves: out of my sight, out of my way or I'll sic the dogs on you.

SISTER Brother: He fills empty bowls with blood and fulfillment, happiness and song. Let the three of us strike the harp, tune the voices for a heavenly trio.

SOMEONE Let us three shine in the ether. Shine in the heavenly triumvirate.

BROTHER Am I betrayed? Doesn't the ground tremble? Doesn't the earth shake? Doesn't the dog bark? He howls for a long time – is it for a dead person? – Am I the dead person? Jester – it's you!

SISTER Brother, speak: Brother I understand, since I've grasped him, I understand you better too.

SOMEONE Do I have my sister? Do I hold my brother? Did I walk in vain – through the woods? I gained perfection in scourging and kindness. Am I at my end? Am I finished?

SISTER Brother – we love –

SOMEONE Brother – we're alive.

SISTER Let us be alive!

BROTHER Night has come. The fish are blurry. The death-worm is already pecking. The sun fell from the roof like a bundle of burning straw. The toad sneaks through the kitchen and the cellar, and the owl rejoices so loudly.

SISTER My brother – you speak as if in a fever – night air harms the frail lungs. Come inside – the kettle boils. There are eggs and ham on the table, mail lies under the napkin. Asia and China send you fairy tales, send you adventures and greetings.

SOMEONE I'd be happy to help with your work – catch butterflies and arranging beetles, guarding the pupating caterpillars and feed the newts into the jar.

SISTER He'd be happy to help you – help him too – he is better than any human being. Want to love him! Want the will! And the gods bless us three!

BROTHER Two remain two and do not become a trinity.

SOMEONE God is three and one at the same time.

BROTHER My love feels betrayed.

SISTER Your love – loves only yourself.

BROTHER Ha: I hate – (*an echo I love*) Which echo? Which falsification! God humbles himself to perform a miracle!

SOMEONE Are you not the eternal miracle yourself? Mysterious feverish lord.

BROTHER Magician! Pickpocket! You were sent by God, the eternal bungler, to provoke me. But he provokes me – only to laughter (*laughs*). Go to the heavens that gave birth to you.

He rushes toward him and strangles him with his hands.

SISTER Brother! Murderer! Brother murderer!

She throws herself onto the corpse.

BROTHER (*Takes back his fishing rod*) I am going now... fishing... It's a full moon... the fish bite well then... when they see the bait... so well... I will take the boat... and row out into the lake a bit... I will tear my eyes out of my head... and fish with them. For what do I still need to see?
I'm going to cut my heart out. Because why do I still need to live? Good moon – are you truly good? And are you really... truly?

Scene Eleven

Street in Moonlight.

SILVIUS (*Moonstruck, dancing on the roof*) Dear Sir — What does that mean: Dear Sir? I don't quite understand your form of address. If I were as you portray me... disintegrated and incapable of self-control: There wouldn't be much to honor about me, and since you see me as a theatrical villain, you should have immediately labeled me a scoundrel. These somewhat light-hearted words shouldn't deceive you. That I feel I am the one to be despised... It is not fitting for those who waver and stagger to call someone who stands firmly on the ground a loser. Cornelia... if it were possible for you to love a bad person — how bad you yourself must be. Why are you, at this moment, as far removed from me as Sirius? You are one of those stars whose rays we poor humans still see — although they have cooled down for millennia... Cornelia: Close your eyes! Remember every word I've spoken... every glance I've exchanged... all our embraces... all my poems... And then this!... I'm beside myself... and it seems to me as if I were never in myself...

I have never struck a woman. But if you dared to say this to my face: that I didn't love you — I might be tempted to split your face open with a single blow of my hand... Judge not, lest you be judged. I am the one who, if he should ever meet you, will wield the sword of judgment.

A gentleman and a lady on their way home

GENTLEMAN There's a moonstruck man walking up there.

LADY Where?

GENTLEMAN There – above that gable –

LADY For God's sake, not so loud, or he'll fall down...

GENTLEMAN God forbid...

LADY Yes: God forbid...

GENTLEMAN Hey, you: Golden crane! Light-drunkard! Intermediate between the earth and the moon, laughing angel, comet's tail, ball lightning, fixed idea star – wake up.

SILVIUS vanishes into the wings

LADY He won't fall...

GENTLEMAN He walks straight ahead like a recruit on the parade ground.

LADY Like an enthusiastic suitor asking for a lady's hand.

GENTLEMAN He has a good constitution.

Scene Twelve

Garret.

CORNELIA *(In bed)* I dream of home every night. Mom is wearing a new black silk dress embroidered with tears. Dad always walks around in a top hat, Arwed, your brother is constantly demanding satisfaction from you.

SILVIUS Can't you bear me anymore? Misery frays the heart. It wears down the rock. My hands are shaking. I think my hair is falling out.

CORNELIA Don't I always carry you around with me – beneath my heart – oh, I feel the child leaping like a dancer. Will it be a boy or a girl?

SILVIUS That is tragedy: When you want to fly – and you are pressed to the ground by your own weight. When, as soon as you look at the sun, you go blind.

CORNELIA *(Puts both hands to her head)* I see you – and am blinded, but – God willing – I am not blind.

SILVIUS *(Violence tearing herself away)* Tell the truth, girl.

CORNELIA I always tell and believe the truth.

SILVIUS Tell the truth *(tapping on the bedspread)* Is this child truly mine? Oh, I understand what it means to become a father. I sometimes hammer my skull with my fists and cry out to heaven: Help that the child is mine...

CORNELIA (*stands up straight*) Silvius – have I ever loved anyone but you?

    Silvius: (*Roaring*) The dead man! You loved the dead man! Can't the child be the dead man's? Every night he rises from the grave with his clattering bones that sound like castanets and shamelessly lies down in bed between you and me. His jaw chatters up and down – he swears eternal loyalty to you – beyond the grave – only when the morning glares green through the panes like the bleary-eyed face of a drunkard does he depart – taking a sigh from you – a curse from me – with him on the way. How I hate him; the dead man: Ever since you felt like a mother (*he shakes her*) Tell me: Is the child the dead man's? How horrible that you can't kill the dead again. They live, the dead, forever and ever. They pass through you as if you were glass and they were rays. You can't grasp them, you can't hold them: they are floating smoke and butterflies.

    I love you because I come from the moon... and you are my sun. Why must we both endure black clouds obscuring us? Say: Will you bear a Jupiter? Will it be my son?

CORNELIA It is your child, as sure as I live.

SILVIUS (*screaming*) You're lying! You're no longer alive! You're dying! I see you dying, I feel you dying, the increased torment of having doubled, even tripled, and of enduring every pain three times over. Through you, through me, through the child — but you don't know if it's my child. Can the mother, who obviously had two lovers, one living and one dead, know which of them the child is from? She can't know... she can only hope that it's — from the living...

CORNELIA There's a knock at the door.

SILVIUS It's the deathworm, thumping in the wood.

CORNELIA (*shuddering*) Wake up, there's someone at the door. I see his shadow.

SILVIUS The dead man... (*goes to the door and opens it. A student enters, very elegantly dressed, wearing his colors*).

STUDENT If I may — Rebbach.

SILVIUS And? – What do you want?

CORNELIA Arwed! Brother!

STUDENT I come on behalf of my family to negotiate with you regarding my sister Cornelia, whom you have abducted.

SILVIUS What do you mean: negotiate? Am I a delicatessen merchant?

STUDENT You are not considered fit for satisfaction. Therefore, we offer you ten thousand marks in cash on the table if you swear under oath – your word of honor does not suffice – to entirely relinquish your influence over Cornelia, allow her to return home unmolested, and never again attempt to approach her. The so-called marriage will be declared invalid.

SILVIUS You are an amusing young man and could, just as you are, perform on a tightrope. But I do not wish to insult you. After all, I am not considered fit for satisfaction. Nor do I wish to harm you – spiritually – assuming you have a soul. The only question is whether in the trap you've touched upon — not: ham, although that would be a logical metaphor — but: trap: That is to say: whether Cornelia might not also be capable of giving you satisfaction.

STUDENT I request clarification. I seek elucidation of the situation.

SILVIUS Cornelia's situation is, depending on how you look at it: horizontal or vertical. And therein lies the conflict of her and my nature. We can be viewed from above and below. We suffer from the parallelism of all human and earthly appearances: that never is there just one, but always two, or three. Do you understand?

STUDENT I took logic under Professor Dessauer and occasionally attended his lectures. I do not understand you. You seem insane.

SILVIUS I seem insane. Emphasize the first word: seem, shimmer, sparkle, glow.

STUDENT We are straying from the essentials —

SILVIUS No: we are approaching the essentials.

STUDENT So in short: I am pressed for time, I must attend brunch – what do you mean by saying that my sister is not fit for satisfaction? And what answer shall I bring to the family council?

CORNELIA Arwed! Be kind to me...

SILVIUS I mean to say that your sister is expecting a child...

STUDENT (*startled*) That significantly changes the situation... We will then have to insist on an official civil wedding in the German style... and then immediately initiate a divorce.

SILVIUS But what if the child Cornelia is carrying is not mine?

CORNELIA (*cries out*)

STUDENT I – perhaps – do not quite – understand you?

SILVIUS Oh, you understand me perfectly. The child Cornelia is carrying is not mine...

STUDENT But whose then?

SILVIUS Her second lover's.

STUDENT (*correctly*) Cornelia has a second lover?

SILVIUS As surely as I stand here...

CORNELIA Beloved, you are killing me –

SILVIUS Then you will all the sooner be united completely with your lover...

STUDENT I have no further business here. My mission is complete. (*approaches* CORNELIA *'s bed*) Harlot! (*gives* SILVIUS *a short bow*) Sir. (*exits*)

Scene Thirteen

Under an arch of a bridge. Berlin. Early, around 5 a.m. Light pink and yellow clouds, which also scatter a little light over the Spree. Houses in the distance.

SILVIUS (*sitting on the bulwark, fishing*) A new day is rising over the mountains of houses. The first trams chirp like nightingales. Rotten puddles from yesterday's rain lie on every corner. Pools of melancholy. Black eyes in the pavement. Ah... I'm tired, 18 years have made me tired. I've barely gotten out of bed when I'm overcome by a longing for the past. For yesterday, for yesterday. For the twilight of an evening that I no longer need to leave, to plunge my poor arms, torn apart by the feeling of divinity, darkly into a new light. I hurts me to breathe when I inhale the morning air. The gray dew attacks you like soot. Why am I not brainless and cityless, a faithful animal, born in the forest, with the only thought of the stars in my open eye at night? A metallic beetle, honestly clinging to a blade of grass? Able and willing to dig my own grave and pass away without suffering or pity, alone like a cloud in the blue, otherwise cloudless sky?

I am human. I am a weak human. Loneliness calls me with a thundering trumpet: I am afraid of it. It terrifies me.

I am a human. There is no distance greater than that between one moment and the next. Firmaments revolve between two eyes that strive to find each other. A wall of heavens towers between them. A luminous, impenetrable golden veil of stars conceals each chamber from the other. Armored lies stand at their gates. Imperfection is the gatekeeper. The mice of malice undermine the ground. The eagles of pride nest on the battlements.

Where is a person that I may sink into their breast? Drown in the stream of his heart? Take his hands in holy brotherhood? I have lived to be 18 years old, and I know so little of the world that the dawn always runs down my cheeks like shame. Didn't I fly for many years on a ship called the "Seagull" over a thousand rivers? I furled the hawsers. I tied the sails. I cooked the meager meal, which always consisted of dead fish. Then they gave me the helm: braids adorned my blue sleeve, and I was called: Mr. Helmsman. I steered the ship past towns large and small, meadows undulated along the banks, villages ran colorfully like children part of the way, girls waved blood-red cloths, cloths that they had bathed in their own blood - I see them approaching, standing still, and disappearing, and even today I don't know where I'm steering the ship.

The sun has risen. The moment it begins to shine, a beautiful woman slowly crosses the bridge; in a violet gown that sparkles against the pale blue backdrop of the sky. She resembles CORNELIA.

She pauses briefly, leans over the bridge's railing, and looks down at SILVIUS. Then, suddenly, a thought pulls her away: SILVIUS looks up, sees her for a moment before she disappears.

SILVIUS Cornelia.

From the right, an elegant young man hurries onstage. Top hat, evening cape. He looks a little surprised. He gazes attentively across the bridge. Notices SILVIUS at his feet.

YOUNG MAN Did you not just see a young lady?

SILVIUS The sun has just risen.

YOUNG MAN I asked about a lady, do you not understand?

SILVIUS I understand nothing. Least of all myself.

YOUNG MAN Then listen to me: I am searching for a woman —

SILVIUS Who isn't looking for her!

YOUNG MAN Who may have crossed this bridge —

SILVIUS We all must cross this bridge. It leads to another shore, where even the ivy is said to bear blossoms the size of plates. Where myrtle and laurel are twined around the lowliest brow. Eternal pain deserves eternal glory. And what person does not suffer always and forever?

YOUNG MAN I suffer because you do not answer me.

SILVIUS You are asking the wrong question. I am very happy to provide any information. Ask!

YOUNG MAN The lady?

SILVIUS Came from the east and went west.

YOUNG MAN Across the bridge?

SILVIUS Across the bridge!

YOUNG MAN Then I know the way. It leads to her. I will follow it. (*He moves to leave.*)

SILVIUS Stay. I gave you information. Now help me. I will ask. I will set questions like bird traps. Answer them, if you please.

YOUNG MAN What do you want?

SILVIUS Your help. Where do you come from? From the night. Pleasure radiated electricity through me. Artificial light flowed into my eyes. Inflated rubber dolls sat at my sides. Their fake seaweed hair smelled of rotten fish. Their hands stuck like jellyfish. Only one smiled — humanly, she moved among instruments. She wore a purple dress: And her blondness shone like an anticipated sun. She danced with no one. I sent her a glass of champagne through the waiter. She didn't touch it. But she smiled — forgiveness. I fell to my knees in the ballroom. Everyone laughed. Like a thunderstorm made of tin in the theater. But I felt no shame.

SILVIUS Where are you going?

YOUNG MAN Into the day. Into the dream. Across the bridge of the desiring heart.

SILVIUS You are stepping into life?

YOUNG MAN Into life. I have awakened.

SILVIUS What is this: life? A fish that cannot be caught because no one knows the bait it will bite?

YOUNG MAN Life means: To recognize the sun.

SILVIUS I have a request for you.

YOUNG MAN Speak.

SILVIUS Take me with you.

YOUNG MAN Where to?

SILVIUS Into her life. I gather my fishing tackle. The factories are already whistling. Workers hurry ghostly through the still-deserted alleys. Shop girls sprout from the asphalt like poppies. The bridge arches promisingly. Let's search for the lady. Perhaps. Perhaps she is your beloved, perhaps she is mine.

>   *Both slowly walk over the bridge.*

Scene Fourteen
Garret.

CORNELIA (*alone*) A little flower blooms blue... that means do not forget me... how sweet the song the maids sang. The fountain in the courtyard murmurs. Flies buzz over my head. I keep thinking of the moon. Good moon! Silvius, stroke my forehead... ah... I no longer have a forehead. Where my forehead was, a city stands in the glow of sunset — and burns. Why did I leave our solidly built dwelling and go into a house without walls? Where the wind whistles in from everywhere? No shady roof protects against the blazing midday sun? Someone is playing the harp on my ribs. I resound softly. I was always pious. I always went to church: knelt before the wooden Madonna. Confessed such minor sins every year at Easter that the priest smiled and said: My dear child, you are forgiven... Wish to God there were nothing worse to confess than a mocking word in the street... defiance towards my mother... teasing the black cat (*stands up*) I shudder. I hear an owl hooting. The air trembles. I breathe a strange scent. There is someone in the room. He is walking towards me. On tiptoe. Now he is standing by my bed. Who are you? Oh, a little child? Who are you, boy?

CHILD I am your child... death...

CORNELIA Where do you come from?

CHILD From heaven... from God...

CORNELIA You are beautiful, like I have never seen a child. Let me kiss your blond head. How happy Silvius will be when he sees you...

CHILD He will never see me... for he is blind to me...

CORNELIA What are you babbling about, child? Silvius, should your father actually be blind to his child? He will love you and kiss you. He'll let you play hopscotch and buy you toys: a rocking horse, a crossbow, and a steam engine that makes real steam...

CHILD I hear him groaning – outside the door...

CORNELIA He dreams of you... of your future, Thunder-walker... Speak well of him! Stay with me! I'm shivering... Pull the blanket up a bit... I'm freezing...

Scene Fifteen

Stairwell outside SILVIUS's small room.

SILVIUS sits on a step. The wind whistles through a crack in the floor.

SILVIUS I'm shivering. The wind hits me, hot as the breath of hell. It's a foehn... My stomach hurts like a child's that's eaten too much semolina porridge. I have to hold my head with my hands, otherwise it'll fall off and roll down the stairs like a potato falling from the market woman's overflowing basket. Oh dear God, there are so many potatoes. So many heads. But instinct tells you: Don't lose your head! Don't become headless! Ha! The wind! It almost singes your hair. (*A scream from the small room*) Why didn't I poison her, to free her and myself from our torment? (*Takes a small bottle out of his pocket, strokes it*) Dear Poison (*Puts it back in his pocket*)

The door opens. A figure appears.

MIDWIFE Psst... young man...

SILVIUS (*Turns around, startled*) What's that supposed to mean?

MIDWIFE Well, don't be so miserable! Cheer up! Just don't lose your head!

SILVIUS You're thinking like me, dear lady. You're a philosopher; you should be offered a professorship to help your clients have bowel movements.

MIDWIFE Don't babble! Pull yourself together.

SILVIUS Your face reminds me somewhat of the waning moon. It once whispered to me as well: Let not your mind be poisoned by deeds left undone! How truly you speak, plump spinner of fate!

MIDWIFE Do you have the money to call a doctor here? I can hardly manage it alone anymore. Your female is suffering greatly. I've never seen such a young mother who's also married. It's a shame —

SILVIUS How?

MIDWIFE To get married so young... when you have no money. Better to have illegitimate children. Still more practical. Still cheaper. In her class it costs 20 marks a month.

Silvius You see, that would be an idea — couldn't you artificially make the legitimate child illegitimate? Declare it, as it were, outside of marriage, existing entirely on its own? Immaculate conception? From a dead man?

> *A scream from the room*

Midwife I'm coming... You're exhausted! Go to sleep! I've seen people sleep on harder wood than the one on these stairs!

Silvius Yes... in a coffin.

Midwife Why don't you lie down on the divan?

Silvius (*shakes his head fanatically*) I can see people striving — but how children come into the world — to watch that is beyond my strength...

> *Long-drawn-out screams from the room.*
>
> *The* Midwife *enters*
>
> *after a short while, exits again, agitated*

Midwife You have to get the doctor... there's no help for it... It's a matter of life and death...

Silvius I've known for a long time, that life and death are at stake in this world.

Midwife (*shakes him*) Listen up... washcloth... he collapses like a bundle of old clothes... The doctor lives right around the corner... run, run...

Silvius (*tearfully*) I can't... I can't... my feet are cast in lead. Wooden poles run through my arms like a scarecrow's. My heart beats like hammer and anvil.

Midwife (*contemptuously*) And that's what a man wants to be — (*tuns down the stairs*). I'll be back in two seconds — I'll get the doctor myself...

Silvius I don't want to be a man at all... (*suddenly straightens, looks down the stairs, listens, grabs the vial of poison in his pocket, and rushes into the room. After a moment, he rushes back out and collapses in his previous position by the stairs.*)
She was thirsty... I gave her a drink of water...

> *Someone stomps up the stairs. It's an invalid with a wooden leg and an accordion.*

Invalid A poor defender of the fatherland, shot in the war for the Emperor and the Empire, asks for a charitable donation.

Silvius (*angrily*) What does that mean: defender of the fatherland? What did they defend? The fatherland? Was it even in danger: The fatherland – and did it need their defense?

Invalid I've never thought about it, because I'm a patriot.

Silvius Then I'm not a patriot, because I first consider whether my fatherland has a good cause to defend – and then I defend that good cause. Suppose my fatherland, in my conviction, served and sacrificed for a bad idea – I would refuse to serve my fatherland, desert, commit so-called treason, and fight against my own fatherland – for the sake of the good idea.

INVALID I don't know what that is, a good idea. The fatherland is as good to me as it can be. It pays me a small monthly pension and, with a business license, it gives me permission to play the harmonica in people's homes.

SILVIUS So they play... here's my last mark...

> *Screams from the room*

INVALID (*Plays: Youth is beautiful in happy times...*)

> *The MIDWIFE and the DOCTOR rush up the stairs*

DOCTOR What's all this fuss about? Someone is dying here.

SILVIUS You mean sick of life, sir, sick of life.

DOCTOR Are you the man?

SILVIUS Yes, sir.

DOCTOR Coward! (*to the MIDWIFE*) Come on! (*Both go into the room*)

INVALID (*Puts down the accordion in surprise*) Now that's an energetic man.

> *The GENTLEMAN IN YELLOW suddenly appears on the stairs*

GENTLEMAN IN YELLOW Here I finally find you... You haven't shown your face at the cabaret since the night before last. Is this your gratitude to me? Is this how you maintain your principles? You've broken your contract. You fulfill your commitments to the utmost — even at the risk of collapse. That means: duty, ethics, standpoint: Ask the defender of the fatherland here. He had to endure enemy fire until the order to cease fire or retreat was given.

INVALID Yes, sir.

GENTLEMAN IN YELLOW Did I give you the order to retreat?

SILVIUS (*jumping up*) I was putty in your hands. You wanted to mold me, but now I'm frozen into stone — in a terrible pose... and can no longer be molded. Forever I must carry this stony smile, these marble tears, these coral eyes through the world. I wanted, still a child myself, to be immortal in my child. This child should have another child! Grandfather! I wanted to be a great-grandfather! Now, in revenge, because of my defiance of him, because of my bitter struggle with him, Death has fathered a child with my daughter: (*Last cry from the chamber*) Oh, I know, I don't need to be told: The child my wife is giving birth to is a dead child. And this dead child is not my child. For if it were my child, it would be alive! (*Collapses*)

> *The DOCTOR emerges from the room, sleeves rolled up, in a scrubs.*

DOCTOR I must inform you of the unfortunate news — according to God's inscrutable decree —

> *The GENTLEMAN IN YELLOW and the INVALID take off their hats.*

— Where is the man — (*sees him on the floor*) — collapsed — nervous shock — modern youth —(*The MIDWIFE enters. To the MIDWIFE*) All right

— I'll write the death certificate for mother and child immediately.

Scene Sixteen

Garret.

Silvius stands at the window, looking out into the dreary day. Rain beats against the panes. Two workers are in the middle of the room, busy nailing shut the poor coffins — paupers' coffins — of Cornelia and her child.

First Worker (*hammering in a nail*) There... now they can finally have some peace from each other... She won't slip away again... This nail will hold... The coffin is watertight... I can guarantee that... Even if it's just a pauper's coffin... our city council doesn't skimp.

Second Worker Not every poor man is lucky enough to have his wife and child die on the same day. He should be grateful — now he only has to take care of himself. These are hard times. A pound of beef costs four marks. Where's a man supposed to get four marks? Even nailing and hauling corpses now has to be done on credit. These are hard times.

First Worker Good thing we don't have to load these hard times onto our cart as well. A hard time like this must weigh a good thousand kilos, I'd say.

Second Worker Five flights of stairs! Impressive! He lives pretty far up! Loves the view, huh? A rather high-and-mighty fellow, isn't he?

First Worker Don't worry, we'll manage... Which corpse do we take first?

Second Worker Open the door... There... I'll strap the little corpse onto my back... Give me a hand... Hup... That's it... there... now let's lift the big one together... gently... careful not to bump it... we wouldn't want her to hurt herself against the hard chest of drawers... Slowly now, watch the glass... don't stumble... no rushing... we'll get to the cemetery soon enough... to the morgue... No need to hurry with the burial. (*They exit.*)

The door slams shut. Silvius is alone in the room. He turns around, rubs his eyes.

Silvius My eyes are inflamed... I haven't slept for seven nights... I think I've forgotten how to sleep... (*He steps up to a mirror that stands at the center of the back wall.*) Is this a human face? Repulsive pimples spread across my forehead. My matted hair harbors lice. Breathing — it hurts! Swallowing — it feels like an iron ball rolling down my throat. I must have laryngeal tuberculosis. I cough like a crow and whimper with the technique of a second-rate actor. Let's see if I can cry when I want to. (*Fake crying that turns into real sobs.*) What a bad actor I must be, that my role moves me... and fake tears give birth to real ones... What is there left to do?

He reaches into his pocket, pulls out a revolver.

Aha... the item from yesterday's break-in at the gun shop. I smashed the display window... just like a seasoned heavy criminal... Isn't it true that nowadays every noun comes with the adjective "heavy?" Heavy criminal... heavy times... heavy distress... My heart feels so heavy... How a common phrase can, at times, physically grab you... with fists... How a word becomes deed... How yearning becomes action... intoxication... Peace... just to have peace... to be able to sleep... to have peace... (*He grabs his head, pulls at his hair.*) If only one could tear off one's head — it would be a blessing to see one's own blood shoot from the neck... It should flow forever... and drown the whole world in it... in my blood... It would be a red flood... and Cornelia would hover above it, my dove... (*He listens.*) What's that noise? Oh, it's raining. It's been raining day and night, night and day. Since Cornelia... left, I haven't seen the sun by day, nor the moon by night... Should I notify my parents of my death? By telegram, perhaps? They probably don't care. Better not to remind them of my existence just as I am ceasing to exist. They disowned me. It was their right — just as it was my right to despise them. (*He raises the revolver to his forehead.*) My steel friend... Your cold mouth rests on my forehead, still mindful of Cornelia's warm kisses. (*He puts the revolver down. Looks into the mirror.*) Who are you? I recognize you — my wild adversary, my staggering double! If I sway, you sway. If I grin, you grin! When I embraced Cornelia, you too lifted your shimmering arms. I climbed the mountain — you panted, silently, beside me. I looked at the moon — and saw my own furrowed peasant's face. I, a little man of Earth! I, the Man in the Moon! Cursed to a double existence. I wrote a poem — only to find it already printed in your works. I loved Cornelia — and you had already sired her child. The only difference between us is that you live in two dimensions — and I in three. You are the dead one. I am the living. That is all. And nothing. I want to come to myself. If I lift the weapon (*he does so*), you lift it too. We must destroy each other, for I harbor an endless hatred for you. Fire! (*He pulls the trigger. A bang. The mirror shatters into pieces.*)

> The GENTLEMAN IN YELLOW *enters from the left, carrying a wreath with a ribbon. He places a hand on* SILVIUS's *shoulder.* SILVIUS, *with an exalted expression, turns toward him.*

GENTLEMAN IN YELLOW Come to your senses! Boy! Earthling! I love you and shine upon you with eternal mildness! Look at them: they cannot die (*he takes the revolver from* SILVIUS's *hand*) — no matter how much you rage against yourself and your destiny! No matter how you strive to debase yourself, to drag your soul through the dust — look at them: they are rising, they are soaring like a silver bird to the stars, their brothers and sisters.

SILVIUS Cornelia is dead... I did what I thought I should — I believed, she shouldn't suffer... like I did — Was that thought... evil?

GENTLEMAN IN YELLOW I dedicate this wreath to Cornelia.

SILVIUS The child... is dead...

GENTLEMAN IN YELLOW Let me tell you — and believe me: It was your child —

and not the other's.

SILVIUS (*sobbing*)

GENTLEMAN IN YELLOW But they were not yet worthy... of their child.. of immortality... and so the child died, because the dead one overpowered them. They have fought — not without honor — and yet they have been overcome by death, by the dead. Now fight for your life! Cast off the boy's defiance: Become humble — like a man. He who hates himself as you have — how great must be his capacity to love!

SILVIUS I loved Cornelia...

GENTLEMAN IN YELLOW But your love was dark — and it killed her. Become clear... like the moon in blue autumn nights... Become conscious... Submit to the community! Do not scorn the cripple: he sees himself as a member of a greater whole, as a stone in a building — and he served. Learn to serve — not as a soldier with a weapon, but as a human being with a heart.

SILVIUS What should I do?

GENTLEMAN IN YELLOW Your gaudy revelry is at an end. You will turn your back on the cabaret and its flaming misery. I have secured a position for you — as a servant on a noble estate nearby. Humble before principle, you will receive the reflected glow of happiness. You will rise at 5 a.m., raise the shutters when the sun rises, clear the path for light and air, tidy the master's study, dust his library, his books, his precious vases. At 6 a.m. you will bring his breakfast to his bed. At 7 a.m. you will saddle the horse for his morning ride. At noon, serve the silver dishes at table. After lunch, mend the livery, brush the riding boots. In the afternoon, sit next to the coachman on the box seat, cap in hand, fling open the carriage door, help the master and mistress to alight. In the evening, serve again, and at 10 p.m. sink into deep, dreamless sleep, the blissful sleep of fulfilled duty. Have you ever known this word: Duty? You have a mission. It is not enough to be human. You must earn it. Work, not dream, is the goal of humanity, the measure of its worth. Perhaps I should first send you to a servant's academy — but I trust you will not disgrace my recommendation. Pack the bare essentials into a small suitcase. Come.

Final Scene

Suburban Station. Patrolling railway official. SILVIUS with a small suitcase and the GENTLEMAN IN YELLOW pacing back and forth.

GENTLEMAN IN YELLOW (*Pulls out his watch*) The train will arrive soon. Here's your ticket. Don't lose it!

SILVIUS How can I ever thank you!

GENTLEMAN IN YELLOW With a good reference for your service and character, since this is your first job.

SILVIUS I'm going to behave very awkwardly.

GENTLEMAN IN YELLOW You'll try your best, and the Count will be pleased with you.

SILVIUS (*Looks along the track*) Up here, it seems as if these shimmering rails must run side by side forever, always at the same distance. But back there, before the bend, at the curve, they meet flaming and merge into a single beam. (*half to himself*) I'll see Cornelia again. I will have another child, and it will — I know it, I sense it with joy — live.

GENTLEMAN IN YELLOW In that direction they are traveling — to where the two parallels meet... into infinity.

SILVIUS (*Looking into the distance*) Yes... infinity lies before me, the great plain... sea and earth in one.

GENTLEMAN IN YELLOW In an hour they will reach their destination. The count's coachman will be waiting for them at the railway. Recommend me to the count. We spent a delightful winter in Copenhagen. I knew his daughter when she was still in diapers. Later, during a brief visit, I was able to admire the fifteen-year-old, half-grown girl. I fell in love with her. She has certainly developed into an enchanting creature. How old will she be now? — Wait — about 18.

SILVIUS (*holding his breath*) And what is her name?

GENTLEMAN IN YELLOW (*simply*) Cornelia.

SILVIUS (*breathing deeply*) I knew it.

GENTLEMAN IN YELLOW Attention... be careful... don't get too close to the tracks... your train is arriving...

> The train is arriving: just a ghostly shadow, no one is getting off

CONDUCTOR Aboard... all aboard... wait a minute...

SILVIUS (*Has put down his suitcase, hugs the man in yellow*) My fatherly friend!

> A man in a gray suit and a policeman in uniform rush out of the underpass

GENTLEMAN IN GRAY (*To the CONDUCTOR*) Stop... don't let the train depart. The train has to wait until I give the signal... Official order from the police commissioner (*approaches SILVIUS*) Are you Silvius Lang?

SILVIUS Yes.

GENTLEMAN IN GRAY By order of Privy Councilor Rebbach, the coffin of his deceased daughter, Cornelia, her former wife, was officially opened. The forensic examination of the body revealed that your wife did not die of natural causes during childbirth. The remains of a lethal poison were found in her body. I hereby declare you under arrest as a strong suspect in the poisoning of your wife.

GENTLEMAN IN YELLOW (*approaches the GENTLEMAN IN GRAY*) You are mistaken. This young man is innocent. He is the victim of my experiments. I request that you handcuff me. I was the one who poisoned Cornelia... Take me away!

GENTLEMAN IN GRAY Your name?

GENTLEMAN IN YELLOW You will record it at the police station.

GENTLEMAN IN GRAY (*to SILVIUS*) So I release you... go wherever you wish...

SILVIUS (*shocked*) You are sacrificing yourself... for me...

GENTLEMAN IN YELLOW I am sacrificing myself neither for you nor for myself. I only want justice! Go with God!

SILVIUS They are robbing you of your freedom!

GENTLEMAN IN YELLOW No one can rob me of my freedom. I carry it within me. But you must first conquer your own. To do this – I will pave the way for you. Clear the stones... of prison out of your way. Fear nothing! You will meet me again on your journey!

CONDUCTOR All aboard... aboard

SILVIUS (*kisses the GENTLEMAN IN YELLOW's hand*) I will then strive to become worthy of you! Farewell!

GENTLEMAN IN YELLOW Become worthy of your own existence! Farewell! And die well! Moonstruck! Sleepwalker! Up! Into the day! Into the sun!

> *SILVIUS falls, climbs in, the train begins to move. The GENTLEMAN IN GRAY and the POLICEMAN lead the GENTLEMAN IN YELLOW away.*

Part Seventeen:

Dialogue on Politics and Poetry

"Dialogue on Politics and Poetry" was published in the magazine "Young Germany," 1918.

Dialogue on Politics and Poetry

Characters:

Pausanias – Socrates

PAUSANIAS It is fortunate for me, Socrates, to have meet you just now.

SOCRATES What is on your mind, Pausanias, or whatever is on your lips?

PAUSANIAS This: or, Socrates, mocks me. Have you ever found me to be insincere?

SOCRATES Certainly not, Pausanias, I was joking. For the serious cannot be spoken of lightly enough. Let me hear what draws you onto my path. For if it pleases you, we can continue walking together.

PAUSANIAS I feel as though I am groping in the dark concerning politics and political affairs.

SOCRATES Entrust me with your power, and I shall gladly be the moon that illumines it.

PAUSANIAS I have just come from the Acropolis. There Eusymachus, the poet, spoke about ostracism. He threw his hands in the air just like an eagle does its wings. He screamed so loudly that his voice echoed all the way to the Tyrrhenian Sea. A few, mostly beardless youths, applauded him vehemently, while the majority of his listeners shook their heads and said that the poet should concern himself only with poetry, sing of the nymphs and Orpheus's gray descent into Hades, and keep his hands off the things he understands nothing about, namely politics. Politics, they said, was an unmusical occupation, and a poet should never, under any circumstances, be a politician.

SOCRATES Hold on, Pausanias: what, in your opinion, are politicians by profession? For if they are not politicking, they must have a profession, like Eusymachos, you, and I?

PAUSANIAS They are lawyers, leather traders, grain sellers, generals, buffoons, professors of science, and so on.

SOCRATES So then you admit that in addition to one's profession, one can be a politician?

PAUSANIAS Most certainly.

SOCRATES Then how can you reproach only the poet for being a politician? Is politics then a science, like astronomy or zoology, or a trade like butchery?

PAUSANIAS No.

SOCRATES What is it then?

PAUSANIAS It seems to me now that it is the occupation of humans with their external relations to one another.

SOCRATES Precisely, Pausanias. It concerns itself — and note this word carefully: to act! — with the objectification of the subject. So that we speak together, instead of killing each other like wild animals — this is politics.

PAUSANIAS So politics is based on knowledge.

SOCRATES Most certainly — and should a poet possess less knowledge of human relations than a leather merchant? When it is his very duty to know mankind?

PAUSANIAS But doesn't politics require certain specialized knowledge: of economic and legal systems — sciences in their own right?

SOCRATES Certainly, Pausanias: but this knowledge is secondary in politics. The primary is conscience: the granite cornerstone without which even the most scientifically constructed building must collapse upon itself.

PAUSANIAS So you believe that politics must be governed by goodness, if governance is to endure?

SOCRATES The spirit must govern, and virtue must rule through the spirit.

PAUSANIAS Then would you wish that the poet, when engaging in politics, should write only of political matters?

SOCRATES Certainly not, Pausanias. Do not cloud yourself after I have just managed to clarify your darkness. There is a difference between a poet being a politician, and poetry being political. Goodness lies immanently within poetry; otherwise, it would not be poetry at all. Therefore, poetry has no need of lyrical programs to bring forth the good. I heard a young writer exclaim: The time of poetry is past. The thesis, the program, the pamphlet — these are the demands of the hour. The demand of the hour may appear to him to require the slumber of the Muses. But he shouldn't forget the commandment of eternity. For eternity desires the work, not merely its effect. He who speaks into the wind today will have his words vanish by tomorrow. But he who writes upon tablets of bronze will have his words endure — through the storms of time.

PAUSANIAS The poet, then, should act in the political sphere, for this is something that befits everyone, by virtue of their soul and their insight — but let him continue to dream his dream of words. For these are more real than many a hastily performed deed.

SOCRATES That is it, Pausanias. Let the poet be good, act well, and write well. From this trinity grows his perfection. Just as the leather merchant's excellence lies in being good, doing good, and knowing how to properly tan leather. For everyone should do right within their circle — thus justice will prevail.

Published in *Young Germany*, 1918.

Part Eighteen:

The Gravedigger

"The Gravedigger" was published in 1919
by the Publishing House of Beautiful Rarities.

The Gravedigger

Figures:

Old Gravedigger
Young Gravedigger
The Young Gentleman
Coffin Bearer

In Memory of My Angel

Young and old gravediggers are digging at a grave.

YOUNG GRAVEDIGGER: Summer raised its blue wreath
    Of shining cyan onto its head, smiling.
    Dreamily the first banners of autumn flutter,
    The white threads, dusted with sun's joy.
    Blessed, the golden ears sway in heavy heat,
    Laden with the gentle burden of their fruit.
    Those once turned blissfully toward the rays
    Now bend the knee where they once lay as children.

OLD GRAVEDIGGER: The sun is filled with the cries of seagulls,
    The brown leaves tumble drearily to the ground.
    People like to walk in pairs,
    With September's grim demeanor.
    A dog barks canine-like from the barren pothole,
    Surrounded by eerie loneliness.
    Above the people, the clouds wander white
    And know nothing of autumn and death and life.

YOUNG GRAVEDIGGER: Autumn is sweet. I drink it like wine,
    Ah, one day I too shall be dark and possessed,
    Eaten away by worms and larvae,
    The poor brother of this sister.

OLD GRAVEDIGGER: Ten years now the leaves have been rustling
    While I dig among graves like a miner.
    And I conduct myself, smiling, comporting
    In the taverns like a proper townsperson.
    No shadow falls from these black crosses
    Into the comfort of my room.

When ravens, owls, or screech owls
Scream all night long outside my window,
I merely wake to blow my nose at most,
For I am immune to the call of owls.
My youngest child overcomes it in dreams.
The death worm does not tick in my room,
And fear ebbs away from me like waves of foam.

YOUNG GRAVEDIGGER: But I shudder when the ravens caw,
 And when a shadow stands in the moon at night.
 I breathe heavily. And my sighs groan,
 Until they are blown away by a smile from the wall.
 There, in the pale light, in the golden frame,
 My symbol and constellation hang to which my gaze is drawn.
 I will never tire of doing good,
 I am more and more inclined toward goodness.
 If only her brow shines for me, the eternal lamp,
 And if I bask in the suns of her gaze –
 Charon recedes and the Styx evaporates,
 I only listen for her steps on the gravel,
 I prick my ears like the hare Lampel;
 A small cloth once slipped from her head,
 I stole it, to revere it as a host.
 In every church it casts me onto the bier,
 In all alcoves, I build altars for her.
 Yes, the joys of earth and heaven bloom everywhere,
 For everywhere I worship the Madonna!
 Must I not praise life in psalms,
 Since she lives in the light that shines for me?
 It is she who adorns my heavy melancholy,
 With butterfly-like, gentle gestures.
 Let my arm, which swung the shovel heavily,
 Rise as light as a bird in the golden autumn air.
 Sing, dear soul, your funeral song:
 She has lived for a thousand eternities,
 And I will live for a thousand eternities!

OLD GRAVEDIGGER: Have you measured the length and width
 Of the grave to see if it complies with regulations?
 There are strange people in the magistrate's office.
 When an ill-tempered old man gets the itch,
 He will measure the grave for you! So measure and step carefully
 You stride too far for me – and don't even realize it.
 Grave work requires careful workers,

So that everyone finds their proper resting place.
How would the good citizen feel
If he were in a grave much too large,
With his robe billowing and restlessly
Forced to master an enormous space?
His is the wooden, rigid duty,
That breaks prismatically against the walls.
Five steps long, two narrow steps wide,
Is the well-bred citizen's desire.

YOUNG GRAVEDIGGER: But I, if I were to die, would whirl and wish
    The whole Earth as my burial place!
    So that as a spirit I might frolic into the deepest depths,
    And that my round skull would roll
    From the deepest sea to the highest Ararat.
    Today, fish would swim between my ribs,
    And tomorrow, the moon would hang in my bones,
    Today, moths would flutter on my lips,
    And tomorrow, I would be a pathway for worms.
    Even in death, it would be my holy endeavor:
    To bring the living to life!

OLD GRAVEDIGGER: So speaks the youth, still moved by sighs!
    To him even the gray fog approaches magically.
    The dark path of darkness seems to him
    To still lead into the brightest brightness.
    Old age knows, when it casts earth here,
    That it digs in vain for the bottom.
    We throw earth, with earth: grubs,
    How many piles of earth have I tossed in already!
    I know for sure, my grandson will still
    Always throw earth into the air.
    For what? To cover decayed bodies!
    We live, alas! Only to perish.

YOUNG GRAVEDIGGER: You lie! Death is a black gateway
    That lead us, veiled, into new spaces.
    Like someone traveling through a cave,
    Whose belief in the light had withered,
    Suddenly praises deliverance with joy;
    Barely trusting his brightly blinking eyes:
    A purer heaven wishes to delight him greatly!
    So death is surely another kind of life.
    We might become clouds. Stars. Maybe even animals.

But know, old man, we are always us,
And whatever may happen to us,
Whether we gather dust or rise with the vines
Blooming in the new spring:
The spirit that makes this heart beat here,
Always calls anew for the Feast of the Resurrection.

OLD GRAVEDIGGER: Don't forget the shoveling! In an hour
A black coffin will be lowered here.
Already the young gentleman is making his rounds
And checking to see if his beloved is laid to rest.

YOUNG GRAVEDIGGER: I hear frogs calling, owls hooting.
But it's a blue day, isn't it? And why is
The sun darkened by a pale veil of mist?
Has its torch not still shone brightly?
Who might have extinguished it in the sand?
A harsh curse freezes on my lips –
But it's up to us to comfort the young gentleman.

OLD GRAVEDIGGER: He shall be comforted. For the gentle spirits
Released his wife from eternal suffering.
A hot summer was dedicated to happiness;
Autumn has cut down this happiness like a sheaf of wheat.
How long will it last, my friend, believe me,
Until another head rests in her bed,
And if the first was blonde, now this one is brown.
Who can remain unwed for half his life
And be half-souled and almost half-dead?
Prudence hinders digestion,
Holding a warm woman in your arms at night
Is better than growing cold in a cold grave.

YOUNG GRAVEDIGGER: (*to the passing* THE YOUNG GENTLEMAN:)
Forgive me, for my duty compels me
To cover your dearest light with earth!
If I were a nail, riveted to that coffin,
I wouldn't shy away before the burial!
I would be hired until the last day
To guard the limbs until they renew. –
I can only stammer poor words
And gather tears to water the grave.
I am a shy person like you, born

From a mother who cried out in labor.
And I am chosen to be the gravedigger of her happiness
And I am lost in this wild pain
Senseless and sensual like an animal.
Forgive me, sir, and believe
That I share your torment like a twin,
Yet warmly I dwell in your heart.
And that for all eternity I will never
Forget the misery of this day.
This earth indeed weighs upon my chest.
Which I am condemned to heap upon their happiness –
I'm a heretic! Will no god rebaptize me?

THE YOUNG GENTLEMAN: I hear the music we danced to,
    I hear your blue silk dress.
    On which towering domes did we not plant
    The banner of bliss.
    I cannot grasp this empty shell,
    Which I once carried full through palaces.
    There have been so many sighs here in this hall,
    Since I asked you for your lips.

OLD GRAVEDIGGER: Wake up! You are floating in realms
    From which often there is no return.
    Remember that you dwell on earth,
    And that many souls still love you,
    And you have duties imposed on you
    To perform your work honestly day and night.

THE YOUNG GENTLEMAN: Many verses called out your name,
    And many painters have painted you.
    Painfully pale, they came to your smile,
    They walked away singing, illuminated by you.
    Even the heaviest wounds healed easily,
    The poor sinner was no longer condemned,
    And in the best of their dark hours,
    You flared up in their eyes.

YOUNG GRAVEDIGGER: Oh, how I understand you, that you stumble!
    That your dry lips babble like a child!
    A terrible forest of crosses stands
    Here in the graveyard. Bare wreaths dangle,
    And some wreaths crack like a whip.

On some graves wild rye grows.
From others loud bells ring.
And many tombstones sway like penitents.
The carnival of death is so eerie,
And more than you, Lord, I pity the executioner,
The poor person must transform into angels,
By beheading them like flowers with billhooks.

OLD GRAVEDIGGER: Do not regard as presumptuous
The request to remember the heartbeat.
Climb inwards! Inside yourself,
The root of oblivion is already sprouting,
The lungs already yearn to breathe deeply again,
In their breath, the loveliest scents dissipate.
You walk from the grave through the bustling streets,
Many hands will tenderly reach for you.
Perhaps you have a small poodle,
The little poodle must be tended to.
Perhaps a cheerful group of children
Playing with hoops will enter your grief.
The milkman shouts. The chimneys smoke gray.
I know: you will forget your pain,
For if there were no forgetting on Earth:
Not a single person would be born!

YOUNG GRAVEDIGGER: It is no consolation to the man to whom the messenger
Called out the dark news across the floor.
How is it suddenly autumn? Where did the red
And wild vines come from, which still slept in summer?
They carry a dead woman through the rooms
Where yesterday she still walked lightly and smiling.
Ah, when humanity's only human is stolen –
how he is completely covered in the earth's ashes.
I have no choice but to seek you
In world and meadow, midnight and forest.
Do I hold your shadow here among the beeches?
Ah, I embrace a phantom.
I breathe you in scents and whispers,
I hear a laughter that echoes from you.
Where are you, angel? Give a golden sign
That my words may reach your throne.
I am certain: one day
The longing will tear me completely apart,
I am just a vessel of tears and lament.

A faint reflection of your radiance,
I wish I could reach into the clouds,
To be close to the noble dance of angels.
Beseech your god of love,
That he may lift me out of the crowd to you.
Wherever I look, I see your lines:
The birds there moving in flight,
They nestle against those black pines
And form that smoke on the Gotthard train.
You dreamed of Germany. But in Argentina
There is a church that bore your image.
In the Madonnas of Italian masters
Your spirit rules and the spirits that are yours.
The God to whom we owe our bliss,
Denied us the greatest happiness:
To be entwined like vine tendrils
Wandering through the rainbow's yoke.
Why didn't our young, slender bodies
Not sink together into the dark abyss together?
At your grave, I clear the weeds.
The survivor dies many deaths.
Let me languish paler in my pain,
So I die blissfully. Blondest one, by you.
How snail-like the dreary days crawl!
How slowly the breviary turns its pages!
Will I smell the new spring in the bushes?
Winter beckons me with white sheets.
I tune the final notes of my harp:
Oh, quench my thirst for death and take me!

YOUNG GRAVEDIGGER: Tell me about your young wife,
So that I fill myself with tears like a honeycomb
And that I bury her deep
Into my heart.
That I see the world
Only with your tear-stained eyes.
Grasp her with your petrified fist.
When we hold hands like brothers,
We are better able to form, recognize and shape
The noble mind, the noble brow
Of the fair queen.

THE YOUNG GENTLEMAN: They brought her, the fairest of them all,
To the hospital a week ago.

I heard her laughter echo once more,
Then it suddenly snapped like a rope.
I had to fall to my knees sobbing
And gazed into an unfathomable valley.
And my torn eyes wandered
In a depth they couldn't understand.

OLD GRAVEDIGGER: I am familiar with the symbolism of this kind.
It often appears when parting with relatives.

YOUNG GRAVEDIGGER: But do they not speak, sir, saying: Blonde?
Is it not true: Bathed in an eternal sun?
And her eyes, like spring, are blue?
Ah, sir, I too love a blonde woman!
I too am bathed in the blonde moonlight,
My windows are painted blue as well.
My hands often wander in strands,
That she considers as light as spiderwebs.
My ears also listen to the footsteps
Of the angelic, like the sound of cymbals.
Although I timidly pursued the reality
Of first love's anxiety.
But my longing has utterly delighted me,
I searched, barely seeing, I was delighted
And entirely removed from my dark trade.
Ah, the awareness that the eternally blonde one,
The fairest blonde in my thoughts, lives,
Revive me when Death stands on his rounds
By the graves that despair digs.

THE YOUNG GENTLEMAN: Keep peace in your mind!
My peace has vanished since she departed.

YOUNG GRAVEDIGGER: What's the name of the blonde, sir, who was your wife?
Who was your echo, your second self?
Let me know the rapturous name:
I will mention it next to my beloved!

THE YOUNG GENTLEMAN: Her name was like a lark singing
From a bowstring instead of an arrow.
It was like a trumpet. And like autumn wind moaning
At twilight. Like young roosters, it greets
The morning glow that adorns its call.

YOUNG GRAVEDIGGER: The name, sir?

THE YOUNG GENTLEMAN: My girl's name was Irene.

YOUNG GRAVEDIGGER: (*cheerfully*)
>   Irene! Lord! That's my girl's name too!
>   (*stopping abruptly*)
>
>   Forgive me for disregarding your sorrow.
>   As I thought of my beloved's happiness.
>   As I laughed the name in joy
>   Like a cheeky boy, like a fool.
>   If a woman named Irene
>   No longer burns as the torch of this life,
>   How can I then ally myself with life?
>   As a servant of death, I should only proclaim death.

OLD GRAVEDIGGER: (*halfway from the background to the* YOUNG GRAVEDIGGER:)
>   Oh, may a good angel guard you.
>   To witness your downfall.
>   When your beautiful girl grows old,
>   She will be a strange mirror.
>   The young ones are pale and swollen like saints.
>   Wrinkles are often a sign of witches.

YOUNG GRAVEDIGGER: Where was the temple that you built for her?

THE YOUNG GENTLEMAN: Here, close to the gravedigger's building. I inherited
>   That house shaded
>   By that dark elm tree.

YOUNG GRAVEDIGGER: You drag and pile up stones
>   So suddenly they almost crush me,
>   Am I confused? Lost? Perhaps delusion
>   Crows in my brain like a rooster gone astray?
>   The flood is rushing, and swans emerge from it,
>   I feel as weak as a little child.
>   In that house also resides Irene,
>   For whom my thoughts constantly yearn.
>   Surely, you must know the residents,
>   (I never asked the woman's full name,

Her image sufficed for my temple:)
Two women lived there, both named Irene.

THE YOUNG GENTLEMAN: There was only one woman in that house,
     At night, she often stood stargazing
     At the window facing the graveyard.
     She looked at the star from which she was once sent.
     (*pulls out a picture*)
     See this picture of her!

YOUNG GRAVEDIGGER: (*shouting*)
     It is her, it is Irene...

     (*Pause*)

     Give me your arm, so I can lean on you.
     You are my closest brother now. I must
     Love you and embrace you for every kiss
     With which this lovely being blessed you.
     I must love you, because married to you,
     She found the fulfillment of her soul.
     A red ribbon runs from you to me,
     Stained with blood: dyed with her blood.
     As I feverishly carved her name
     In that elm, I became related to you.
     Now that in the grave, blood of my blood
     And flesh of my flesh will rest henceforth.
     Only now does this courtyard become my homeland.
     Did her blessedness bear you a child?

THE YOUNG GENTLEMAN: A son!

YOUNG GRAVEDIGGER: So he is my son too, and for him in joy,
     I will drag the corpse of my life
     Over thousands of marble steps,
     Until one day at her angelic throne,
     We kneel arm in arm before the Madonna:
     We lived only for you,
     We died only for you,
     So accept us!

     (*Pallbearers with a coffin approach from afar. Light twilight. Sunset.*)

You helped her to live. And I helped her die.
Her coffin approaches. The sunset flares up.
The old man has left. Take the fallen shovel
And join the gravedigger's clan.
The ones we love most among humans:
Let us bury the sister fraternally!
What remains of the wine press for us? The dregs.
This is the ultimate plight of humans:
We are the grave diggers of our own lives.

(*The pallbearers lower the coffin. The two begin to shovel.*)

THE YOUNG GENTLEMAN: (*pauses in the grave*)

You, who are always surrounded by death,
You know how to seize life like a master.
But I am so weak and must feel ashamed
That my lips, like a fountain, spew
Such empty words, even though they may shine
And resound in the most delicate cadences.
I know the insignificance of my nothingness.
Like a divining rod, I feel it tremble.
(*points to the grave*)

My heart after this death – after this life.
How soon winter snows its flakes
Upon your and my humble memory!
To your arms I entrust this legacy:
The child: The magical time of the future!

(*into the grave*)

You became the most consuming chimera,
I whimper like a wounded dog.
I gave you my God and my honor,
So, dreadful one, give my mouth back to me!
With my limbs already sold to death,
I stagger onto the bridge of your body.
Oh, may I in my smallness only reflect
The love that I lay at your feet!

(*short pause*)

(*looking up*)

Give my eyes their paths once more!
Once more let my fist have control!
In humility, the Savior's grace appears,
And renewal blossoms in our breath.
Many a man, dismayed, turns the wrong wheel.
They lack the blood's lightning: fervor.
Only from the heart, that sweats iron,
Does the holy, the hard spirit emerge.
I want to understand myself only from within.
The clock stands still. The sandy hour runs out.
Mountains may whiten sideways,
In caves, the eucalyptus wind dwells,
The books will ripen like apples,
When the south just begins its sunbeam.
Oh valley of sorrow! Timid place!
The mists rise. Farewell is at hand.
Let no one try to hold me back.
The cloud beckons. I have chosen freely.
I already feel my marble forehead cooling,
And I feel my hands almost steeled.
I ask you to manage my small legacy.
The brother who is not lacking in dignity.
And my heart's last cantilena,
My last sigh rejoices: Irene!

YOUNG GRAVEDIGGER: The cemetery shows me a hundred sarcophagi,
In every sarcophagus, you rest.
Oh, close my lip's meager lament
With your pure angelic kisses.
Appear once more in this second
That calls me away, in holy radiance.
And let me die gently on your lips.
So gladly will I be utterly destroyed.

THE YOUNG GENTLEMAN: Who will believe that in my pain
I wasted away thirsting for you?
People today have hearts of metal;
Their God is their serpent that crawls.
They read heretically of great myths,
Of Hero, who entrusted herself to Leander.
They marvel that once humans flourished,
That once a human lip sang.
In disbelief they read that the lover

Could not bear to part with the beloved.
That he was scattered as dust to the four winds,
That her death struck him with lightning.
It ends with me like a dream.
Irene calls for holy serenity,
And our love shines like a legend
Into a better and golden time.

(*The Young Gentleman: collapses at the grave*)

Young Gravedigger: (*leaning on the shovel*)
The moon stretches its pale dead hand
Into the graying day. In bright ocher
A small sky still glows in the west. Loosely
A heap of female breasts lies on the land.

(*pauses for a moment*)

Now you are dead like them: And from your side
Red blood seeps into black sand.
Even over gods, Ananke rules
With a relentless, stern hand.
God and man are nailed to the cross of this life
And the dream of both: the hero.
Eros, the holy spirit of hellish death
Harnesses you to his war chariot.

(*He begins to dig a second grave next to the first.*)

Everyone honors the god that suits him.
Spirit is found wherever there's a derriere.
And he, a beloved drinker,
Sipped deeply from the cup of living.
This is the truth; otherwise, there is none:
Two was one and shall become one again.

(*He digs, the curtain falls.*)

Part Nineteen:

The Awakening

"The Awakening" was published as individual scenes in 1919
in the magazine "The Revolutionary." In this play, Klabund demonstrates
the inhumanity of war, a work he had been composing since 1917.

The Awakening

Dramatis Personae:

Sergeant – Lieutenant – Adjutant – General –
Lieutenant of the Reserves – Young lady from Lille – Foreign Legionnaire –
Two Wounded – Rosa + Erna + Paula, Three Girls – Young Worker –
Brothel Madam – Deaf-mute – Blind man – Lame man – Madame de G. –
Concierge – Young gentleman – Waitress – Old man – Director – Agent –
Senior Student – Two Dead – Hussar – Infantryman – Some Workers –
Women – Children – A Picket Line of Soldiers – Non-commissioned Officer

Trench

SERGEANT A bird is singing...

LIEUTENANT Good morning...

SERGEANT You were sleeping?

LIEUTENANT Badly...

SERGEANT Were you alone... in your dream?

LIEUTENANT Infinitely lonely and alone... no one left in the world... only me... the earth devastated: no more cities, villages, forests, fruit trees, cathedrals... only shell holes and trenches... thousands of trenches... dug one after the other... ever denser, ever denser... like the rings of a lunar crater... and no soldiers in them: only empty tunics decorated with sticks and rifles like scarecrows. The artillery: set up as if to deceive enemy airmen: just old stovepipes placed on peasant carts. The gunners: jolly ghosts. In the rear: scarecrows. At the division headquarters: scarecrows. At the army group headquarters, the generals: scarecrows. Scarecrows that no sparrow feared anymore. Tits nested in their headless helmets. The general staff maps were soiled and defaced by the young birds, but that didn't make them any less improbable or different. Here, the droppings of a swallow signified a fortress with its towers; there, those of a finch: a troop encampment. I walked from the front to the rear, from the rear I thought I was returning home: I came to a new front, then to a new rear, to a third front, a third rear. Everywhere these scarecrows. And I, infinitely lonely and alone: the only human being... Can you interpret this dream for me?

SERGEANT I'll dare to say it: because it shakes me to the core. The dream: that is our life. The scarecrows: are us. But the human being, the one truly living human being — he's missing... (*Silence. After a while.*)

LIEUTENANT You think the same people live over there as we do?

SERGEANT Yes.

LIEUTENANT With bones, longing, ulcers, nervousness, smiles, intestinal catarrh — like us?

SERGEANT Yes.

LIEUTENANT You're knee-deep in dirt...

SERGEANT Like you...

LIEUTENANT You have lice in your fur...

SERGEANT Like you...

LIEUTENANT You're afraid —

SERGEANT Of what?

LIEUTENANT Afraid of eternity —

SERGEANT Afraid of eternity... like us...

LIEUTENANT They send greetings home to the enemy pilot flying over the lines...

SERGEANT Like you...

LIEUTENANT They have wives, children — like us. And over there is one — oh, I know, his name is Marcel Canquoi — a strange name, isn't it? He's exactly the same age as me, to the day and hour... 29 years old... he sells felt, hair, and straw hats: the latest style, tall, with a narrow black band — sells hats: just like you... he has a boy, like me, who just got his first pair of trousers... and proudly shows them off to his comrades on the street...

SERGEANT The first pair of trousers, my dear fellow, are imitation soldiers' trousers...

LIEUTENANT Oh, if only we could one day keep the colorful coat away from our children, the colorful coat soaked in blood — that's the only reason it's so colorful... Children should play with flowers and salamanders, fish, and butterflies: no more fake flags, wooden rifles, fake heroism. Instead of French toy soldiers, they should play with French beetles. They also have red trousers... and are alive...

SERGEANT You're right: the toy soldiers are to blame for the war. They must be eradicated. When I return to Germany, I will set fire to all the tin and lead soldier factories in Nuremberg. How will it flicker when millions of tin soldiers melt in the flames of the new era?

LIEUTENANT Children harbor murder in their little hearts. They're poisoned by the tradition of "heroism." In school, they always learn: First Punic War, Second Punic War... First Coalition War, Second Coalition War... They should never, ever learn: First World War... Second World War... this war would be organized madness if it weren't called the last.

SERGEANT In this war, concepts fell along with the people. Reason fell along with the concepts and became a whore, duped by all... and cheated yet further for her filthy coin.

SERGEANT Slogans, erected in place of the old barriers, resounding — shrill —

on the streets of the country, are what make it happen... Germany ahead in the world... the fight against Tsarism... England, the shopkeeper... Italy, the traitor... Siegfried Line, U-boat peace...

SERGEANT Do you believe in a breakthrough at the front?

LIEUTENANT Which front? I don't know any front... I only know an 800-meter-long, muddy trench. Wire fences in front of it. Spanish cavalry. Listening holes. The so-called front over there, I imagine, won't be longer than 800 meters either.

SERGEANT Who's facing us — do you know that?

LIEUTENANT Yesterday a deserter arrived. They're territorial family men like us. We prefer to leave each other alone and are glad when the higher-ups leave us in peace.

SERGEANT Yes, if it weren't for "the higher-ups." Then suddenly the army command asks: why hasn't anything happened in this sector for weeks? Why is it so quiet in Sector C? Order: Combat reconnaissance... Well, we shoot, they shoot back. We shoot each other's good friends dead. We get angry with each other. The French set up a post at night. The next night we do the same. We get to the daily report. The captain gets the Iron Cross first... Then we play tarot or skat for another eight days...

LIEUTENANT But after eight days, someone comes up with the idea of tying an empty can of food to a cat's tail. No sooner said than done... Laughter... and a twinkle in the eyes. The cat races around the barbed wire obstacles, clattering with the can. As if a cavalry lieutenant had suddenly gone mad and was dancing around with his trailing saber... the French think God knows what's going on... They're firing like mad. The artillery starts to spark... It's getting closer and closer... damn, now the grenades are coming: it's a real curtain call... Where are we going to get the rations from behind tonight: herring and bread... I feel sick just thinking about those cold fried herrings... A mutton chop with green beans: that would be something before death... We lie, dead tired, in the dugouts. The sentries left behind in the trenches are watching to see if they're coming... At dawn, something cracks in the wire barriers... It's the enemy engineers, cutting through the wire with their pincers like stag beetles... Hand grenades fly at their skulls like firecrackers... The metal buttons of the enemy assault troops bounce from the trenches beyond... Machine gun fire 200 meters... taktaktak... No one can get to our trenches... A few French engineers hang like flies in the cobwebs of the wire barriers... One shouts: I'm thirsty... thirsty... We throw him a beer bottle... It falls, three meters away from him... His eyes become hands, long polyp arms pulling the beer bottle towards him... I think it's Marcel Canquoi... 29 years old... exactly the same age as me... Chapellier from Toulouse... (*Silence.*)

SERGEANT Where is your Iron Cross?

LIEUTENANT I've worn it long enough – like Jesus wore his. I hung it on a dead

Frenchman.

SERGEANT Why?

LIEUTENANT I'm still honoring him with it... It was no longer an honor for me: to boast or show off. I was on duty at the rear. Every cook at the goulash cannon had it. Every orderly who served in the officers' mess. Yesterday a letter came from my father. That was the last straw. It ripped the Iron Cross right out of my buttonhole. I couldn't, I didn't want to wear it anymore.

SERGEANT What does your father's letter have to do with your Iron Cross?

LIEUTENANT My father received the Iron Cross first.

SERGEANT Congratulations. Did you have your congratulations telegraphed to him?

LIEUTENANT Congratulations? Why wish him luck? He's lost his. I laugh at his vanity... his parrot-like senility... his impotence...

SERGEANT What is your father?

LIEUTENANT A colonel...

SERGEANT Where is he stationed... in the West... in the East... in the Balkans?

LIEUTENANT He's nowhere... not even firmly on his two feet. It's the old days that are wavering within him.

SERGEANT But the Iron Cross?

LIEUTENANT He's a station commander in W:... Do you know the latest order? All officers from major upwards who don't yet have the Iron Cross are to be submitted for the Iron Cross as soon as possible. The Iron Cross has been demoted to the marksmen's festival or choral society medal. We front-line soldiers need no outward symbol: a high flame burns on our foreheads. The holy fire of boundless brotherly love, which no longer knows border posts, descended upon us like the Holy Spirit, fiery to inspire us.

SERGEANT I have long since been cured of the delusion that one could annex the heart of the country along with the land. Love... is won through loving. It is not blackmailed.

LIEUTENANT All of us at the front, on all fronts, want to tear open our shirts, the dirty, lice-ridden ones, and show each other our bleeding, scarred chests. We will then fall into each other's arms, weeping, realizing too late that the other's wound is also ours...

Room in the headquarters of the Xth Army

ADJUTANT The telephone, Your Excellency.

GENERAL Who is it?

ADJUTANT Command post of Division Z.

GENERAL Well?

ADJUTANT The division has attacked as ordered.

GENERAL When?

ADJUTANT 7:15 sharp.

GENERAL It's now?

ADJUTANT 9:30.

GENERAL They've reached it?

ADJUTANT The forest of C. Some buildings of N. are in their hands.

GENERAL Buildings of N.? Who ordered them to take N.?

ADJUTANT No one, Your Excellency. An explicit order even contradicted it.

GENERAL The division is being flanked. It is needlessly sacrificing at least one battalion. Who is the recalcitrant divisional commander?

ADJUTANT General Z., Your Excellency... I may speak freely, Excellency.

GENERAL You may... Speak...

ADJUTANT General Z. is ambitious.

GENERAL Certainly... Certainly...

ADJUTANT He knows that disobedience to superior commanders, when it results in success, is credited to their advantage.

GENERAL General Z. can achieve nothing in N. N. will be flanked immediately.

ADJUTANT General Z., Your Excellency, is the only divisional commander in the 10th Army who has so far been denied the Pour le merite. It would not matter to him to sacrifice his entire division... to the Pour le merite... I was permitted to speak freely, Excellency...

GENERAL Telephone: Division Z. is immediately turning back its left wing. F.'s Regiment of Brigade D. is assisting it. I will request the Pour le merite from His Majesty for General Z. Otherwise, the gentleman will get us into trouble again... despite all his abilities. At the outbreak of a war, senior officers should be awarded all higher decorations, Iron First, Pour le merite, etc., immediately, so that their ambition for the decorations doesn't play stupid and... immoral tricks on them. What do you think, Adjutant?

ADJUTANT I agree, Your Excellency. I may speak freely, Your Excellency?

GENERAL Speak!

ADJUTANT Shouldn't such officers be hanged according to the laws of war?

GENERAL We should... but we lack the necessary number of gallows... we are all... scoundrels. We should all be hanged.

ADJUTANT I agree, Your Excellency... I was allowed to — speak freely, Your Excellency...

A Street in Lille

LIEUTENANT OF THE RESERVES Good day, Mademoiselle.

YOUNG LADY FROM LILLE Good day, sir.

LIEUTENANT OF THE RESERVES Where does the road lead?

YOUNG LADY FROM LILLE Into the world.

LIEUTENANT OF THE RESERVES It's not far – a mile in any direction, and it ends.

YOUNG LADY FROM LILLE You're speaking in riddles, sir.

LIEUTENANT OF THE RESERVES You speak in arabesques of silence, Mademoiselle. Only your parasol is writing strange symbols in the air.

YOUNG LADY FROM LILLE I don't understand you.

LIEUTENANT OF THE RESERVES Well, do you have a special pass that allows you to leave the city limits of Lille?

YOUNG LADY FROM LILLE No, sir.

LIEUTENANT OF THE RESERVES You see: the world is a target for you – one that you shoot at, a target, only, thank God, the English don't hit with every shot.

YOUNG LADY FROM LILLE Lille is my heart. If it were infallible! How gladly I would bleed to death!

LIEUTENANT OF THE RESERVES The market square of Lille is the center of the disk. From there: ten kilometers — and you'll hit an iron wall.

YOUNG LADY FROM LILLE I'm not so foolish as to bang my little head against an iron wall.

LIEUTENANT OF THE RESERVES You are clever, Mademoiselle.

YOUNG LADY FROM LILLE Not as clever as I seem, not as clever as the sun shines. It shines on an inconspicuous woman.

LIEUTENANT OF THE RESERVES Philosopher!

YOUNG LADY FROM LILLE Philosopher and mercenary... a pretty idyll.

LIEUTENANT OF THE RESERVES Tell me, girl and man — a purer one!

YOUNG LADY FROM LILLE A gray skirt — and swoons?

LIEUTENANT OF THE RESERVES A gray skirt — and floats!

YOUNG LADY FROM LILLE I'm ashamed.

LIEUTENANT OF THE RESERVES Why?

YOUNG LADY FROM LILLE I'm so heavy...

LIEUTENANT OF THE RESERVES So light! You're hanging in the air like a dragonfly!

YOUNG LADY FROM LILLE I'm a coward...

LIEUTENANT OF THE RESERVES Cowardly?

YOUNG LADY FROM LILLE Yes, I have no courage — and unfortunately, no talent for spying either. It would surely be my duty to spy for my country...

LIEUTENANT OF THE RESERVES You're honest, Mademoiselle... How do you know I'm not informing?

YOUNG LADY FROM LILLE You're an officer. An officer is a gentleman. A gentleman doesn't inform...

LIEUTENANT OF THE RESERVES Do you live on this street?

YOUNG LADY FROM LILLE Yes, the third house around the corner. Up two flights of stairs; would you like to accompany me to my room?

LIEUTENANT OF THE RESERVES With pleasure, Mademoiselle.

YOUNG LADY FROM LILLE It's a bit dark in the hallway. You'll have to excuse me. We have to use gas sparingly because coal is in short supply.

The Girl's Room

YOUNG LADY FROM LILLE So, take off your coat, make yourself comfortable. Do you like it here with me?

LIEUTENANT OF THE RESERVES You have a lovely room, all white with gold, absolutely charming.

YOUNG LADY FROM LILLE Actually, you shouldn't have been allowed up here at all... in uniform... don't you think?... visits... to someone like me... are forbidden, aren't they?

LIEUTENANT OF THE RESERVES So many things are forbidden that God has commanded us to do. But war, unfortunately, is still not forbidden.

YOUNG LADY FROM LILLE It forbids itself...

LIEUTENANT OF THE RESERVES But people refuse to see it.

YOUNG LADY FROM LILLE Oh là là! You, a Prussian officer, take off your tunic in the company of a lady of gallantry, and reveal yourself as... an anti-militarist. You wear your heart hidden beneath the uniform... like a locket.

LIEUTENANT OF THE RESERVES Do you think we've forgotten how to be human?

YOUNG LADY FROM LILLE Sometimes one might believe it: in Belgium, in one city, they shot 123 civilians in a single day... 123 civilians. In one city. In one day. Did you know that?

LIEUTENANT OF THE RESERVES I didn't. That sounds sensationally exaggerated to me.

YOUNG LADY FROM LILLE Exaggerated... yes... inflated by the winds of despair...

LIEUTENANT OF THE RESERVES Mademoiselle...

YOUNG LADY FROM LILLE Lieutenant?

LIEUTENANT OF THE RESERVES You have tears on your lashes... may I kiss them away?

YOUNG LADY FROM LILLE Kiss... kiss me... I want to close my eyes and believe: repentance kisses despair. Love near weakness... humility strong...

LIEUTENANT OF THE RESERVES My... girl... how long it's been since I kissed a girl...

YOUNG LADY FROM LILLE Blue-white-red... black-white-red... the colors blend into one another... Man, my man... I love you... do you see the rainbow above us?

Trench

A Foreign Legionnaire has defected. He waves his French cap, shouting:

LEGIONNAIRE Germany! Germany!

SERGEANT Don't shout, or they'll shoot from over there. You can praise Germany quietly too. We've always been yelling "Germany! Germany!" at the top of our lungs, and all we got for it was the whole world coming down on us because of that senseless blaring.

LEGIONNAIRE My heart is so full... I'm with you now, comrades... I speak German, I hear German... The German language sounds like nightingales singing.

SOLDIER You must be thirsty...

ANOTHER Here, drink...

LEGIONNAIRE Thank you! Thank you!

SERGEANT You're a Foreign Legionnaire?

LEGIONNAIRE From the Sidi-Bel-Abbès regiment. I've served for seven years. I wasn't a human being anymore. I made corporal. My only longing: a quarter liter of red wine after duty... Now the rock splits open... the spring gushes forth... Germany! My heart pours out... pours... roaring like the Rhine... I have to laugh... with joy... laugh... laugh...

SERGEANT You laugh well... like a laughing dove... so rapturous. We only laugh like parrots now: an imitation of laughter that still echoes in our ears from earlier times. We can't laugh like you... We can't defect... where would we go... maybe backward... because behind us lies Germany...

LEGIONNAIRE I ran forward... before me shone the star of Bethlehem, Germany: the dome of Cologne Cathedral.

SERGEANT Germany: we love it madly, or we wouldn't be lying here in the dirt.

But, comrade, I hope you haven't come here to fight at our side against your former friends. Stay connected to them. Like an umbilical cord. Seven years is a long time. Remember the camaraderie in Africa a little, with gratitude too. Not everyone becomes a corporal in the Foreign Legion. We'll send you back home, to some office desk. There you'll be in Germany. But you can't stay here in the front trench. If the official French catch you, they'll hang you as a deserter and defector. Don't be a true traitor. You stand between nations: don't betray the soul of humanity. Fight no one more than yourself. Take off that uniform... here's a field-gray jacket... You'll still have to account for yourself to battalion command... say hello to Germany... it lies far... far behind us... farther than you think... I'd like to hear the rain in the Thuringian Forest again... or the buses on Friedrichstraße in Berlin... or the bells of the Church of Our Lady in Munich... not always this eternal air raid alarm... farewell, comrade...

Field Hospital

FIRST WOUNDED MAN What's your name?

SECOND WOUNDED MAN Nameless. — And you?

FIRST WOUNDED MAN Someone or other.

SECOND WOUNDED MAN Your father?

FIRST WOUNDED MAN No one.

SECOND WOUNDED MAN Your mother?

FIRST WOUNDED MAN A woman.

SECOND WOUNDED MAN What kind of wound?

FIRST WOUNDED MAN A gut shot. — You?

SECOND WOUNDED MAN Lung.

FIRST WOUNDED MAN Grenade?

SECOND WOUNDED MAN Shrapnel. You?

FIRST WOUNDED MAN Machine gun.

SECOND WOUNDED MAN You're alive?

FIRST WOUNDED MAN A little...

SECOND WOUNDED MAN Are you afraid of death?

FIRST WOUNDED MAN Only the doctor.

SECOND WOUNDED MAN The doctor?

FIRST WOUNDED MAN He's cruel. Has knives and forceps. Rough hands, like a butcher.

SECOND WOUNDED MAN But the nurse?

FIRST WOUNDED MAN Smiles sweetly.

SECOND WOUNDED MAN Like a statue.

FIRST WOUNDED MAN Like a lilac bush. She's a doe. Walks so slenderly through the forest of our beds.

SECOND WOUNDED MAN Where did you fall?

FIRST WOUNDED MAN In the assault on Bixschoote... We went in without artillery. The general wanted it that way... we charged... kept charging... sea breeze over the ocean... the artillery didn't follow... wouldn't come, just wouldn't come... I jumped and jumped... hopped like a hare across the field... In the end, there were only four of us left beside me... "Forward," I shouted, "Comrades, forward... to the farm... we have to take it..." We crept closer... there stood our own, the Saxons... they'd shot up our whole regiment... all volunteers... fresh-faced students... we four were the only survivors... I collapsed two steps in front of the Saxons... with a stomach wound... I had to hold my intestines in... so they wouldn't fall out... My own brother was with the Saxon regiment. He shot me in the belly... I'm sure of it.

Brothel in Leipzig

In the reception room three girls sit in sheer gauze dresses.

ROSA We haven't had business like that since the first days of the war... like in the days of the dozens of declarations of war... not since then.

ERNA Yes, back then things were really wild... the young men needed an outlet for their enthusiasm... for their daredevil spirit... and we gave them a chance to blow off steam for relatively little money.

ROSA With us, their attacks weren't life-threatening either.

PAULA On the contrary, we saved more than one life by giving someone gonorrhea. They couldn't be sent to the front for months and sometimes ended up declared unfit altogether if it dragged on long enough.

ROSA Oh... the first days of the war... I still dream of them sometimes, when I've eaten well, which happens rarely enough; you have to go barter in the countryside now...

ERNA Back then, all our rooms were decorated with black-white-red flags... the Iron Cross was embroidered into the bed linens... and in every room, a gold-framed picture of the Kaiser hung...

ROSA While we danced with our friends and clients, the young soldiers and war volunteers, or offered them the arts of our bodies for a fee, the gramophones played: Germany, Germany above all... and: A call rings out like thunder...

PAULA Back then... when Austria joined our side... I marched with the crowd, it was quite late at night, to the Austrian consulate. A drunk baker's apprentice led us, waving a hastily made Austrian flag in his hand. We shouted: Stand firm in the storm! and behaved like madmen. That night, I gave myself to a young worker for free, without asking for anything. I still get angry about it. I was out of my mind...

ROSA It's gotten lonely here... lately... I haven't had a man in so long, I could almost fall for the first halfway decent one who walks in. And I swear to God, I couldn't care less about so-called love...

ERNA The men don't get enough to eat. And they have to work too much. Feed a man beefsteak and eggs and let him do nothing for three days, I guarantee you, by the second day he'll be knocking on our door.

PAULA Beefsteak and eggs, don't be ridiculous. Beefsteak and eggs, now in the third year of the war!
> *The bell rings. The girls jump nervously and adjust their ribbons and skirts.*

ALL THREE A man!
> *The YOUNG WORKER enters the brothel, a little disoriented, led in by the MADAM.*

MADAM Just pick one, go ahead, don't be shy... (*She exits.*)

YOUNG WORKER Good evening, ladies... may I come closer?

ROSA Good evening, sir.

PAULA Please, have a seat.

ERNA Would the gentleman care for a drink?

YOUNG WORKER Yes, wine, please.

ROSA Perhaps some champagne?

YOUNG WORKER Yes, champagne, please.

PAULA May we each have a glass?

YOUNG WORKER Yes, of course.
> *ROSA exits to fetch the champagne. She soon returns with champagne and four glasses.*

ERNA (*sitting on the YOUNG WORKER's knee*) You're a handsome boy...

YOUNG WORKER You think so? The girls in the factory say that too...

PAULA You seem like quite the rascal! I bet you've gotten up to all kinds of things... with the factory girls, right?

YOUNG WORKER Oh no... not really... I have a fiancée!

ROSA A fiancée? And you cheat on her so easily with us, just like that?

YOUNG WORKER I'm not cheating on her... I just couldn't be with her today... she... she's been crying all day...

PAULA Oh... poor thing... but you're not even drinking...

YOUNG WORKER Cheers, ladies...

PAULA Why is she crying... the poor girl... surely because you were cruel to her?

YOUNG WORKER I've always been good to her...

ROSA But a girl doesn't cry for no reason.

YOUNG WORKER (*drinks*) Cheers, ladies... no, she doesn't cry for nothing. She cries because there's a war...

PAULA Because... there's a war? Well then, we should all be crying...

YOUNG WORKER (*seriously*) We should all be crying... because we're all to blame...

ROSA Blame — for the war?

YOUNG WORKER Yes... blame for the war...

ERNA I don't recall being to blame for the war...

PAULA He's right... back when I marched with the crowd to the Austrian consulate and shouted "hooray for war," "hooray for war" — I made myself partly guilty for all the misery...

YOUNG WORKER (*stroking her gently*) You're a good person, miss... better than you might think...

PAULA Don't say that... I'm an animal...

YOUNG WORKER We're all animals, miss.

ROSA So why did you come to us... Cheers... go on, drink?

YOUNG WORKER I was drafted today... and found fit for duty... and that's why my fiancée is crying... and I couldn't bear to see it anymore... but all the women in the street had the same face as my fiancée... so I came here... I thought, surely here they don't know the war... here, the women have no brothers, no souls, no husbands... here, maybe they still know how to laugh... (*to PAULA*) But I see now, I was wrong... Even here, they know about the war...

PAULA (*spreads her arms*) Come upstairs with me... I want to love you... truly love you... as I've never loved a man before... Yes... until now, I wasn't capable of love... You've taught me remorse... and love... Come. Come... I'll pay Madame for you with my own money... even the champagne... You mustn't give me a thing... (*exalted*) Come... come! (*They exit together, embracing.*)

At the Veterans' Convalescent Home

A garden. Trees. Sunshine. Lush greenery. A DEAF-MUTE plays the hand harmonica. A BLIND MAN man and a CRIPPLE with a wooden leg dance to the music.

CRIPPLE More swing... (*yelling*) more swing...

DEAF-MUTE (*smiles uncomprehendingly and keeps playing*).

BLIND MAN Hopsassa... hopsassa... what else is life for?

CRIPPLE (*stomping with his wooden leg*) Rhythm, rhythm! I used to be a wood-cutter, that puts rhythm in your limbs... now that's music... woodcutting... a different music than what this deaf-mute squeezes out of his torture chamber... (*shouting*) Bounce! More bounce!

BLIND MAN I much prefer it when you dance softly. Look, like this... (*dances alone*) N...ta-ta...n...ta...ta...n...ta...ta... (*bumps into a tree*) whoops...

CRIPPLE (*laughing*) You should see yourself, the way you hop around... like a crane in an oil salad... (*imitates him*) n...ta...ta n...ta. Nah, that soft-as-butter stuff isn't for me. A man's got to have marks, I tell you, marks and pennies...

BLIND MAN (*hooks his arm through the CRIPPLE's*) Tell me, what do you see today...?

CRIPPLE What do I see?... You... the deaf-mute... the trees... the house... What are you getting at?

BLIND MAN I mean, isn't it a beautiful day today? I can smell the sun all the way here in the shade. It must be made of gold today, like the good fairy in those children's storybooks... Give me a little sunshine in my hand... There... just so I can have my hand in the sun. You see, because I'm blind, I see with my hands... Dear sun!

Hotel Lobby in Geneva

MADAME Is there a telegram for me?

CONCIERGE Here you are, Madame.

MADAME (*opens the telegram, glances over it, walks downstage left to a table, sits in a club chair. She takes out a cigarette case. A bellboy offers her a light. She blows the smoke toward the ceiling. She notices, opposite her at the table to the right, an elegant young gentleman and begins to flirt with him... At the table behind the young gentleman sits an older white-haired gentleman reading the Frankfurt Newspaper.*)
YOUNG GENTLEMAN Garçon!

WAITER Sir!
YOUNG GENTLEMAN It's very hot today. A mineral water, please!

WAITER What would monsieur prefer: Fachinger, Harzer Sauerbrunnen, Gießhübler...

YOUNG GENTLEMAN That's all Boche... I don't drink Boche soda...

WAITER Perhaps Passugger? Swiss spring. Swiss bottling.

OLD GENTLEMAN (*has jumped up*) This is outrageous! Am I in a neutral country or not? Will you immediately take back this insult to Germany? Will you take back Boche at once?

YOUNG GENTLEMAN For you, sir, very gladly. I can tell by your accent, you are German. I take back the word Boche in regard to you, with which I insulted the mineral waters. But in general, the Boche as a species still exists for me.

OLD GENTLEMAN You insult Germany all over again! This is unheard of! In a neutral hotel, one has to put up with this! Director!

DIRECTOR Sir, I beg you not to take this little incident too seriously.

OLD GENTLEMAN My bill! Immediately! I am leaving this instant. Where is my valet?

DIRECTOR He is having dinner in the servants' dining room.

OLD GENTLEMAN You will have him summoned. He is to pack at once.

DIRECTOR Sir, I deeply regret this. I ask your forgiveness in the name of the hotel. May I perhaps telephone the Grand Hotel Beau Séjour to reserve you an apartment? It is already late in the evening.

OLD GENTLEMAN When does the night train to Montreux leave?

DIRECTOR (*checks his watch*) In an hour, sir...

OLD GENTLEMAN I'm going to Montreux...

DIRECTOR (*bows, goes to the young gentleman on the right*) I don't understand, sir. Tact should have prevented you from making such remarks... loudly enough to be overheard at the next table. Do you know who the old gentleman is? He is the owner of Germany's most prestigious champagne house, Bratt & Co.

YOUNG GENTLEMAN (*bows*) Thank you, that's all I wanted to know. (*He ascends the grand staircase with a smile.*)

DIRECTOR directwatches him, astonished, then exits.

MADAME (*who has attentively followed the entire scene*) Garçon...

WAITER Madame?

MADAME An ice cream soda...

WAITER Very well, Madame...

A very elegant young man enters the hotel lobby, slightly dramatic in his movements; he is a German secret agent.

AGENT I am delighted, my dear, to see you again so soon in Geneva. (*He hands his hat and cane to a bellboy. Sits down.*)

MADAME You're strikingly handsome, my boy. Today as always. My lips haven't forgotten yours.

AGENT (*kisses her hand.*)

MADAME For your... profession, it would be quite sufficient if you were merely handsome. The striking part... could be left out.

AGENT I only stand out to women... and that is absolutely necessary for my... profession.

WAITER Your order, sir?

AGENT Whisky.

WAITER With soda?

AGENT With ice water.

WAITER Very well.

AGENT Madame...

MADAME Sir?

AGENT What news do you bring us from Paris?

MADAME News... the latest... the best kind...

AGENT Let's hear it...

MADAME Since the 15th — that is, four days ago — a new newspaper has been appearing in Paris... that finally... strikes a decent, human tone...

AGENT Who owns the newspaper?

MADAME I'll tell you.

> *Music begins to play – a one-step.*

MADAME Music!

AGENT An element of our future life...

MADAME There's a small evening dance going on. Do you dance?

AGENT With the greatest pleasure.

MADAME (*rises, places her arm in his*) Then come with me!

Gymnasium (Senior Year)

SENIOR STUDENT Next week is the University Entrance Exam. God and the headmaster willing, we will all pass it. Listen up, guys, there are some among you who, now in the fourth year of the war, after the goddess of war has long since unveiled herself as an old whore, still want to volunteer for war service. Decision of the sergeant council of the secret student fraternity Markomannia, to which you all belong: whoever volunteers for war service in the fourth year of the war commits treason against the fatherland. You are all needed as volunteers for peace. We recently read the political remarks of Lichtenberg, a German writer of the eighteenth century, in our literary reading circle. Remember what he said: I would give anything to know exactly for whom the deeds were actually done, of which it is publicly said that they were done for the fatherland... (*Thunderous stamping of feet.*) We love our fatherland with a burning heart. (*Thunderous stamping of feet.*) But we see it forged in chains before the tribunes of an ambitious military party and an imperious principality. Germany has been silenced under the unlawful law regarding the state of siege. Gags have been shoved into all our mouths. We are only allowed to babble. Our arms are not free: we are only allowed to use them according to certain rules, as in gymnastics class. We are only allowed to see what is permitted to us: tyranny forces rose-tinted glasses onto our noses so that we see the world in the rosiest light. But the rose-red will turn blood-red. We will see the world blood-red... as it is. Friends! We have a secret meeting tonight in the pub "Green Path 1" at nine o'clock. Let no one be missing! Our girlfriends Lilli, Margrit, and Iris will be present. (*The bell rings.*) The school attendant is ringing the bell. Homer begins immediately. Don't forget your Lichtenberg! I certainly cannot say whether things will get better if they change; but this much I can say, things must change - if they are to get better... (*Thunderous stamping of feet.*)

Battlefield

FIRST DEAD MAN Spring is coming. Can you smell it?

SECOND DEAD MAN Violets.

FIRST DEAD MAN And blood. The spring offensives are starting.

SECOND DEAD MAN A tin can... with fresh greens.

FIRST DEAD MAN I'd have preferred young peas and carrots — if I were still alive...

SECOND DEAD MAN I'm glad I don't feel hunger anymore... it was always a fatal sensation between the ribs...

FIRST DEAD MAN I'm glad I no longer have to think philosophically. My head is as empty as a drum. Wind and moon debate behind my eye sockets. The moon burns like a candle in my skull. The wind wants to blow it out. That's what you call a pleasant conversation.

SECOND DEAD MAN Such a light, airy skull – a comfort I wouldn't want to do without anymore. It floats above you like a child's balloon. Our brains dragged us down into the muck. Since we lost them — and we'll be sure not to go looking for them again — we've finally been happy... that is: dead...

FIRST DEAD MAN Would you like to go back to life?

SECOND DEAD MAN God forbid... I'm not curious...

FIRST DEAD MAN What was your profession?

SECOND DEAD MAN Aviator... believe me, the earth looked no better from above than it does from down here. A stewed hospital prune... dried fruit...

FIRST DEAD MAN You were closer to the sun!

SECOND DEAD MAN And to the clouds...

FIRST DEAD MAN You could take in millions at a glance...

SECOND DEAD MAN Loving... tormented with sorrow... I saw millions: a twitching heart... gripped by a polyp... then everything went black before my eyes... I lost control... I crashed... and here I am...

FIRST DEAD MAN I was a gunner on a submarine... I torpedoed some merchant ships, a few grain barges... I enjoyed it... but then came the intensified U-boat campaign... I trained the barrel on a passenger steamer... it was night... from over there came laughter, dancing, drunkenness... I heard a small child crying in its sleep... an older one calling for its nanny... two lovers stood embraced at the railing... they went up in a burst of flame, rising into the heaven of their love... I blacked out... I requested a transfer to the naval infantry. So here I am. An Indian stabbed me. The very moment I struck him. He lingered around here for a while afterwards. I think the English buried him. A pity, he was a fine fellow. A clever head. Even without a lower jaw.

SECOND DEAD MAN Shh... quiet...

FIRST DEAD MAN What is it?

SECOND DEAD MAN A medic dog barked... good night... the moon is high... let's sleep...

Prisoner-of-war camp in Africa

A black sentry paces back and forth in the background.

HUSSAR I've been squatting on this same spot for a year and a half now, my ass glued to the ground like a termite queen.

INFANTRYMAN How many times have I counted the uniform buttons on my jacket? And the individual planks of the fence! And the minutes of an hour — they're countless...

HUSSAR That black girl the other day wasn't bad... Eyes like agates... Breasts like earthworms... Teeth like the jagged edge of a sawfish... I paid for the pleasure with twenty-five strokes of the cane... I loved getting beaten... I thought, if only the guy doesn't stop — twenty-five is such a small number...

INFANTRYMAN I don't know what I'd do if I hadn't caught syphilis from a creature like that last year. I'm downright grateful to that little ferret for her kind infection. I'd die of boredom if I didn't have the pox. It gives me some discomforts, at least something to deal with. A little sore, you can pamper it till it grows as big as a hazelnut. Then it bursts... and boredom comes crawling back, disgustingly creeping across your chest on spider legs.

HUSSAR I'm glad we've got a black guard detail... just a few white sergeants... The whites... they're the real barbarians...

INFANTRYMAN The blacks join us in obstructing the white sergeants. They help us whenever they can. They've got bright hearts in black chests. Maybe one should marry a black woman, just to finally escape the white race...

HUSSAR Do you remember Lyon? A troop transport heading to the front jabbed their bayonets for fun into the cattle cars, where the defenseless, helpless people crouched like rabbits.

INFANTRYMAN I despise that nation!

HUSSAR How I pity them, the poor ones who thought they were hurting us and only tortured themselves with hatred.

INFANTRYMAN Women and children threw stones at us and spat on us.

HUSSAR When I was in the hospital, the nurse painted the words Vive la France! on my chest with iodine...

INFANTRYMAN I was starving, and French officers threw me bread from horseback into the dirt, I pounced on it, desperate...

HUSSAR Lord, forgive them, for they know not what they do...

INFANTRYMAN To hell with forgiveness! I wish the plague or cholera upon every last one of them.

HUSSAR Can you still read?

INFANTRYMAN Not a single line. Hardly any letters from home anymore. That seems strange to you, doesn't it? But ever since I was at the front, I know it's all a sham: the printed and the written, the poetic, the dreamed, just as much as the supposedly revealed truth. It all disgusts me, because it's all a sham. The only real things are: eating, drinking, whoring, and killing...

HUSSAR I'll give you five francs if you'll let me sleep in your bed for once. You can sleep in mine.

INFANTRYMAN Why do you want to sleep in my bed? It's crawling with vermin.

HUSSAR That's exactly why, I'll catch them all for you...

INFANTRYMAN What are you waving in the air like a flag?

HUSSAR It's a child's shirt... I found it in a château in northern France and carried it safely through all dangers. I can't part with it anymore. Look, there's a count's crown embroidered on it, it must have belonged to a noble child...

INFANTRYMAN Come on... stop with the foolishness... A filthy child's shirt won't bring your dead child back to life...

HUSSAR I don't want to bring it back. I'm glad it's dead. At least that way, it can't be shot to death.

INFANTRYMAN Or tortured to death while still alive...

HUSSAR Cheer up, brother, cheer up, got any dice? (*With tears in his eyes.*) Let's play merry sevens...

INFANTRYMAN Sad sevens, my boy, sad sevens...

In Front of the Town Hall of a Large City

A tumultuous crowd. Workers, women, and children.

WOMEN Bread for our children! Bread for our children!

CHILDREN Bread! Bread!

WOMEN You lied to us.

OTHERS Lied and cheated.

WOMEN You promised not to reduce the bread ration again. You reduced it. You promised us potatoes. We got none. You dangled turnips in front of us. But they were inedible. We would feed our children with mother's milk. But our sagging, dried-up breasts no longer produce milk.

OTHERS Give us bread! What good are bread cards if there is no bread!

WORKER You said: Just a little more patience. We must hold out.

OTHERS We've been holding out for three years...

WORKER You said: Just two more months. In two months, England will be brought to its knees by submarine warfare. In two months, it will have to sue for peace...

OTHERS The two months are up. England can starve like us. Where is the peace?

WOMEN Where is the peace?

ALL Where is the peace?

A WOMAN I have seven children. My husband is dead.

ANOTHER My father is dead. My two brothers are dead. I prostitute myself to officers. Nothing matters anymore.

WOMEN Our husbands are dead! Our brothers are dead!

CHILDREN Our fathers are dead!

OTHER WOMEN You murdered them... for what?

ALL For what? For what?

WORKER We thought we were defending our homeland — and we were defending you, you gentlemen up there: you gentlemen landowners, you gentlemen arms manufacturers, you gentlemen princes... We defended you, stupidly, proudly, and wretchedly. We've withered into skeletons. Each of us is a walking corpse. But you have gorged yourselves on our flowing blood. You have become fatter and more powerful than ever. The laws are hung around your bellies like warning signs: "Do not touch," "Inviolable," "Imperial Authority," "Autocratic," "By the grace of God." Everything is forbidden to us. To you: everything permitted. You are... legally esteemed. But we will strip you of your license. You have only rights. We have only duties. Give us justice!

ALL Give us justice! Justice!

WORKER We want to decide for ourselves whether we shall live or die.

ALL The people shall vote on whether they want war or peace...

WORKER The Kaiser must no longer appoint ministers autocratically. The will of the people must prevail...

ALL Our will shall rule...

WORKER The will of the people is absolute... The ministers are accountable to the people. We're sick of having lackeys as ministers. Long live the new German people!

ALL Long live the German people!

WORKER Down with the government!

ALL Down with the government!

> *Excited young workers raise a straw dummy with a helmet, a martial mustache, and a white cuirassier's coat on a rope up to a streetlamp.*

ALL Down with the Kaiser! Down with the Kaiser!

OTHERS (*mockingly*) Up with the Kaiser! Up with the Kaiser! String him up!

VOICES The police are coming! Soldiers are coming! Hold your ground! Women and children in the middle! No one is to move!

OTHERS Tear up the paving stones. Bring stones! We won't be gunned down like dogs...

> *A military squad, led by a lieutenant, marches up with fixed bayonets.*

LIEUTENANT OF THE RESERVES Platoon — halt. Stand at ease. (*He steps forward with drawn sword toward the crowd.*) People! I have orders to restore the disturbed peace. I ask you to support me in my difficult duty. Disperse and go home calmly. This square must be cleared within five minutes. In five minutes, no civilian is to remain on the square. Anyone who defies my order is guilty of insurrection. Insurrection is punished under martial law with death by hanging. Be reasonable, people. I'm checking the time (*pulls out his watch*) if the square is not cleared in five minutes, I will give the order to fire.

> *A threatening murmur. No one moves. The LIEUTENANT OF THE RESERVES stands with the watch in his hand. He puts it away.*

Attention...

> *Oppressive silence. Not a sound.*

Load weapons...

> *The squad loads their rifles.*

Take aim...

> *The squad takes aim. At that very moment, the eldest non-commissioned officer steps in front of the squad.*

SERGEANT Lower – arms.

> *The squad lowers their weapons.*

At ease...

> *The squad stands at ease. The SERGEANT steps in front of the LIEU-TENANT.*

SERGEANT Lieutenant, sir, we will not shoot our brothers and sisters, our wives and children...

LIEUTENANT OF THE RESERVES You refuse to obey?

SERGEANT At your command, Lieutenant.

LIEUTENANT OF THE RESERVES Soldiers, you disobey me?

THE SQUAD At your command, Lieutenant.

LIEUTENANT OF THE RESERVES (*breaking his sword*) I submit my resignation. I... thank you for disobeying me... You've shown me the right path...

> *Cheers from the crowd. The soldiers unload their rifles. The cartridges roll onto the cobblestones. The bayonets are sheathed. Rifles and weapons are piled together. The crowd lifts the soldiers onto their shoulders in jubilation.*

Part Twenty:

The Strange Guest

"The Strange Guest" was published in the magazine "The Dame" in February 1922.

The Strange Guest

Drama in a Monologue

The stage is dark. Then laughter and talking are heard. MARGRIT enters through the portière, switches on the electric light, and pulls the pale gentleman in an evening cape along behind her.

MARGRIT Come in... look... this is where I live. Quite charming, isn't it? The furniture and the wallpaper... so simple in color and lines... and yet that touch of quiet eccentricity... Klaus had a marvelous sense of taste... he designed the entire interior of our apartment himself... for hours... for days... he discussed it with the furniture makers, with the wallpaper dealer... Won't you sit down? But first, won't you take off your cape? What, you don't want to? You only want to stay for a few moments? (*She looks at him.*) I hope... that these moments stretch into eternity... I want to keep looking into your eyes... I don't know what draws and compels me toward you... that I, who only met you today... who should be a complete stranger to you, spent the whole evening dancing and laughing and drinking champagne with you... and yet I feel this strange bond... or kinship between us... immediately... from the very first moment... What even prompted me to go to a ball today, on the first anniversary of his death, to laugh, to dance, and drink champagne? You probably think I'm a bad, frivolous woman... am I? I spent the whole year in tears... I beat my breast like a mourner... I didn't harbor a single unfaithful thought... But tonight, when I stood before his portrait... and wanted to bring him flowers... then... the frame was empty... the frame was empty... completely empty... the picture vanished... And can you believe, from that moment on I could no longer remember what Klaus even looked like... I tried hard to recall what color his eyes were... how they looked... I tried to picture him... but I couldn't anymore... the shape of his head — how was it, really? It had once seemed unforgettable to me... his forehead had seemed indelible... and now... now I had forgotten everything... when I thought of his head, I suddenly saw a turnip or a pumpkin or some other ridiculous thing... I tried to listen for his footsteps in his study... at night, when he was working, he would restlessly pace up and down in there... back and forth... and those footsteps... I heard them all year long... in my lonely, eerily silent nights... but today... today I heard them no more... I couldn't breathe anymore... well, the fit passed... maybe I'm hysterical... all widows are supposed to be hysterical... and suddenly, I was seized by a wild cheerfulness... I laughed... laughed and spun around and danced through every room... and when I reached the bedroom... and saw myself in the big mirror, dressed in black from head to toe... I tore off my mourning clothes... and then... then... then... I started rummaging through the dressers and wardrobes... pulled out my finest lace lingerie... my most beautiful crepe de chine dress and adorned myself like a bride... I even tried on the myrtle wreath before the mirror... the one I wore on my wedding day with Klaus... and it suited me so well, just like back then... Then I saw the evening newspaper lying on the nightstand, and right at the top, the announcement for tonight's ball at the German Theater. I clapped my hands like a child, I was so delighted... yes... I wanted to dance again... dance... dance... until I dropped. So I took a cab... went to the ball... and met you in the foyer... in the cloakroom! You approached me... and even though you never introduced yourself — you still haven't — you only looked at me... you fascinated me... yes, you fascinated me. You may smile at the confessions I'm making... It's not very smart for a woman to do this... certainly not... but perhaps I don't have time anymore to be smart... yes... you charmed me with your elegiac gestures, your melancholic manners, your dark eyes, and your unspeakably pale, slender hands (*she takes his hand*). I always looked at men's hands first... hands reveal more about someone than the face; because you can't disguise your hands... hands don't lie. Yes, I love your hands... I'm not afraid to say it... (*She kisses them softly.*) Show me — turn your left hand over — I want to read your fate... and maybe mine too. (*She bends over his hand.*) You have no life lines... how strange... as if you weren't truly alive... as if you weren't even really here... and I — maybe I'm no longer here either... oh, what foolish, ridiculous things I'm saying... I must have drunk too much champagne... I'm not used to it anymore... I haven't had champagne in a year... Back then, I even brought him a glass of champagne to his deathbed... the doctor had ordered it... to stimulate his heart... Wait, there should still be half a bottle left... I left it standing in the bedroom ever since... just as it was then... I'll fetch it... and we'll drink a glass together... to celebrate the day... (*She quickly exits into the next room and immediately returns with a bottle of champagne and a glass.*) Drink... it's the glass he drank from too... You won't? Why so distant, my friend? (*She raises the glass.*) Then I'll drink it: to my love! (*She drinks.*) How beautifully it burns in the blood... the blood itself begins to burn... I feel the fire rising to my head... my hair is already burning... and my eyes are burning... (*Music, a Chopin waltz, later turning into a gallop.*) Do you hear the music? How sweet! Come, let's dance... (*She dances. He remains motionless.*) Oh, how you lift me... how you carry me... I'm floating like a silver bird... I drift like a cloud... I... dissolve in bliss. (*The dance becomes faster and faster, then suddenly stops; at the same moment, she collapses. The gentleman removes his top hat, stands motionless for a moment, then puts the hat back on and disappears behind the portière, while a few bars of Chopin resound once more.*)

Part Twenty-One:

The Models of Phidias

"The Models of Phidias" is a play fragment, an undated typewritten carbon copy
with handwritten corrections by Klabund. Composed around 1922.

The Models of Phidias

Act I. Scene 1.

When the models come in front of the curtain, the 1ST MODEL says:

1ST MODEL You're right to ask: who are we? You'll hear in a moment: one, two, three.

CHORUS We are the models here in the house!

The curtain rises.

PIRAEUS Well, ladies, what brings you to the studio of my famous lord and master Phidias?

1ST MODEL We already told the audience. But since you weren't there, we'll gladly tell you again. (*to the conductor*) If you please: We are the models of the house.

PIRAEUS You spend so much time here that you don't need to hang around Phidias too. When I see you standing around like this, I know exactly how the market is doing. No amount of dialectic will help.

1ST MODEL No, only your dialect will help.

PIRAEUS Is it that noticeable, my dialect?

1ST MODEL Oh, only if one listens carefully...

2ND MODEL Nobody in Athens speaks like that.

PIRAEUS Nobody in Athens knows the Bean-Language either... the "Vindo-Bean-Language." I'm from Vindobona.

2ND MODEL Where's Vindobona?

PIRAEUS Vindobona is a city in northern Austria, right next to Grinzing. I wouldn't be surprised if it became famous in history, especially because of its strudel — its apple strudel.

1ST MODEL Vindobona? Grinzing? Strudel? Austria? Never heard of them.

PIRAEUS What? Vindobona, the old Vienna, the crown of cities?

1ST MODEL Ah, the place of the crown!

2ND MODEL Thank you, that's enough ethnological explanation, Mr. Piraeus.

PIRAEUS You can just call me Pira, for short. A name my father found for me: He didn't want me to be called Aristides or Xenon, he wanted to show a very special taste, and so he had the brilliant idea To name me: Pira.

2ND MODEL Potato purée!

PIRAEUS Don't mock! With a noble back line, one can get away with a lot. Allow me to run my rough hand along that delicate line.

2ND MODEL Leave it be! This isn't public transport!

PIRAEUS Let's leave that undecided. Many have surely ridden down that line to the knees already.

2ND MODEL Wrong. If you want to get to the knee, you have to take the C-line.

3RD MODEL Or O and W.

4TH MODEL Oh dear!

2ND MODEL (*pointing to a futuristic statue*) What's that supposed to be?

PIRAEUS Don't know? You'll solve the riddle easily: the first grazes in the grass, a four-legged, hoofed animal. The second brings you all joy, and usually shows up just when you want it. The third is a disgusting dish. The whole thing is Phidias' latest style.

2ND MODEL That's obviously another outrageous indecency!

PIRAEUS No, it's not indecent.

3RD MODEL I know what it is, and it is indecent.

PIRAEUS How so?

3RD MODEL Oxtail soup!

PIRAEUS No, it's neither oxtail soup nor indecent. Let me tell you: the first grazes in the grass, four-legged and hoofed — The cow!

3RD MODEL Oxen.

PIRAEUS And what do you all enjoy? Not the tax collector, but the "bite-kiss" — the bite in a kiss, which often even demands a fee. (*to which the models say "ouch"*)

2ND MODEL Cubism?

PIRAEUS And what was spread on your war bread during the great Peloponnesian War? Mush.

ALL MODELS Cubism!

PIRAEUS And Phidias has that on his conscience.

3RD MODEL I still prefer oxtail soup.

PIRAEUS Shame on you, girl. What you prefer doesn't interest us.

1ST MODEL Mr. Pira, we're leaving now.

ALL MODELS Goodbye, Mr. Pira!

PIRAEUS Take care, children.

1ST MODEL Master, may we quickly ask you one more thing?

PIRAEUS Make it quick.

1ST MODEL Tell us, what kind of model is Phidias looking for these days?

PIRAEUS What Phidias needs, you all lack, despite your youth.

1ST MODEL What is he looking for?

PIRAEUS He's looking — for virtue.

2ND MODEL Then he'll be searching for a long time.

3RD MODEL He won't find it anywhere in Greece.

PIRAEUS Yes, I know, it's not easy. We even placed an ad in the A.Z. — the Athenian Newspaper — five double-columned, nonpareil-sized lines — a fortune to advertise: "Sought: Prime Virtue, etc."

PIRAEUS Fi-FI. But who answers ads! You think that discourages me? On the contrary, I need virtue — I will find virtue. I must have virtue.

1ST MODEL So you're looking for virtue here, and meanwhile, we'll go to the Romance Café — uh, the Roman Café.

2ND MODEL By the way, the real reason we came: Would you place 2 drachmas on Ptolemy for me? Sunday is race day.

1ST MODEL For me too.

2ND MODEL For me too.

3RD MODEL For me too.

2ND MODEL For me too.

4TH MODEL For me too.

PIRAEUS Win or place?

ALL MODELS Win.

PIRAEUS If I were you, I wouldn't bet on Ptolemy — I'm betting on Foxtrot.

Models exit.

Scene 2.

PIRAEUS These good children might not be entirely wrong. But where am I supposed to find virtue? I've been to all sorts of boarding schools, girls' schools, dance halls, Hermaphrodites, and Wertheim — everything but virtue. Ah, virtue is something I struggle with.

Scene 3.

PHIDIAS Well, you simply have to make a virtue of necessity.

PIRAEUS Pardon me, Herr Phidias.

PHIDIAS Has my wife asked about me?

PIRAEUS Yes, she did: on several occasions.

PHIDIAS And what did you tell her?

PIRAEUS I answered her: His Excellency Pericles is expecting you.

PHIDIAS That's a very fortunate turn of events, which I would ask you to maintain in the future.

PIRAEUS In the future.

PHIDIAS Whenever a lady asks after me, longs for me, you shall say:

PIRAEUS His Excellency Pericles is waiting outside.

PHIDIAS And no other visitors, no interesting ones?

PIRAEUS No, only those with "interests." You understand, it's not so easy to find both virtue and beauty in one person. What one woman lacks, another also lacks in a different way. The women with good figures have bad features, and the women with good features have bad figures — it's a *circulus vitiosus*.[15]

PHIDIAS Where did you learn your Latin?

PIRAEUS I did finish the fourth year of High School.

PHIDIAS I see — and yet a model must be found. Just yesterday Pericles sent me a letter of reminder. I can't put it off any longer — you know what I'm looking for:

PIRAEUS Virtue: it must be full of charm and grace, a complexion like apricots, two tender breasts, sweetly shaped like oranges, two eyes full of soul, from whose lips the song of Philomela resounds, a small foot: shoe size 31. Ah, sir, I could not find her.

PHIDIAS Then you did not search diligently enough.

PIRAEUS Oh sir, I searched; I ran up and down stairs, but it was always either the chest or the bosom that was lacking, sometimes the neck, sometimes quite the opposite, sometimes there was a hump, sometimes a bad leg, most already suffered from gout and rheumatism — Sir, a perfect virtue — I could not find.

PHIDIAS You seem untalented to me.

PIRAEUS Let's not lose hope.

PHIDIAS I met the most beautiful virtue tonight. As beautiful as Aphrodite and shy as a dove.

PIRAEUS I hear the message clearly, but I lack belief.

PRA Dear sir, I fear you have fallen victim to a small error.

PHIDIAS I encountered such an enchanting innocence. Oh, such a dear love. Speaking of love — have you found a model for that yet? Pericles, after all, commissioned not only the statue of Virtue but also one of Love from me.

PRA Yes, I know, the commission for the group reads: Virtue and love united, found domestic happiness.

PHIDIAS I have the Virtue; you must find me the Love.

PRA Yes, I had a young man for that, one who seemed not unsuitable.

PHIDIAS Well then —?

---

[15] vicious circle.

Pra He also showed the warmest interest in the matter.

Phidias Well then —?

Pra Yet when I spoke with him, I felt strangely uneasy. He had a certain way of viewing things — from behind, as it were — And besides, we could not agree on the price.

Phidias Then one must find another love.

Pra Master, it's not so simple to find an impeccable Love. A Love where everything fits. Would you like a great Love, a small one, a moderate one, a fat Love, a thin Love, a neighborly Love, a platonic Love, brotherly Love, childlike Love, or monkey Love?

Phidias I want a pretty love, a nice love, a sweet love.

Pra Very well, sir.

Phidias Don't look at the price, but look at the feet.

Pra I'm in the picture.

Phidias And don't forget to deliver Venus and Victory today. They've already been complained about three times.

Pra People make you nervous. If they hadn't complained so much, Victory would have been delivered long ago.

Phidias But dust them off again first; Victory has already kicked up enough dust as it is.

Pra So Venus to Madame of Samothrace and Victory to Herr Milo.

Phidias No, no — the other way around: Venus to Milo, Victory to Madame of Samothrace.

Pra Aha, Venus to Milo, Victory to Samothrace — done. I'll make sure to deliver the statues to the right excavation sites. I know what I owe to posterity. (*exists.*)

Scene 4.

Aspasia Herr Phidias!

Phidias Aspasia, my child. How lovely that you are so punctual.

Aspasia Yes, my watch is broken. (*She looks around the studio.*) My goodness, what charming little trinket-figures you have here! (*She points at the Venus de Milo with her umbrella.*) What kind of shop girl is that?

Phidias That girl has been standing in my shop for quite a while. But now I've found a buyer for her.

Aspasia How interesting, how enchanting!

Phidias This must be your first time in an artist's studio?

Aspasia No, I work in a studio myself, a tailor's studio.

PHIDIAS What a coincidence!

ASPASIA Actually, there's not much difference between your studio and ours. You carve out the ladies; we take them for a ride. Prices, prices we have — you wouldn't believe it. A simple spring dress made of gabardine or cheviot: 4000 drachmas. What do you say to that?

PHIDIAS I would love you at any price. Where do you work?

ASPASIA At Gerson's.

PHIDIAS Already?

ASPASIA Gerson, 600 years before Christ, of course.

PHIDIAS You're priceless. (*He tries to embrace ASPASIA.*)

ASPASIA I'll scream, hands off.

PHIDIAS You won't escape your fate.

ASPASIA (*Pointing at a picture hanging on the wall with her umbrella.*) "Kindly refrain from touching the sculptures on display."

ASPASIA (*Fleeing from PHIDIAS and accidentally knocking the arm off the Venus with her umbrella.*)

ASPASIA Oh dear Zeus, I got a little too close to the shop girl.

PHIDIAS It doesn't matter at all, just a little accident. It's not the first shop girl someone has gotten too close to.

ASPASIA I'm beside myself, such a thing had to happen to me. Can't it be fixed? Or glued back on with Syndetikon?

PHIDIAS I'll see what can be done.

ASPASIA I'm miserable. Maybe there's still a way out? Couldn't you knock off her legs too, and sell her to our tailor shop as a dress mannequin? I could ask Herr Gerson —

PHIDIAS I'll keep that in mind.

ASPASIA Besides, this is all your fault.

PHIDIAS You accuse me unjustly.

ASPASIA If you hadn't insisted on kissing me, none of this would have happened.

PHIDIAS But who's blaming you?

ASPASIA You say that, but deep down you're angry with me. Put yourself in my place: you come closer, I move away. You come even closer, I move even further. You raise your hand, I raise my umbrella — and whack (*she accidentally knocks the head off the Victory of Samothrace*). Oh dear Zeus, another one! That silly goose had to be so sensitive and lose her head immediately! Everything's happening head over heels! Yes, misfortunes never come alone. Things always come in threes. First the watch, then the shop girl, and now the good lady with the wings. What must you think of me?

PHIDIAS I think it's lucky you have such a small clumsy hand.

ASPASIA Was it important, what I just smashed?

PHIDIAS It was a Victory.

ASPASIA Now it's a Defeat.

PHIDIAS Oh, it doesn't matter, I'll just think of a new Victory, never speak of it, always think of it.

ASPASIA Your magnanimity shames me, Master.

PHIDIAS Oh my child, don't call me Master — call me Phi-Phi. When you call me Master, you cut off all possibilities.

ASPASIA All of them? Ah, because I'm a seamstress?

ASPASIA (*Singing.*) The melody is very pretty. But nobody understood the words.

PHIDIAS We can afford that. (*Sings.*) May I explain the contents to you? (*He tries to approach her.*)

ASPASIA What are you showing off again?

PHIDIAS The summary.

ASPASIA You're getting a little too detailed for my taste.

PHIDIAS Aspasia, you're getting me all worked up.

ASPASIA Whether directly or indirectly — you won't get worked up that easily here.

PHIDIAS Do you have any idea how beautiful you are?

ASPASIA Ah, empty words. An artist is easily inflamed. Artist's love!

PHIDIAS You have something so unspeakable, something that speaks so much for you... (*Pause.*) Why don't you say anything?

ASPASIA Why should I? I already have something that speaks for me.

PHIDIAS May I tell you something?

ASPASIA Oh, you can't sweet-talk me — I know your fairy tales well enough.

ASPASIA Sir, what did you think of me?
I am horrified and must speak in verse.
Mama would never have allowed me
To enter this house of vice.

PHIDIAS It's no house of vice; it's a house of joy, where all the girls undress with joy. It's a house of art, devoted to noble craft.

ASPASIA I came here, sir, to act with virtue; you, however, wish to seduce me with all your art.

PHIDIAS Why all the grand talk? I only wish to admire your beauty. I'm no rake, no lecher, no rogue. Because I long for unadorned beauty, in every naked woman I see the goddess; by their forms, I shape the gods in stone. When I see the goddess, I don't think of the bed — It's not desire that lures me, only the art itself.

ASPASIA What's the short version of your long speech? I am and remain a seamstress.

ASPASIA You have made a mistake with me, my lord. I must ask you for some distance. You were concerned with decorum when I met you — but not distance. I am still a virgin, chaste and simple. You barge in like a bull in a china shop — is that decorum? Proposing the finale before the overture!

PHIDIAS Aspasia, I swear sacred oaths — By Zeus, you're going too far.

ASPASIA Not as far as you, sir.

PHIDIAS I swear it to you — I will leave you in peace — By Zeus, Apollo, Styx, and Hercules (*he raises his hand to swear*).

ASPASIA Put that hand down, it's making me nervous.

PHIDIAS You move before me as if on lofty stilts!

ASPASIA That's no reason to make such a fuss. You can say everything calmly.

PHIDIAS How could I ever attempt anything improper? Yet when I come close to you, I am inspired by the work of art that you are.

ASPASIA Everything you say is just words blown into the wind. You should be ashamed of yourself.

PHIDIAS I would like to... I want to... I should...

ASPASIA ...Put your hand down.

PHIDIAS But I fear that passion will get the better of me. I have hot blood. I'm no cold frog or lizard.

Scene 5.

FRAU PHIDIAS enters

FRAU PHIDIAS Mealtime.

PHIDIAS Now we're in a pickle. Every man for himself! (*to his wife*) I'm completely innocent, just listen to me. I ordered a model.

FRAU PHIDIAS I suppose you're looking for your models among minors now.

PHIDIAS I wandered through the woods alone, seeking nothing, my intent unknown. But scarcely had I seen this maiden's fairy-tale legs, when I knew: this is virtue — or nothing else.

FRAU PHIDIAS Just you be quiet. I know perfectly well what I know. And you, young lady, what are you still doing here? Off home with you!

ASPASIA You're shouting so loud it echoes through the whole house. Making scenes for your husband. Since I don't care for such performances, I'll make my exit now. (*exits*)

PHIDIAS Well, that's a fine how-do-you-do. Now I've gone and lost my virtue.

FRAU PHIDIAS You must really think I'm pretty stupid. That girl — to represent virtue? Do you even know what that is? That's one of your silly hu-hu-hu-humanitarian sentimentalities, taking a woman like that for it.

PHIDIAS But I didn't even take her.

FRAU PHIDIAS That's all that was missing.

PHIDIAS I'd really like to know how you would behave in such a situation.

FRAU PHIDIAS I'll tell you right now.

Couplet

FRAU PHIDIAS You dare to intrude into my house!

PRINCE I thought this was the house of the sculptor Phidias! I wanted to pay a visit to his studio. I bless the chance that unites us here.

FRAU PHIDIAS Consider, if Phidias were to come, what would you say!

PRINCE Good day; I would say I wish to buy a statue. This one of marble — or that one there (*points to FRAU PHIDIAS*). I would pay any price for the pleasure of viewing it.

FRAU PHIDIAS I fear that remark needs some correction. You speak very gallantly, but it will do you little good. You'll hardly get your money's worth here. I have no doubt that when gold jingles in the chest, many a beauty would gladly fall into your arms. But I live with my husband in the honeymoon phase; I have never, never broken faith with him. I beg you, sir — there is the door: I am virtue itself, you've had bad luck with me.

PRINCE Then my victory will be all the greater. If I may confess: virtue itself shall be mine. I do not love victories without a fight. One crosses glances, and soon crosses swords; the enemy fights bravely and boldly, until at last he sinks to his knees, until one swings over the ramparts, and with the banner held high, the victor storms the fortress.

FRAU PHIDIAS I find your imagery rather militaristic.

PRINCE Oh, I am a pacifist.

FRAU PHIDIAS Yes, once the battle is over.

PRINCE Sweet is the peace you will grant me. I shall be blessed, the happiest on earth. I will not leave this place, I will stay near you.

FRAU PHIDIAS Fine, stay. But that's all, I am leaving.

PRINCE You flee the battle and won't stand your ground?

FRAU PHIDIAS I'm afraid.

PRINCE Of me?

FRAU PHIDIAS Of... myself. Goodbye. (*exits*)

PIRAEUS (*enters*)

PIRAEUS Has His Lordship selected a statue?

PRINCE Yes... no... that is... allow me: Erotocles, Prince of Syria. (*hands him money*)

PIRAEUS From Wieringen?

PRINCE From Syria.

PIRAEUS This visiting card is enough for me. Allow me to shake your paw — pardon — your hand. The gold is real — you are a true prince. How may I serve you?

PRINCE Oh, I find everything here simply delightful, everything delights me exceedingly.

PIRAEUS Take your pick — a rare opportunity. This Diana of Ephesus, top quality.

PRINCE (*distracted*) Very pretty, very pretty.

PIRAEUS Buy, Your Highness — it's White Week! I'll let you have this Apollo here with a 10% discount. This Venus has had her hands a bit knocked off, but that doesn't matter — you can get her on installment. But if you'll excuse me a moment — (*goes to the telephone*) Hello, exchange? Alexander the Great? Please, 22 22. Is that Totokles' betting office? Piräus here, valet to Academy Professor Phidias. Please place 600 drachmas on Ptolemaios to win. Ptolemaios. P as in Parthenon, T as in Themistocles, O as in Osiris, L as in Leonidas, E as in Emil, M as in Marathon... Got it? (*to the PRINCE*) Would you like to take the pieces with you right away? Shall I pack them up, or have them sent to your house?

PRINCE I would like to...

PIRAEUS The housewife? I'm afraid I can't sell her to you at any price. She's priceless. But — I'll give her to you as a gift.

PRINCE I will not lose heart in trying to win her.

PIRAEUS That's the spirit! Chin up — after all, as a prince, you surely belong to the League of the Upright.

Couplet

ALL MODELS We are the models here in this house,
    Every morning always punctual at our post.
    We pose nude, late and early,
    For Herr FiFi.
    And yet posterity will not know us,
    Every art historian will only mention his name.
    The whole world talks about FiFi.
    He alone is the genius — never us.

1ST MODEL Completely headless, I offered my head to the Winged Victory of Samothrace.

2ND MODEL I enchantingly offered my back to the goddess Artemis.

3RD MODEL I gave my arms — oh, poor me — to the glory of antiquity. I was once called Venus de Milo and now stand in the Louvre of Paris.

4TH MODEL I will cause the historical scholars a lot of headaches one day, because I will only pass on to posterity with my most honorable values.

CHORUS OF MODELS :
>We have lost everything
>To that cursed horse.
>If only that beast had never been born,
>We're in terrible shape now.
>Alas, Clotho, the Fates,
>Brought us bad luck in the lottery, Oh!
>You dear old Augustin,
>All our money is gone.

CHORUS OF MODELS :
>Will Ptolemy be the victor?
>Will he win the race?
>Our hearts beat only for him,
>In sleep and in waking.
>If only that perfidious wretch
>Does not ride us into ruin.
>You yourselves wagered
>All of Mr. Phidias' money.

>Our imagination already sees him
>Twenty lengths ahead,
>And from the stands the applause
>Is already roaring loudly.
>Tumult upon tumult,
>Rapture of victory and cheers,
>Hip hip hip hip,
>Hip hip hip hurrah!

Couplet

>Of the amusing counting game
>I and you
>The miller's cow
>Even the ancient Greeks already knew a lot.
>The miller's donkey — that is you.
>When the animals no longer suited them —
>Fox and cat
>Mouse and rat —

They threw them into the toy chest
And made room for new games.

First, they plundered the flowers in the pots,
Then counted on the buttons of their vests,
Until the youth and the maid
Cried out lovingly to the gods.
And following the old Greek custom,
They longingly counted off the gods:
Bacchus, Hera, Aphrodite,
Eros, Dionysus, Apollo.

Later times will no longer know
I and you, the miller's cow,
Will burn incense to new gods —
The miller's donkey — that is you.
One day, to everyone's amusement,
There slumped already
On the throne
That Zeus abandoned in horror —
General Director Davidsohn.

On Olympus, once the shepherd sang his song;
Today, he plays an extra in a film company.
Who still speaks of Venus and her companions?
Their times are over.
In ten thousand years people will read:
Germany's gods once were —
Asta Nielsen, Henny Porten,
Hella Moja, Mia May.

Couplet

I've long known all the stories
That Grimm and Musäus have told us.
Ghosts haunt the night,
When no one is awake anymore,
The brownies comes, far and near —
Papa snores in his sleep and stretches,
Mama lies awake and longs —
But suddenly the brownie is here.
Et cetera, et cetera.

Papa, Mama,
What fairy tales you tell, aha!

Who still believes in the old story
Of the nightly house-elf glory?
The ghosts
Mostly
Turn out to be a family friend.
When Dad wakes up in the morning,
All the work is already done.

Who nowadays still believes
In the tale of the cooing doves?
Those who, night and day,
Killed themselves for love
In a tender amorous struggle.
Fidelity now is lazy sorcery.

Therefore, you must pat the dove's tail.
When he stretches his neck out of the marital cage,
According to old custom, sprinkle some salt.
Only a little salt.

Papa, Mama,
Then the bird will stay faithful,
If you follow the fairy tale's rules,
He won't fly off to other birds.
Gallant,
Charming,
He'll eat from her hand.
The male stays true to his female
If she handles tings even halfway right.

Couplet

I was coming from Alexander Place.
A young brat followed me.
He looked as divine as Apollo.
He was barely 18 years old,
But he wanted
To escort me home by force.

PIRAEUS His Excellency Pericles is waiting there.

FRAU PHIDIAS One moment, I am coming immediately.
    He followed on my heels
    And spoke to me in verse, intoxicated,
    But full of unrhymed lines.
    The stock exchange is already visible at the corner,

As he leans tenderly toward me.
And the dollar rises and rises.

PIRAEUS His Excellency Pericles is waiting there.

FRAU PHIDIAS One moment, I'll be right there.
We were already at the opera –
Sir, you're taking a liberty,
What kind of operas are you talking about?
At the Brandenburg Gate he continues to follow me,
And he whispers into my ear:

PIRAEUS His Excellency Pericles is waiting there.

FRAU PHIDIAS One moment, I am coming immediately.
Why do you always follow me, you wretch,
Do you not consider the consequences,
Leave me this instant.
He begged: Just one kiss –
Then I jumped into the bus
And drove to the Department Store of the West.
Whom do you think I saw there?

PIRAEUS The young man was there again.

FRAU PHIDIAS That's how it really was.
I was at a loss,
And I fled to the tearoom.
Hardly did I take the cup in my hand,
When — who do you think came running up
Until he stood before me, longing –
Whom do you think I saw there?

PIRAEUS The young man was there again.

FRAU PHIDIAS Then I became furious
At this impudent male creature,
I'd lost my patience.
I wear size ten gloves.
I swung, then the clock struck ten,
Without even turning around
I landed one on him with a thump.
(*slap in the face*)

EROTOCLES The young man was there again.

Finale

ASPASIA Aspasia

PERICLES I, Pericles.

PHIDIAS I, Phi-Phi: We protest.

FRAU PHIDIAS How we've been singled out here.

PRINCE To the mockery of the whole world.

ALL For our holy glory has become a fuss.

FRAU PHIDIAS History has given itself to you.

PRINCE In all its glory.

ASPASIA Fritz and Rieke think in amazement.

PHIDIAS Who has honored us until now.

PERICLES That's antiquity.

PIRAEUS Hold your breath, be brave.

ALL TOGETHER I think the whole gang isn't worth a penny.

PRINCE Hold your nose.

ASPASIA Aren't you a bubble too?

FRAU PHIDIAS Do you believe that skirts and trousers?

PHIDIAS Symbol of morality —

PIRAEUS Get into your car.

ASPASIA But we Hellenes, oh, are dreading it.

ALL Of your godless and godforsaken times.

Couplet

> What must you be in life? Stupid, stupid, stupid
> Be stupidly happy here on earth.
> So that no one turns up their noses.
> We five embody happiness here
> The happiness and peace of the house

FRAU PHIDIAS I am the woman.

ASPASIA I am the friend.

PHIDIAS I am the man.

PRINCE I am the friend.

PERICLES I the patron.

ALL In every play
> You can see all five of us
> Where, how, and what it may be.
> We five are always there.
> We are in the quintet
> Of every operetta

We accept every bet
At Caiman, Strauss, and Fall
In Syracuse and Crete
You see us early and late
And everyone cheers: Look there
You can find us everywhere.

Couplet

Oh dear sir, forgive me, forgive me,
Forgive me. I'm still completely beside myself,
Completely beside myself, completely beside myself.
Please excuse me very much.
I'm talking so much nonsense here.
I'm still quite breathless.
I'm still completely stunned.
Please excuse me very much.
I'm talking so much nonsense.

PIRAEUS Don't get so worked up, madam, you're getting more and more depressed.

ASPASIA I've never been so hopeful.
I've just come from Lady Pythia.
There's a blond gentleman there.
I'll be his wife. He's taking me with him
to his palace at the Grosser Stern.

There's still a dark lady standing
before our future marriage bed.
That's surely the quite infamous
Lysistrata from the Nude Ballet.

She laid the cards perfectly for me.
My luck is truly evident.
I'll be someone in the Republic:
Who knows? The President's wife.

I'll stand in a noble pose
In Ullstein's World History
And for the whole future thing
I'll only pay twenty marks and ten.

Oh, dear sir, forgive me.

Couplet

When I look at the newspaper,
What do I care about politics?
I want to see if there's a dance in Wannsee
And what kind of ballroom music.
I couldn't care less about the state treasury.
I need a treasure for the state.
I'm the craziest, craziest doll
On Lacedaemonian Square.

I only read the sports section.
The latest Athens W scandal.
The latest fashion, the latest murder.
I couldn't care less about anything else.

I'm enthusiastic about the Six-Day Race.
And the Six-Night System.
Homer's novel makes me want to cry.
Of One-Eyed Polyphemus.
I read every ad from
the marriage agencies.
But with Plato's feature sections,
There's very little going on these days.

I only read the sports section, etc.

Couplet

That is the law of the spheres.
No matter how high you are placed,
Sometime you must come down from your heights.
For everything falls in this world.

The snow sometimes still falls in March.
Sometimes the barometer drops,
The virgin sooner or later.
And the heart sinks into the trousers.

Before the leaves fall from the tree.
They wanted to end the great war.
But leaves can also turn.
Now they cut down wood – it was a dream.

The dollar doesn't fall far from the tree –

Shareholders' capital.
The knight falls for his honor.
Faints when the Sipo comes.

Many a man falls in with money.
Your eyes close in bed.
The curtain falls at the end of the operetta.
If it doesn't fall first.

Couplet

My friend Fi-Fi, don't make such a silly face.
Listen to the wisdom speaking to you from my lips:

They say only the naked truth can
enchant men. But I say
The truth is a matter of toiletry questions.
It's better to wear something.
Only nature tempts,
In silken clothing.
For only the image tempts
Which is half-veiled.

Furred with skunks.
Shod with little pumps.
Skirted in the latest style.
Such a lady, such a lady has always enticed gentlemen.

Sweetly perfumed
And sophisticatedly coiffed
Manicured and athletically trained
Such a lady, such a lady, has always seduced men

I know that men tell you
In this regard, everyone is equal
That a woman who is truly beautiful
Will look good in anything

That a hat for twelve marks eight
Will turn you into a goddess,
That your complexion will shine brightest
Powderless and without makeup
If you follow this advice, then things will end badly for you
Because he'll take another woman who'll cost him a fortune.
Because she's done it to him

Just because she's done it to herself:
Covered in skunk fur

I know well the man tells you
In this respect, everyone is the same
That a real pearl necklace is far too ostentatious
Because you yourself are a real piece of jewelry, a true pearl
If you believe a single word of it,
You're already on the wrong track.
Leave the wrong track, take the path to your jeweler
To the hairdresser, to the seamstress – don't listen to the gentleman.
At first, he seems disgruntled,
But then he agrees with you:

Couplet

When God created the world in seven days
He showed great talent for the profession.
Sun, earth and the fruit of the Hesperides
He created everything here below as a sphere

When Adam once made his way through the bushes,
He saw Eve carrying two fruits,
Aware enough of their beauty.
And she shyly confessed to him:
Take the fruit from the tree of knowledge.
Pick the golden fruits.
When they glitter before you.
When they beckon you.
In the green blossom.
When they hang plump and
Ripe in the sun.
And push their way to our mouths.
Through the branches,
Let us pick the ripe fruits.
That bring us such sweet joy.
The Garden of Eden blooms.
Even today for everyone.
Who has not lost paradise.

As I walked through the streets in summer
Twilight was already hanging over the houses
A beautiful girl offered me a basket full of apricots
with a carefree smile
She had starry-blonde hair

I asked her the price of the goods
I asked her how old she was
Sixteen years was her confession
And I made my pleading confession to her.
Give me the golden fruits
Quench my thirst
Quench my desire
To bliss
When they are plump and etc.

Couplet

Oh, Athena, graciously hear my plea,
Who, full of shame, bares herself in the light of day.
You have often relieved me from heartache.
My husband has often seen me this way.
May you kindly consider in my prayer
That if I do not, another would.

Indeed, it is called a sin to stand fully naked
In the light from head to knee before the holy chest,
But it is half as bad when it is full of harmony,
When the chest swells sweetly, and the legs are arrow-straight.
May you kindly consider, etc.

I must confess to you, it makes me embarrassed,
That it pulls me toward my husband with longing.
Does he not see how young and beautiful I still am?
Should other women arouse him to lust alone –
May you kindly consider, etc.

Finale.

PHIDIAS Oh, should my happiness really depart so soon? Aspasia threw a harsh "no" at me. Should I perhaps write her a few lines by post? The postage is too high. I'll leave it be.

PIRAEUS Don't worry about it, sir!

PHIDIAS But who is that boy?

PIRAEUS The sir wishes to be recommended as a model.

PHIDIAS Then let him quickly take off his tunic, So I can have the full view of him.

EROTOCLES What does the man want?

PIRAEUS Please, you should try To take off your coat and pants, So that he can see your figure.

EROTOCLES This is, I must admit, an amusing place. What can happen? I'll take my clothes off.

MODELS Come, children, take a quick look, At the latest model. What a model indeed! What a frame indeed! Not too thick, nor too thin, But right in the middle. He seems to have The necessary qualities, The young man is a real catch.

PIRAEUS He could do The craziest things.

PHIDIAS I'm very unwilling about this method.

EROTOCLES Among the models That are posed here, I am the latest fashion. Every limb is trained in me, My muscles are made of iron. If the ladies are not ashamed, I'll gladly prove it to them.

PHIDIAS No, with such a swan-like neck, He will be chiseled by me as:

CHORUS What?

PHIDIAS The God of Love.

CHORUS The God of Love.

EROTOCLES This is to the shrine, What can it be? The good man wants me to practice the position As the God of Love here, What a strange ambition. Well then, if you're interested, I am predestined for the job. I think I have a lot of talent for this position. I know every position known in the field of love. It is a great honor for me to practice my art at any time, I always take myself out of affairs to total satisfaction. Love, love is my only passion. I have studied it thoroughly, Studied it with Venus in person. Love, love, Has smiled brightly at me (*laughs*), Day as the sun, Night as bliss, Day and night. In this work, endurance is key. The most important thing is to hold on, as long as you can. I have often been in the position of the model, And I always finish the assignment I undertake promptly.

PHIDIAS Now announce your name and your origin as well, For that is the custom of this land.

EROTOCLES Master, my name is simply, plainly, and cheekily: Erotocles.

CHORUS What a name, plain and cheeky: Erotocles. How much does the name alone promise? Doesn't every lady like the name? Doesn't every lady like it? In it, it sparkles and shines. Erotocles. The name advertises itself — Erotocles.

EROTOCLES I am just a model, not a plaything for you, my beauties. If you continue pampering me this way, Phidias will be angry with me.

PHIDIAS Well, if the guy is so silly, I'll pay him below the rate.

CHORUS He's a toy for fooling around with,
With whom I'd happily sleep.
We stroke him,
We flatter him,

We love him,
And in the chorus, it chirps: Erotocles.

Waltz – Duet.

FRAU PHIDIAS You caressed me tenderly.

PRINCE You were my only happiness.

FRAU PHIDIAS You flattered me with kisses.

PRINCE You returned the kisses.

FRAU PHIDIAS You know the most tender games. You are thoroughly familiar with them.

PRINCE In the old Doric style, I feel at home there.

FRAU PHIDIAS You bravely stole my heart.

PRINCE You spoke words that were forbidden.

FRAU PHIDIAS I had to perish, perish, pleading.

PRINCE You fought bravely with sword and thrust.

FRAU PHIDIAS But you also wounded me.
I had to surrender to both death and life.

PRINCE No more talk of the past.
The flag of the future is raised,
Let us think of the joy
That still awaits us –

In a suburb, we will rent
a room, you and I.

And we will love each other
Every day from five to seven.
There are cushions of every kind
That will gently do us good.
Embroidered on them: After a job well done,
It's good to rest.

FRAU PHIDIAS And in my veil I creep to you,
Knock on the door
And you open it for me.

Let me, let me, let me, beloved
Listen to what speaks from within you,
From the locked chest
You lifted my heart to the light.

In the sea of love
I want to drown in bliss,
Starfish sparkle,
Let me sink,
But remain silent.

Waltz.

ASPASIA Leave me, leave me, leave me in peace.
To listen to what speaks from within you,
From a locked chest,
You lifted my heart to the light.
In the sea of your eyes,
I want to drown in bliss,
Starfish sparkle.
Let me sink.
But remain silent.

Like a sun, you burn hotly.
Draw your circle around me.
And with the tenderest rays,
You send ever new torments.
No longer can I withstand the fire.
Your hand
Fans the blaze.
No longer can I escape
That it draws the bow.
And your arrow aims at my breast.
And my heart's blood flows, and I die from desire.

PRINCE Leave me, leave me, let me find the peace
that I lost.
Open your chest.
Lift up the treasure.

BOTH In the sea of your eyes, I want to drown in bliss.
Let me drown,
Let me sink,
But remain silent.

Finale.

PIRAEUS Isn't this duet really nice?
That the author wrote from the soul
Even something like this appeals
In this area
Not even in the whole song
Did the lovers sing: I love you

MODELS To escape our gaze
They withdrew in peace
And closed their curtain.
What does that mean

Oh, oh, one makes jou jou in broad daylight

PIRAEUS More discretion, my dear children

MODELS Oh, if only we, oh, if only we
Had a ladder here at hand
You see better looking down from above
Than looking up from the shelter.
Just take the chairs, quick, quicker
Take the chairs for this

PIRAEUS What indecent pleasure. That's insolence personified.

MODELS That's a grumpy patron.

PIRAEUS That's insolence personified.
You take possession of everything.
You won't leave me the slightest crack.

MODELS If that's all it is,then do not grieve.
And put on a friendly face.
What we see here, what we spy,

Pirae, we'll tell you. Oh, Oh.

PIRAEUS So what?

MODELS Sweet and gallant, Oh, how piquant.
He wants to caress her.

PIRAEUS Well, what then?

MODELS The hand.
Now danger threatens.
He even wants to kiss her tenderly.

PIRAEUS Well, what then?

MODELS The hair.

PIRAEUS That doesn't sound very interesting.
Hand and hair, hair and hand.
More, more —

MODELS Nothing more.

PIRAEUS But what is Erotocles doing?

MODELS It's very hard to see.
It's a mishap.
Now you can see clearly.

PIRAEUS Well, what then?

MODELS Nothing more.
Dreaming close to him
She smiles there
Whispers half asleep

PIRAEUS Well, what then?

MODELS Mama.
Her face shines, transfigured —
Love knows what it wants.
And she sighs: I am blissful
I have never felt so sweet...

PIRAEUS Quiet

Act II.

PIRAEUS Let's have a look and see what's new. Can't you wait? You're tearing the whole newspaper apart. I have here the *Athens Newspaper A–Z* from midday, the sports section, just a moment (*he reads*): "The Spartans attacked with full force. A fierce struggle ensued until after 15 minutes the right wing of the Athenians broke through and, with full vehemence, hurled itself at the surprised Spartans."

1ST MODEL Oh God, how terrible! I didn't even know there was a war between Sparta and Athens.

PIRAEUS "The Spartans had bad luck with their shots. Almost all were misses. Five minutes before noon, it came to hand-to-hand combat."

2ND MODEL Please stop this horrifying depiction of a civil war!

PIRAEUS "A wild tangle writhed on the ground like an inextricable chaos. Blood splattered."

3RD MODEL Water! I'm going to faint!

PIRAEUS What's the matter with you all? Who said anything about war? This is the sports section — it's the report of the latest big football match between Sparta and Athens! (*reads on*) "After ten minutes Athens makes a pass to the half-right Hahn, who from 2 meters away pushes the ball into the goal. A corner kick is beautifully placed in front of the guest team's goal, headed against a post, and then fortunately deflected in." Do you understand that?

MODELS Not a word.

PIRAEUS Yes, it's strange what kind of Greek people speak these days.

MODELS The race! The race! What about the race report?

PIRAEUS (*reads*) "Auction of Castan's Panopticon..." No, that doesn't seem to be it. Here: "The big race." "It was an international event."

MODELS Ah!

PIRAEUS "The society of Athens was present in full. The eye was delighted by the splendor and magnificence of the uniforms and the latest spring fashions. Among the attendees, Lysistrata was noticed, in a delightful dress of crepe georgette."

MODELS The winner!

PIRAEUS "Crepe georgette seems destined to become the new fashion. Also noticed was Xantho in a gown of silver-gray tulle with Brussels lace."

MODELS The winner! Who won?

PIRAEUS "Polype, the famous general, was recognized; he wore the full dress uniform with raspberry-red General Staff piping. Among the press figures, Diogenes, editor-in-chief of the Lantern, and Prometheus, publisher of the radical weekly The Chained Man, were noticed."

MODELS The winner!

PIRAEUS "At exactly three o'clock, a landau appeared, recognizable by the standard of the President of the Republic. Pericles, President of the Republic, was greeted by the cheers of the people. His re-election in the upcoming presidential election seems assured."

MODELS The winner!

PIRAEUS "In the air, the rattling of an engine: everyone turns their heads upward. The well-known flying lieutenant Icarus appears in his biplane. A regrettable incident occurs. The airplane crashes — so unfortunately that it tears the shirt of a man from the people, named Nessus, and strips a lady of her entire outfit including her chinchilla coat: she stands completely naked next to the crashed airplane. An unforgettable sight: she is recognized as Phryne..."

MODELS Ah!

PIRAEUS "Finally, the signal for the start sounds. At that very moment, according to ancient custom, Jupiter Pluvius went into action. A terrible downpour began. Everyone fled to the stands. The ladies' dresses suffered terribly — except for Phryne's outfit, for the reasons previously mentioned. The horses set off. The favorite, Ptolemy from the stables of Augeas, seems to be in brilliant form,"

MODELS Ah!

PIRAEUS "which unfortunately doesn't help him much. There's a collision between Ptolemy and Bucephalus from Alexander's stables. Ptolemy breaks away from the field and ends up in a dead heat. Foxtrot from Mr. Weinberg's stables crosses the finish line first."

Chorus

PIRAEUS I no longer deserve my name; I am a harbor, but I'm high and dry.

MODELS Why?

PIRAEUS I sold all the works of Phidias for 600 drachmas and bet the entire sum on Ptolemy.

1ST MODEL Ptolemy — that's the name of an Egyptian king. I still can't warm up to the Republic. I'm a staunch monarchist. I bet on the king — and lost. Oh, my beautiful money.

MODEL His beautiful money... What will the master say when he finds his statues gone?

PIRAEUS That's the least of it... I'll tell him I sold them.

MODEL But what if he demands the proceeds from you?

PIRAEUS That's just it... if he demands the proceeds from me. Great Zeus... what am I to do?

2ND MODEL Dear Mr. Piraeus, I have an idea!

PIRAEUS Hopefully not a Platonic one.

MODEL Until you find a way out, my friends and I will stand on the empty pedestals and take the place of the missing statues.

3RD MODEL We know the pose of each one — we stood as models for long enough — it won't be hard for us.

PIRAEUS That's a brilliant idea — I'm delighted! How can I ever thank you?

1ST MODEL By paying us the usual hourly rate for posing: 2 drachmas per hour, per person.

2ND MODEL Please pay up — to the cashier.

PIRAEUS There are eight of you — that makes sixteen drachmas. Where am I to get it without stealing? I will remember this Black Thursday forever.

2ND MODEL We'll get ready, Mr. Piraeus.

PIRAEUS Very well, you'll get your sixteen drachmas. But on Sunday mornings, I only pay half price. (*The models strike the poses of the statues.*)

2ND MODEL Come over here, take a look. How do we look? Is the difference too obvious? Any complaints?

PIRAEUS Only about the price you're charging me — otherwise, no complaints. But wait, what's that bruise? (*to one of the models*) I don't recall the Diana of Ephesus having a bruise — Phidias will turn blue in the face when he sees it.

MODEL I bumped into something... in the subway... it was so crowded.

PIRAEUS Oh, you bumped into something, did you?

MODEL But I swear to you, it's not what you're thinking.

PIRAEUS All right, all right.

3RD MODEL It's been four years since I posed for the Venus de Milo.

PIRAEUS So what?

MODEL My figure has suffered a little over the past four years — I'm wearing a bra.

PIRAEUS The Venus de Milo with a bra — that's just what we were missing! What are we going to do now? Sacrament! I hear footsteps, someone's coming. Psst. Don't move — it's Phidias. No, it's Pericles, thank God.

A MODEL All this excitement — I feel sick, I'm going to faint!

PIRAEUS That can wait a moment — here, have a schnapps. (*PERICLES enters*)

PERICLES Good morning. What's the matter with you, Piraeus? You're trembling all over!

PIRAEUS Not all over, Your Excellency, not all! But you gave me quite a fright — I thought it was the master coming.

PERICLES And why the fear?

PIRAEUS Before you, Your Excellency, who are the State itself, there are no state secrets.

PERICLES Our much-revered master is not here?

PIRAEUS Regrettably — thank God — no.

PERICLES I will wait for him and meanwhile take a look at his masterpieces.

PIRAEUS As you wish, Your Excellency!

PERICLES This Phidias — what a talent! One could almost believe this marble were living flesh. At any moment, you expect these statues to open their mouths and begin to speak.

MODELS You're telling us!

PIRAEUS Will you be quiet, you rascals?

PERICLES What did you say?

PIRAEUS The acoustics — I mean the lighting — isn't very good, but it will improve in a moment.

PERICLES How the master has managed to breathe life into marble. Everything is there: even the muscles and veins stand out in relief, you can almost feel the blood pulsing. Marble is usually cold and immobile. But here, it's warm and glowing.

PIRAEUS That's the sun, the sun shining on the marble.

PERICLES Admirable, admirable. Our master has given his statues such an illusion of movement that you expect them to move at any moment.

PIRAEUS No, they won't move. Impossible. They're paid not to move.

PERICLES You think: now they're stretching their limbs, now lifting their legs... now they're jumping down from the pedestal... now they're singing.

The MODELS climb down from the pedestal and sing

MODELS "We are the models of this house..." etc.

PERICLES What on earth is going on here?

PIRAEUS Don't even try to understand it, Your Excellency. There are things between heaven and earth, as Shakespeare will one day say... With common sense, Your Excellency, you can't govern here — although, with your common sense, you've often governed the state. Better occupy yourself with the statutes of the law than with the laws of the statues. One, two, three — they're gone. The statues just left you — they were polite enough to leave us alone — and I would like...

PERICLES You can say what you want — it's strange... I came here to visit the exhibition of the fine arts.

PIRAEUS Yes, fine arts, indeed! I repeat: they were polite enough to leave us alone. And now, Your Excellency, I humbly wish to submit a request.

PERICLES Go ahead.

PIRAEUS Your Excellency is such an excellent horseman, you came first in the race for the presidency. May I ask your advice: how does one win a race, where should I place my bet?

PERICLES Do you want honest advice, or official advice?

PIRAEUS I beg for it!

PERICLES Don't gamble. Never — ever.

PIRAEUS I had a tip on Ptolemy!

PERICLES And? Did you bet? Win or lose?

PIRAEUS Lost... everything's gone.

PERICLES You shouldn't have bet on Ptolemy — you should've bet on your own head. Besides Ptolemy, there were three favorites — what can one horse do against three?

PIRAEUS What can a horse do against three? It can run — that's why it's called a race! But it didn't run.

ASPASIA (*enters*) I'm overjoyed!

PIRAEUS You bet on Foxtrot?

ASPASIA I've just come from the woman of Pythia — she prophesied a brilliant future for me!

PIRAEUS I take my leave, ladies and gentlemen. (*exits*)

PERICLES Mademoiselle, you look fabulous! (ASPASIA *sings a couplet*)

PERICLES What you're singing is outrageous!

ASPASIA Oh, it doesn't matter. I'd just love to know who that young, blond gentleman is that Madame Pythia hinted at.

PERICLES You have no idea who it could be?

ASPASIA Well, Master Phidias... although, he's bald.

PERICLES You don't know any statesmen?

ASPASIA No, I don't know any man you could build a state with.

PERICLES Have you never seen Pericles?

ASPASIA Thank God, no! I'm not curious.

PERICLES Then I wouldn't want to bet with you — you would lose.

ASPASIA I only know that the A-Z sometimes publishes ridiculously boring articles from him around noon. Papa sells the A-Z at the Reichstag building.

PERICLES You agree with his political stance?

ASPASIA I don't even know what that is — political stance.

PERICLES I will explain that to you right away: I will quote some passages from my last election speech: The day is drawing ever closer when the Greek people will have to decide what fate it has placed in its own hands. With a thundering fanfare, the dawn of a new era breaks. It is fitting, then, to both look back and ahead. Far be it from us to knock the bottom out of the Danaides' barrel — the solid ground of facts on which we stand. Come now: Forward and backward — that shall be our slogan! Religion must be preserved for the people, and this can only be achieved through a general lowering of prices and rational dividend policies. The struggling heavy industry, which is already no longer able to appropriately invest its enormous profits, must be incorporated into unemployment relief. The proletariat has many a bone to pick with capitalism! Let us raise our hands — may they wither if we do not speak the truth — and swear that this chicken shall soon be stewing in every worker's pot. We are for the proletarian dictatorship in its moderate form: the constitutional monarchy.

ASPASIA Well, now I know what a political standpoint is, but what interests me about a newspaper is something quite different!

PERICLES And what would that be?
(ASPASIA's *song/couplet*)

PERICLES My gracious lady...

ASPASIA Aspasia is my name!

PERICLES My gracious lady, Aspasia, I am most delighted to have made your acquaintance. I hope that we will not stop at that. (*approaches her*)

ASPASIA Stay right where you are.

PERICLES May I take the liberty of handing you my business card? (*he gives her a brick*) But please, do not look at it until five minutes after I have left, and visit me as soon and as often as you can.

ASPASIA Oh, I can be quick and frequent! When is your regular reception day?

PERICLES Reception day? Ah, I usually receive on Fridays at 5 o'clock.

ASPASIA Oh, that's convenient, Friday is the day of the week when there's warm water!

PERICLES In my salon, half the whole world and the whole half-world come and go. You will meet Aristophanes, a little malicious fellow with a sharp tongue.

ASPASIA I prefer people with a good tongue.

PERICLES Then there's the young Alcibiades, an extremely handsome man.

ASPASIA Oh, that's the one who has a relationship with the so-called philosopher Socrates? That's fabulously interesting!

PERICLES Then there's an innocent, quite amusing storyteller named Herodotus, a young assistant physician at the first polyclinic, who has a great future ahead of him — Hippocrates! And two comedic playwrights of some renown: Euripides and Sophocles!

ASPASIA Oh, they're the ones who wrote *The Rape of the Sabine Women*!

PERICLES You're very well informed!

ASPASIA Well, I'm a messenger girl, after all — though I did fail the entrance exam for the higher girls' school.

PERICLES No, really!

ASPASIA Yes, and it was entirely the fault of one of those two comedians: Sophocles! The topic for the Greek essay was: "In what ways is Sophocles the Schiller of the Greeks?" And I simply could not figure out how Sophocles is the Schiller of the Greeks. Tell me yourself — what does Oedipus have to do with The Maid of Orleans?

PERICLES You are adorable. Until we meet again soon! (*aside*) I would not be at all surprised if, in my life, this little woman were to play a great role. (*exits*)

ASPASIA If that chubby old boy weren't so terribly red-haired, I might wonder whether he wasn't the slim, young, blond gentleman that Madam Pythia alluded to.
(*PIRAEUS enters*)

PIRAEUS My master is running through the entire city.

ASPASIA Has he taken Carlsbad salts? Is he on a cure?

PIRAEUS Only for you, miss, he is searching for you!

ASPASIA A little exercise won't hurt him, he's too fat anyway.

PIRAEUS Phidias loves you — you are so beautiful and young, he holds you so dear and precious.

ASPASIA The younger, the more expensive!

PIRAEUS He can't find another model like you; to him, you are priceless!

ASPASIA I fear so too.

PIRAEUS He cannot give you up at any price!

ASPASIA My chastity commands a very high price.

PIRAEUS Whether Phidias will reach his goal — that is the question!

ASPASIA Yes, it's always a matter of price — whether a woman gives herself.

PIRAEUS You have such a soul, miss — but as for the price, don't worry. Phidias knows how to properly appreciate the true worth of a woman. If I may judge from appearances — you are worth a lot.

ASPASIA You'll soon be able to judge even better! I hope it doesn't bother you if I make myself comfortable. (*she starts undressing*)

PIRAEUS Not in the least.

ASPASIA Don't be embarrassed; if one gets embarrassed, it always ruins the pleasure.

PIRAEUS Oh, I am beyond all prejudices, beyond good and evil. But while you're undressing, allow me to sweep the studio a bit (*whistles "She was a child of noble soul"*).

FRAU PHIDIAS (*approaching PIRAEUS*) Leave us alone. (*examines ASPASIA through her lorgnette*) You are the young lady who was engaged as the model of virtue.

ASPASIA Certainly, certainly.

FRAU PHIDIAS Then leave quickly. My husband no longer values your presence. He decided on you too hastily. He is an artist; even a trifle excites him.

ASPASIA Am I a trifle? But he hasn't even seen my nude pose yet. How can he know whether I am virtuous and beautiful?

FRAU PHIDIAS He saw your physical perfection at first glance. As for your soul — we shall not speak of it.

ASPASIA What has the soul to do with virtue? Virtue must, above all, be beautiful!

FRAU PHIDIAS Well — Let's not argue here about the definition of virtue.

ASPASIA And for that, I almost had to undress. He could have told me sooner.

FRAU PHIDIAS He was too shy.

ASPASIA Him, shy? I must laugh.

FRAU PHIDIAS Move along now! The master places no value on you. Thus, I say again: You are no candidate for the model of virtue. But to comfort you, he says he will definitely call upon you when he needs a model for vice. However, for today, it's over — it's cake.

ASPASIA Madam, you can visit me at the A-reopagus. (*exits*)

FRAU PHIDIAS Perhaps I went too far? And Phidias will scold me for chasing away his model. But heaven knows, I am terribly jealous. Would I dare what she dared? I dare it! Let it be dared!

> *Prayer to Athena*

FRAU PHIDIAS Quiet, my husband! (*she strikes a pose of virtue*)

PHIDIAS What?! My wife, half-naked? The devil's deceit! What does this ghastly spectacle mean?

FRAU PHIDIAS What troubles you?

PHIDIAS The unfamiliarity of the situation, you understand.

FRAU PHIDIAS Once, it wasn't so unfamiliar to you. You would surely prefer that shop girl, that brazen little toad, standing here instead of me. I sent her packing.

PHIDIAS How could you treat the lady so —

FRAU PHIDIAS Often enough in our marriage, you've expressed the wish to sculpt me. But posing as all those Aphrodites — that seemed quite improper for a decent wife. But now that you seek virtue, I say plainly: Before you turn to others, take your lawfully wedded wife. I can't fathom why you resist so. Especially when you've always objected to using other models, and you save five drachmas per sitting with me.

PHIDIAS Even if you save me five drachmas, you spare me nothing else.

FRAU PHIDIAS On the contrary! Just look at me — am I not beautiful?

PHIDIAS Yes, you are beautiful — but now, please dress again. I am ashamed; I cannot bear to look.

FRAU PHIDIAS If the other woman were in my place, would you be ashamed then?

PHIDIAS That's quite a different matter.

FRAU PHIDIAS No woman is naked enough for you — except your own wife, at whom you balk. But if you now insist that I keep my figure hidden under wraps, then just wait until the next tailor's bill — you'll experience a true blue miracle!

PHIDIAS It's almost pointless to argue with you. Virtue has always been clothed. She has always played the same role. As far back as we can remember, virtue wore woolen stockings, and Lahmann underwear. If duty were already a pleasure and virtue beautiful, what would be left for sin? It would have to go begging.

FRAU PHIDIAS Enough of your sayings! I don't care anymore; I am and will remain naked.

PRINCE (*enters in the costume of Love*) Am I permitted? Gods, what a sight!

PHIDIAS Who allowed you to enter without knocking?

PRINCE I have been knocking at the curtain for an hour — no one heard.

PHIDIAS And what brings you here?

PRINCE Love! I am the model for Love — or have you changed your mind?

PHIDIAS No, no, pardon me. (*to FRAU PHIDIAS*) It's the model I ordered for Love. You see what your childishness has led to!

FRAU PHIDIAS Should I withdraw?

PHIDIAS Too late — stay. (*quietly*) That will be your punishment.

PRINCE Pardon me, madam, for my unceremonious entrance. But don't be embarrassed in front of me; it's a sight I'm used to daily, I beg you, as a model.

PHIDIAS But of course.

FRAU PHIDIAS When a model poses, it doesn't like to be watched.

PRINCE Certainly — but since we have to pose together anyway...

PHIDIAS I thought some unauthorized person had entered. But since it's only you, that's something different.

PRINCE Habit dulls the senses; the sight of a naked or half-naked woman no longer excites me. What one sees every day, one gets over. A cook doesn't like to eat his own food, either. We models are immune to temptation. But here I am talking, and we're getting nowhere. I am here to serve another purpose, after all. Would you please instruct me on my position and my role? Should I group myself at the lady's head or at her feet? Maybe it would look splendid if I, like Hamlet, placed my head in her lap? Would you like my arm a little more slanted? Or perhaps my head even lower?

PHIDIAS No, stay as you are now — just a bit calmer, please. Virtue is so agitated — what's wrong with it?

FRAU PHIDIAS Nothing.

PHIDIAS Don't you feel comfortable in your position? A little more devotion, please! You stand so coldly next to the young man, like a wooden idol. Virtue and love are bound together by strong inner ties. You must snuggle up to each other more — you are supposed to embody domestic bliss.

PRINCE I shall embody it.

FRAU PHIDIAS How do you intend to do that? I am curious about your reasons. One moment, I don't feel comfortable.

PIRAEUS (*enters*) Master!

PHIDIAS (*very annoyed*) What is it?

PIRAEUS His Excellency Pericles is expecting you.

PHIDIAS (*angrily*) I can't use him now, I'm about to fly off the handle.

PIRAEUS My God, but the madam is beautifully built.

PHIDIAS Out with you, you scoundrel.

FRAU PHIDIAS Pericles is here and expecting you?

PHIDIAS It seems so.

FRAU PHIDIAS Then go, but hurry — I have no desire to stand around here for hours and catch a cold.

PRINCE We will devote your absence to studying a few original poses.

FRAU PHIDIAS Yes, I will try to be more affectionate, as you wish.

PHIDIAS Goodbye! (*leaves*)

FRAU PHIDIAS How dare you —

PRINCE I dare everything for you.

FRAU PHIDIAS What if I were to betray you —

PRINCE To whom?

FRAU PHIDIAS To my husband Phi-Phi!

PRINCE Then he would throw me out!

FRAU PHIDIAS There would be bloodshed — he would shoot at you with a military revolver. He is a reserve officer.

PRINCE In the transport corps. I was active duty — with the 1st Guards Regiment of Cavalry — nothing ever goes wrong for me. And I would gladly fall in a duel for you. What does my life matter, since I have seen you?

FRAU PHIDIAS You shameless man!

PRINCE I would be damned if I kept silent about the feelings that burn within me for you.

FRAU PHIDIAS So you intend to continue harassing me?

PRINCE Certainly, as long as my love harasses me. What are you doing? You're getting dressed?

FRAU PHIDIAS As a lady, I am ashamed to show myself to you any longer. You could only achieve your aim through a thoroughly wicked trick.

PRINCE If you send me away now, gracious lady, then I know very well that I am not indifferent to you, like an innocent child. Either you stay as you are and treat me like any model, or you dress and send me back to my hotel — and then I can bet that strong instincts and a shy love bind you to me.

FRAU PHIDIAS So if I get dressed now, you take it as proof of love?

PRINCE Certainly.

FRAU PHIDIAS Daring man!

PRINCE I know.

PERICLES (*Couplet*)

FRAU PHIDIAS What shall I do, O Zeus, I do not know.
Oh Aphrodite, show me the path to duty.

MODELS (*enter, pointing toward Mrs. Phidias's room*) It leads that way.

PRINCE Did you hear?

FRAU PHIDIAS Am I dreaming? Am I awake? What miracle has occurred? The stone, the marble, the clay seem to come to life!

PIRAEUS It's just to bring a bit of life into this dusty old lime shack.

FRAU PHIDIAS There stands Bacchus himself, in flesh and blood.

PIRAEUS Well, how did I manage that, eh? The feast can begin — the Bacchanal, the orgy, Plato's banquet — or rather, Phidias's!

> *Ballet. After the ballet, the* PRINCE *approaches* FRAU PHIDIAS *and whispers in her ear.*

FRAU PHIDIAS No... no, no... no... no... no... (*this "no," growing ever softer, finally turns into a "yes."*)

PIRAEUS Virtue is only a chain of many no's, but its final link is a yes.

> *Finale*

Act III. Scene 1.

PIRAEUS (*wakes up, rises*) I must get up — what an uplifting night. This round dance, this ballet, I have to sweep it away. Pleasure — the household. (*He bumps into two models lying on the floor*) What kind of mess is this? We're not in Lesbos here! How can anyone keep order like this? Get up, get up! (*Opens the curtain — daylight*)

ALL MODELS Oh, my bones — I'm dead — oh, my head — oh, my forehead!

PIRAEUS And you still have the nerve to lie around here in front of everyone?

ALL We're only imitating what we saw from Phi-Phi.

PIRAEUS There's nothing to see on Phi-Phi.

1ST MODEL Oh, the things that happened last night!

PIRAEUS What happened is behind us. Let's leave it behind us, let's forget it.

2ND MODEL Yes, but let's not forget that you still owe us the drachmas for yesterday's session.

PIRAEUS Who's still talking about yesterday? Today is today. I'm going to sweep up a little here, and you're going to clear out a little. I'm going to put my last five drachmas on Ptolemy III, who won by four lengths last time.

ALL Then please bet our hourly wages too, the ones you still owe us — for each of us.

PIRAEUS I'll defer your wages — but I would kindly ask you now to disappear quietly and without a fuss.

MODELS (*exit, singing*) We are the models of the house

PIRAEUS (*calls after them*) Quietly and without a fuss — and come back soon.

Scene 2.

The PRINCE and FRAU PHIDIAS enter.

PIRAEUS Is there anything I can do for the gracious lady?

FRAU PHIDIAS Thank you, I have everything I need.

PIRAEUS It is a special honor for us to host such a distinguished guest. Does the gracious gentleman have everything he needs?

PRINCE Thank you, I require nothing further.

PIRAEUS Then I'll withdraw discreetly — there's nothing left for me here. (*exits*)

Scene 3.

PRINCE Do not hide what my eyes long for.

FRAU PHIDIAS I am ashamed — do not despise me too much.

PRINCE Despise you?

FRAU PHIDIAS What we did was wrong.

PRINCE I assure you, it could not have been done better.

FRAU PHIDIAS Why do you say that?

PRINCE Just remember.

(Duet)

FRAU PHIDIAS That would be very nice... but still.

PRINCE You have pangs of conscience?

FRAU PHIDIAS Certainly... certain ones.

PRINCE I see, you're thinking: how foolish I was to resist for so long.

FRAU PHIDIAS Oh no, I regret it.

PRINCE You regret the lost time — don't take it so tragically. We will make up for it all. We will double our kisses.

FRAU PHIDIAS I can hardly bear to look at myself now that I have betrayed my husband, now that I am keeping something from him.

PRINCE What, you're keeping something from him?

FRAU PHIDIAS I believe so...

PRINCE Believe me, you have hidden nothing from anyone.

312

FRAU PHIDIAS You love to joke.

PRINCE I'm not joking, my love.

FRAU PHIDIAS And before...

PRINCE Before, I simply observed that your beauty is worthy of worship from head to toe. Can your husband claim otherwise? So have you hidden anything from him?

FRAU PHIDIAS But then...

PRINCE But then — then you opened the heavens for me — have you closed them to your husband? No. So you have hidden nothing.

FRAU PHIDIAS I always think of it as hiding.

PRINCE Nothing about you is hidden — everything can be seen and admired. Nothing is false, nothing is artificial. Your hair has its natural color, your teeth gleam with natural wisdom, your ankles are delicate...

FRAU PHIDIAS It doesn't matter — I swore loyalty to my husband.

PRINCE That was a mistake; one should never swear an oath.

FRAU PHIDIAS But — but — but —

PRINCE There is no "but." Let us thank heaven that allowed us to meet.

FRAU PHIDIAS Indeed.

PRINCE I have saved you from a lifelong reproach.

FRAU PHIDIAS Impossible.

PRINCE Oh yes — you represent here on Earth a specimen of the rarest female beauty. One would hardly find a second like you, not for the highest price. Do you think all that effort up there was made just to hand you over to Mr. Phidias? Oh no.

FRAU PHIDIAS You think so?

PRINCE With what words do you think Saint Peter would have greeted you?

FRAU PHIDIAS Saint Peter?

PRINCE Good old Peter. "What?" he would have said, "With two eyes like those... with a mouth like that... with legs like those... with that — and you found no better match than that Phidias? Such a beast?"

FRAU PHIDIAS What?

PRINCE Yes, that Phidias, of all people! You can't imagine the embarrassment I've spared you. Thank Zeus it's all been taken care of now.

FRAU PHIDIAS So all women ought to be unfaithful?

PRINCE No, not all — some must remain faithful.

FRAU PHIDIAS Namely —

PRINCE The ugly ones. But to avoid all suspicion — I'd like to propose — that we resume our former stance.

FRAU PHIDIAS What — you think — I wouldn't be ashamed?

PRINCE I don't understand your scruples. What's wrong with it?

FRAU PHIDIAS The feeling oppresses me — that I'm no longer respectable. I have betrayed him.

PRINCE Who is speaking of betrayal?

FRAU PHIDIAS I know, not long ago — I was too respectable. But now I fear I'm not respectable enough, and I fear Phidias will lose patience.

PRINCE If we love each other here, it's not our fault; we obeyed Phi-Phi, not our own impulses — we practiced, out of love for art, the art of love.

FRAU PHIDIAS What was the reason we barely slept last night?

PRINCE We had to immerse ourselves in our roles as deeply as possible! He could hardly have chosen a better pair for love.

FRAU PHIDIAS That's quite true.

PHIDIAS (*enters*) Bravo! I beg you, don't move. That is the grouping I always saw in my mind. You are made by God to pose with others. This is the grouping I always envisioned — the grouping that promises immortality. Astonishing how the lines flow into one another, then pour into the white sea of bodies, perfect in face, perfect in profile.

PRINCE Master, you flatter us too much.

FRAU PHIDIAS I believe I made quite some progress in the art last night.

PRINCE I do not deny that you are very apt.

FRAU PHIDIAS You taught me, the attentive pupil, to fully grasp the laws of art, to dive into the depth of its meaning. Now I can no longer leave the muse, and I shall always bow to her in gratitude. Let my whole future life be lovingly devoted to the service of art.

PHIDIAS Bravo, my child, on your transformation. But now enough of these strained poses — Go out there and rest.

FRAU PHIDIAS What — to my room?

PRINCE I'll go onto the terrace to get some fresh air.

FRAU PHIDIAS Won't you have a cup of tea with me?

PHIDIAS After such a session, one must lie down.

PRINCE If your husband permits — with pleasure. (*exits*)

PHIDIAS What's going on? A completely new attitude from my wife. She doesn't even ask where I spent the night — fortunately. It would not have been very pleasant to explain that I had an adventure with Aspasia last night and that I didn't wake from her arms until rosy-fingered Eos brought the Athenian daily paper.

ASPASIA (*enters*) Good morning, my little Phi-Phi man.

PHIDIAS Good morning, my dear Aspasia, good morning, my dear darling pest, my little Aspasia, already awake — and so changed?

ASPASIA Well, Fiji-Fiji, what do you say to that?

PHIDIAS You won the grand prize?

(Couplet of Aspasia)

PHIDIAS This song — for all its charm — Does not explain the origin of your new gown.

ASPASIA I got married.

PHIDIAS By the Styx, one can't say you're wasting your time. I must confess...

ASPASIA Never confess, listen, my story is short.

PHIDIAS Then allow me to sit down.

ASPASIA You noticed, of course, that for some time now Pericles has been hanging around me.

PHIDIAS For some time? You saw him here for the first time in your life just yesterday.

ASPASIA Either I tell the story — or you do. I repeat: you noticed that Pericles has been hanging around me for some time.

PHIDIAS He was setting traps to bring you down.

ASPASIA Well: everything worked, the trap snapped shut, he got me. But I told him straight away: not with me without a civil marriage ceremony.

PHIDIAS But that's impossible.

ASPASIA I just made the impossible possible.

PHIDIAS Yes, but when, when?

ASPASIA This morning, after I left you.

PHIDIAS Ah, when you left me, of course. Please continue — you're starting to intrigue me.

ASPASIA Pericles is, admittedly, already of a certain age —

PHIDIAS He's even older.

ASPASIA Yes, he's your age. "I'm in a hurry," little Pepi said to me.

PHIDIAS Who is Pepi?

ASPASIA Oh, Pericles — I call him Pepi. "I'm in a hurry," Pepi said to me, "since my days are numbered, I must start counting my nights. Let's get it over with." And so I became Mrs. Pericles. I told you recently that the Pythia prophesied I would marry a tall, blond gentleman.

PHIDIAS But he's red-haired!

ASPASIA He had it dyed — out of consideration for the Pythia.

PHIDIAS That's just like him. These statesmen change their colors so easily — according to need. And you — you are now the wife of the First Archon?

ASPASIA Yes, I'm an Archoness now. As a wedding gift, Daddy will be appointed a commercial counselor by him.

PHIDIAS And you didn't think of me?

ASPASIA Oh yes — Pepi promised you'll be placed in the Pantheon — as soon as you're dead — and they'll give a grand speech about you. They'll inscribe a golden plaque: Je – ka – fi – fi.

PHIDIAS I place no value on that.

ASPASIA How funny men are. I thought the Pantheon would amuse you.

PHIDIAS Yes, but as late as possible — or not at all! Now that everything's over!

ASPASIA Over? On the contrary, now it's just beginning.

PHIDIAS What, you're not pushing me aside — even though you're married?

ASPASIA You think because I've gotten a little married, I'll restrict myself, my doings and dealings? Oh no — especially not: freedom of trade.

PHIDIAS Exactly: no customs barriers, freedom of the seas, free import and export. (*He lifts her onto his knees.*) Did your Pepi deck you out like this?

ASPASIA Indeed, my little Fiji-Fiji, starting today I have control over the assets.

PHIDIAS Oh, then I'm reassured. I know that everything flourishes under your hands.

ASPASIA I urgently ask you not to say anything indecent.

PHIDIAS Why did you marry, then? (*He tickles her.*)

ASPASIA What are you doing there!

PHIDIAS Nothing... I'm arranging... arranging...

ASPASIA (*Rises.*) Your arrangements...

PHIDIAS What's wrong? What are you looking for? Have you lost something?

ASPASIA I'm afraid I'm going to lose my blouse.

PHIDIAS Why did Zeus create you so perfectly,
If he would not allow me this glance?
I have just the right use for you:
To hide you would only be a waste.
Thus I say proudly and free:
What could burn purer than an artist's fire,

One glance reveals to us the whole worth of a woman —
We artists were taught by a god:
By their fruits you shall know them.

(Couplet)

ASPASIA You're ruining my dress.

PHIDIAS That would be a shame — it's very pretty.

ASPASIA (*quickly*) 1500 drachmas.

PHIDIAS Good old Peperl will be delighted.

ASPASIA Of course — he thinks he's married a pearl, a woman who can dress like a princess for nothing.

PHIDIAS Well, you certainly stripped him royally.

ASPASIA It's all about how you do it. I told him: "How do you like this little bargain — seven hundred and fifty drachmas — what do you say? Practically a gift!"

PHIDIAS Didn't you say fifteen hundred drachmas? Are you running up debts?

ASPASIA Not at all. Just a moment — here's the bill.

PHIDIAS For me?

ASPASIA Naturally. You see, my little Fiji man, I'm thinking of you! You have exactly the same rights as my husband — liberty, equality. Have you noticed, Phi-Phi, that all husbands complain their wives are too expensive?

PHIDIAS You're telling me! I'm married myself.

ASPASIA And have you also noticed that mistresses cost their lovers a fortune too?

PHIDIAS (*tries to hand the bill back*) Except soulmates.

ASPASIA (*hands the bill back to him*) That's not what we're talking about now. In any case, I've found a solution of international importance for husbands and lovers alike: I've decided to be Pericles' wife and Phidias' mistress. I'll cost Pericles half as much as a luxurious wife would, and I'll cost Phidias half as much as a luxurious mistress would. You see — I don't demand the full amount from either of you. Pericles thinks he's giving me everything, and you complete the rest.

PHIDIAS Is that a riddle from the newspaper?

ASPASIA I'm not in the habit of posing riddles.

PHIDIAS You're irresistible. So — I complete the whole with 750 drachmas?

ASPASIA Exactly, Fiji. The more a man pays for a woman, the more priceless she becomes to him.

PHIDIAS Yes, bills are binding.

ASPASIA And another thing:

PHIDIAS (*nervously*) Another thing?

ASPASIA Peperl claims I'm an outstanding statue. He insists that you sculpt me.

PHIDIAS But that's what I've been saying all along.

ASPASIA What would that cost?

PHIDIAS Not much.

ASPASIA Seriously — how much? He's willing to pay 10,000.

PHIDIAS Do I have to pay half of that too?

ASPASIA For a bust, I know you charge 5000. But what about the whole figure?

PHIDIAS If I go for the whole thing... Shall we discuss the finer details in my room? I'll give you a special rate.

ASPASIA I'm afraid it'll be a lover's rate.

> *Both exit*

PIRAEUS (*enters, holding a scale*)

PRINCE What are you doing there, my friend?

PIRAEUS I'm weighing, pondering, considering, sir. It's very delicate. I'm weighing the pros and cons.

PRINCE I beg your pardon?

PIRAEUS You see, sir, up to now I've conducted myself like any respectable servant: lying, stealing, smoking the master's cigars, drinking his liqueurs, selling his statues... but beyond that, I can't reproach myself for any serious wrongdoing.

PRINCE My heartfelt congratulations.

PIRAEUS But today, sir, I feel I'm about to commit a...

PRINCE A scandal!

PIRAEUS Oh no — let's call it by its proper name! I'm about to take on a secret I cannot justify.

PRINCE How so?

PIRAEUS Last night, sir, I caught my master's wife — that noble, kind-hearted, great man's wife — in the arms of some scoundrel.

PRINCE And what has that got to do with you?

PIRAEUS What has that got to do with me? Here's where my doubts and conscience pains begin — shouldn't I tell the husband everything?

PRINCE Good heavens, are you mad? Look where that kind of thing leads! You're in debt, aren't you?

PIRAEUS directshouting Crippling debt, sir, crippling!

PRINCE Quiet down, will you!

PIRAEUS Oh sir, that's just the voice of my conscience.

PHIDIAS (*hands him money*) Here — to silence your conscience and balance the scales.

PIRAEUS Thank you, sir.

PHIDIAS And now may I count on you?

PIRAEUS No need — I have complete trust in you. Just, when you leave, make sure you don't take the wrong door. It's the first one.

PHIDIAS Thank you. (*exits*)

PIRAEUS He's gone back to his amorous delights. I may dare to trust the scale — and say with an old proverb, Freshly weighed is half won. But now I must run after my horse. Goodbye.

PRINCE (*enters with FRAU PHIDIAS*) I assure you, we must be careful. We were seen last night. I would even suggest that, to avoid raising your husband's suspicions, you be especially kind to him — don't watch him too closely — in short, turn a blind eye.

FRAU PHIDIAS Oh, should I perhaps put another woman in his bed while you're here? Listen, if you dare suggest that to me one more time —

PRINCE I only meant we should lock the door next time.

FRAU PHIDIAS No, no, thank you. As if it weren't enough that I'm the wife of a cuckold — I won't be the wife of a man who cheats on me, too.

PRINCE In a pinch, wouldn't you allow him to be with a woman less pretty than yourself?

FRAU PHIDIAS Much less pretty.

PRINCE Then I envy your husband — he can have all the women in the world.

FRAU PHIDIAS Allow me —

PRINCE You think that's too much? Let's say: with all the respectable women.

FRAU PHIDIAS So — with none.

ASPASIA enters, embracing PHIDIAS affectionately.

FRAU PHIDIAS Bravo! Stay just like that — that's exactly the scene I've always pictured in my mind.

PHIDIAS (*startled*) Allow me to explain — the lady is commissioning —

ASPASIA — a statue for 10,000 drachmas.

FRAU PHIDIAS Do you dare deny that you betrayed me with this person?

PHIDIAS I admit — appearances are deceptive — the circumstances —

FRAU PHIDIAS I don't recognize circumstances. Did you, yes or no, press your lips to this woman?

PHIDIAS If I did, it was an accident — a slip of the tongue.

PRINCE (*quietly to FRAU PHIDIAS*) She is, indeed, much less pretty.

Scene 4.

PERICLES What's going on here?

FRAU PHIDIAS What's going on here is that my husband is proceeding in a way —

PHIDIAS (*interrupting her*) Allow me to introduce: Mrs. Phidias, my model — Mrs. Pericles.

PRINCE directquietly to ASPASIA

PERICLES Greetings, my dear wife! So you wished to be the first to bring the joyful news here?

PHIDIAS My heartfelt congratulations, Excellency.

PERICLES Have you already spoken with Phidias about the bust?

ASPASIA Yes, we were just in the middle of the conversation.

PHIDIAS Yes, we were right in the middle of it.

PERICLES You were right in the middle of it.

FRAU PHIDIAS AND PRINCE They were right in the middle of it.

PERICLES Bravo, very good — because an idea came to me: instead of personally commissioning your statue, perhaps we could combine it with the group Domestic Bliss commissioned by the Ministry.

ASPASIA How so? And what about the 10,000 drachmas?

PERICLES One moment. The group was commissioned by the state. It will be easy for me to obtain an increase in the agreed price.

PHIDIAS Yes, but what symbol could the gracious lady represent?

FRAU PHIDIAS Perhaps fidelity?

PHIDIAS Why fidelity? Why fidelity? That would be repeating the same idea twice. Oh no, for fidelity we already have virtue!

ASPASIA Wouldn't I make an excellent symbol of thrift?

PERICLES That's it!

ASPASIA (*to the PRINCE and FRAU PHIDIAS*) Where should I stand? Here? (*to FRAU PHIDIAS*) Would you mind making a little room for me?

FRAU PHIDIAS As you command — just not too close to love.

ASPASIA Don't worry, I won't get in your way; I won't get too close to your love. (*She tries to put money into her stocking.*)

PHIDIAS Excellent, please keep that position.

FRAU PHIDIAS Excellent, please keep that position. Thrift stores her fortune in a woolen stocking — what a brilliant group to promote small savers! The whole thing will be called: Virtue and Love United in the Bond of Thrift, Founding Domestic Happiness.

(Couplet)

PIRAEUS Oh lord, lord, forgive your poor servant who comes to disturb domestic bliss. It's over — it's over!

ASPASIA Why? Isn't there still the finale to come?

PIRAEUS It's over for me. It had to end in disaster. Ptolemy IV did not reach his goal.

PHI-PHI So what? (*Models*) What do I see? What's happening to me? My statues on the run!

PIRAEUS No, the statues no longer want the status quo. They are tired of being mere extras. Let me say it: I have sold all your works to this gentleman here. He paid me a fine price — may he be praised! My lord, I could have drunk away the money — that would not have been right. So instead, I gambled it away. I could have won and thrown a feast — that also would not have been right. I lost it all. So I am harshly punished. Zeus has punished me harshly. Ares has punished me. Please, don't be more Zeus-like than Zeus, nor more Ares-like than Ares.

PRINCE There's a way to turn everything for the better: Master, I will allow myself to return your works to you and give the models triple their hourly wage.

PIRAEUS My lord, what charity!

PHIDIAS My lord, you are a prince!

PRINCE Yes, master, a prince who, out of love for art, did not shy away from a ruse of war. A foreign prince, whose currency allows him to make far greater purchases. Like the gracious lady, it was also my dearest wish to become immortal through you.

PERICLES Now that we have restored domestic happiness, we could once again form the group.

PRINCE I'd rather propose that we all go to sleep as soon as possible.

ASPASIA Whereupon I permit myself one very important remark:

Part Twenty-Two:

Cromwell - Two Surviving Scenes of the Lost Drama

"Cromwell" was written around 1926, and Act I, Scene 1 appeared
in "The Bean" in 1926, while "On the Thames Embankment"
appeared in the "Berlin Stock Exchange Gazette,"
August 22, 1926.

Cromwell

(Two Surviving Scenes of the Lost Drama)

Act I. Scene 1.

Court chapel. The body of James I lies in state. To the left and right, a torchbearer and an officer of the Royal Guard in full dress uniform, swords drawn, stand completely motionless. Incense. Organ music. KARL enters quickly through a curtain. The organ music abruptly ceases. KARL ascends the few steps to the catafalque, holding his hat in his hand, and gazes at his father for a moment. Then he snatches the torch from one of the bearers and shines it into the dead man's face.

KARL Dead? Completely dead? Stone cold dead? Didn't the corner of your mouth just twitch mockingly? Are you making fun of me, eh? Why are you grinning? Only feigning death? And tomorrow you'll be up again — drinking the sparkling wine, loving the radiant woman — You've left me a fine inheritance, Anointed of the Lord! The inheritance tax costs more than the entire estate is worth. Was England ever in such confusion? Did you secretly slip away... from the one who made you from dust: God? You were weak, old man, too weak to live by your own theories. A despot with a big mouth. You were afraid of your own fear — and so you acted brave. War, civil war, a steaming pot of soup is simmering at the hearth. Your behind was too fat. You liked sitting on it too much. You didn't like to walk on your short stubby legs. You had flat feet — and a flat mind.

> *From the right, something creeps into the pale twilight, suddenly standing in greenish-white light. KARL recoils — a red-haired fellow with a pockmarked face stands there.*

KARL Who's there?

GRIFFITH Password: Long live His Majesty Charles the First of England! (*He bounds up the steps to the corpse in short hops, lifts one of the corpse's arms, which falls back limply, then returns to the King and bows low three times, court-style, from three directions.*) I am yours! Does Your Majesty not recognize me?

KARL Your face speaks for itself.

GRIFFITH How flattering!

KARL It's the finest gallows-face I've ever seen.

GRIFFITH Charming!

KARL That pock-scarred mug!

GRIFFITH He-he!

KARL That gait of a wheezy little rooster!

GRIFFITH Hi-hi!

KARL That red devil's wig, as if stolen straight from Satan's head!

GRIFFITH Ho-ho!

KARL How did the five years of galley service treat you?

GRIFFITH I'm pleased Your Majesty remembers my humble person at last. After all, I didn't spend those five years in the galley without Your Majesty's help — I mean, I owe this mark on my back, these calluses on my hands, and this eternal buzzing in my head all to you. I always feel as though a thousand bees are buzzing inside my skull, and before my eyes hangs a delicate pink veil: the sky, the bushes, the houses, people's faces, even Your Majesty's royal robe — everything is slightly blood-stained, spattered.

KARL The galley made you reflective. You came out of yourself, saw the world, saw foreign lands, palm trees, parrots, monkeys —

GRIFFITH — and people, people, people — everywhere people, who defile the pure face of the earth, no matter where one goes. I had a tubercular monkey on the galley. I loved him.

KARL (mocking) You loved?

GRIFFITH (unfazed) I loved him. He loved me. We ate nuts together. Then he died and was buried in the ocean.

KARL Quite a grand and noble grave for a monkey.

GRIFFITH There would have been room for me too. I was too cowardly.

KARL You had fewer and fewer qualms about extinguishing the lives of other people.

GRIFFITH True, I've got good lungs, fine breath, and I love to blow out life's little lights — (steps closer to KARL) By whose command, Your Majesty, did I once snuff out a life — a tiny little light, but one that flickered too brightly for your liking?

KARL Be silent if your life means anything to you!

GRIFFITH I value it no more than my death: namely, utterly indifferent. But Majesty should not forget the small services once rendered by a wretched executioner's assistant. Had the firstborn prince lived, he would be ruling today — not you. Who gave the prince lead to taste, which his weak stomach couldn't handle? So, to whom do you owe your throne, eh?

KARL Silence, you dog!

GRIFFITH Cursed be the time when good deeds must seek their reward within themselves!

KARL You overrate the good and evil of your deeds.

GRIFFITH (gesturing to the corpse) To issue that one a ticket to the next world — I came too late. Who was so eager to serve you — or did you yourself find the courage — à la bonheur — gratulor! gratulor!

KARL Shut your mouth, hellhound! His Majesty James of England choked at a state banquet on a turkey bone —

GRIFFITH And no doctor could be fetched in time — blessed turkey!

KARL Silence!

GRIFFITH Oh, I've been silent. And I'll remain so. Bon camerade, bon camerade. I didn't betray you in court or on the galley. I thought: all in good time. Just wait your hour. One day, when Charles the First ascends the throne, the hour will come. Well: he has ascended. The hour has come: voilà! For your sake, I wore rags for five years instead of a shirt. The lice nearly ate me alive, and at night, the rats were fond of me. They nibbled my toes down to the bone.

KARL Become a decent man, Griffith!

GRIFFITH That advice — from you? Wonders never cease!

KARL This place does not bode well for you. Get lost!

GRIFFITH Get lost? On foot? In boots? In socks? I've nothing on my legs but clumps of filth from the long road. And no good wind? A storm? Rain? Fish are liveliest in bad weather — why not me?

KARL Go to Rome, do penance!

GRIFFITH You say that — a Lutheran?

KARL Even Luther went to Rome.

GRIFFITH Gladly would I go to Rome — if Your Holiness would accompany me. For on the path of penance and repentance, we belong together.

KARL Confess to me — I'll absolve you according to the Protestant faith.

GRIFFITH I committed a murder in the name of the King of England.

KARL (*making the sign of the cross over him*) Absolvo te![16] (*Exits quickly*)

GRIFFITH (*left stunned*) There are people possessed by devils. I, for instance. All kinds of vile little demons play their games inside me. But what a pitiful scoundrel I am compared to the one who just left. He'd be capable of possessing a devil — and making it even more devilish. (*He notices a handkerchief on the floor, picks it up*) A handkerchief. (*Lifts it to his nose*) Oh, what a scent! The handkerchief of a noble lady — Parisian perfume — She lost it during the solemn lying-in-state — the queen?? (*Breathes the in scent deeply*) To rise, just once, out of the muck, the swamp in which one's stuck, to have solid ground beneath one's feet. To be clothed in white, bathed, oiled, anointed, to lie in cushions beside the fragrant, radiant body of a noblewoman, loving — and loved. Damn it, I know no other love than... (*He examines the handkerchief*) There's a crown embroidered on it.

The Queen's MAID enters the chapel, searching the floor

GRIFFITH Good morning, lovely child!

---

[16] I absolve you.

MAID (*startled*) What do you want?

GRIFFITH Are you looking for — me?

MAID I'm horrified to find you here. Heaven forbid I should be looking for you! I'm searching for a handkerchief the Queen lost during the liturgy today.

GRIFFITH She was moved by her lord brother the Cardinal's sermon, blew her nose, and wiped her tears.

MAID You've found the handkerchief? Give it here!

GRIFFITH (*waves it like a flag*) I'll give it up — but only to Her Majesty herself. I'm a poor devil, eternally wandering, seeking a modest, stable post, have come down in the world — I mean, traveled the world — I know a bit of science and a few arts. (*performs a few hops*) Dancing, (*mimes playing the flute*) fluting, geometry, astrophysics, palm reading, balancing acts, catechism and idolatry.

MAID My God, you're educated!

GRIFFITH But even in the breast of the learned and the wise beats a heart that feels humanly. (*Approaches her*)

MAID You frighten me.

GRIFFITH Come into that side aisle with me. I'll do nothing to you except what people usually do with pretty, plump girls like yourself. (*Pulls her along*)

MAID You're strong!

GRIFFITH As strong as seven stallions, seven bulls, and seven drakes. Come!

MAID The handkerchief! The handkerchief!

On the Thames Embankment.
Autumn, bare shrubs, fog, rain

CROMWELL Despair is as close to me as the child in the mother's womb. How many more months, days, hours will I give birth? To end it all before I've even begun. I knew an actor once who would only play Caesar on the condition that his director let him die on stage for as long as he wished. And he really died magnificently... a full ten minutes, probably. I too will one day die on stage, but there's still time for that – a lot of time... (*He leans over the water.*) I could jump down there – but from the depths, my accursed pumpkin face is already staring back at me. Someone's already waiting for me down there — me. I can't escape myself – God in Heaven, help me so that I don't find myself up there with you! (*Exits*)

GRIFFITH (*enters*) He went this way. A fox leaves unmistakable tracks. Little fox! Little fox! The wolf is on your trail! 5,000 pounds for a fox's pelt – now that's a tidy sum. One could live on that. What shall I do with all that money? Well then: for 1,000 I'll buy an estate – not too big, not too small. Then I'll marry a woman – a lady, a noblewoman: not too tall, not too short, not too thin, not too fat, well-built. Then I'll build a church to atone for my sins – not too big, not too small. I'll become a respectable man, that is: not too big, not too small – erect myself a tomb, not too big, not too small, with the inscription: Here lies the Honorable Sir Griffith. He stood with both feet firmly on the ground. Traveler, hurry past, lest you wish to be kicked by his corpse. (CROMWELL *suddenly appears beside him in the fog.*) Whoa!

CROMWELL Pardon me, My Lord –

GRIFFITH Pardon me, My Lord –

CROMWELL The fog is so thick you can't see your hand in front of your eyes –

GRIFFITH Dreadful, this London fog.

CROMWELL An unhealthy climate in this city –

GRIFFITH One doesn't live long –

CROMWELL Especially scoundrels don't live long here –

GRIFFITH Is that an insinuation, My Lord?

CROMWELL I don't have the honor of knowing you, My Lord –

GRIFFITH Then you shall come to know me, My Lord – (*draws his sword*) Let the hunt begin!

CROMWELL (*also draws*) Highwayman!

GRIFFITH Land robber!

CROMWELL Pickpocket!

GRIFFITH Seizer of the throne!

CROMWELL Assassin!

GRIFFITH Hypocrite-assassin!

CROMWELL Stand, coward!

GRIFFITH Fall, hero! (*They have been dueling all the while; now* CROMWELL *strikes, and* GRIFFITH *collapses.*)

GRIFFITH Never were 5,000 pounds lost in a more disgraceful way.

CROMWELL Cheater – who paid you to stake your life against mine?

GRIFFITH Not too tall, not too short – here lies the honorable Sir Griffith. (*Dies*)

CROMWELL Griffith?! The King's confidant??? Charles Stuart: you've squandered your last trump card...

Part Twenty-Three:

The Gambler

"The Gambler" is a scene from Klabund's *The Chaotic Decline of the West*.

The Gambler

A Scene

A Scene - published in 1922.

(The Gambler staggers onto the stage in a green tailcoat, green top hat, and orange cloak.)

I have gambled away. I have gambled away everything... I am finished... before I even began... Four queens I held in my hand... Four queens at once... Ha, I thought, at last Fortuna smiles upon you in quadruple form... I bet 10,000... my opponent was a skeleton dressed in the latest fashion... an enormous pumpkin skull... without hair, without flesh... without eyes. Motionless, its bony fingers held five poker cards. "Twenty thousand," squeaked the skeleton, like a poorly oiled handcar. The man, I thought—if he even is a man—is insane, utterly idiotic... I have four queens in my hand, and he wants to outbid me. "Forty thousand!" I shouted, and it sang, it twittered inside me:

To whom the Muse has offered herself fourfold,
He wanders drunken through these meadows,
What do the wives and street women mean to him,
Or the daffodil wind in the glow of evening...

"Eighty thousand!" cackled the skeleton. You must play the card out to the end... You are life, and he is death... You must win the whole world against him... Ah, boundless bliss, if you win eternal salvation... immortality. "One hundred sixty thousand!" I roared. "Three hundred twenty thousand!" echoed the rickety frame. I calculated feverishly... 160 and 80 and 40 and 20 and 10... total 310,000... My whole fortune was in and at stake... What could I put up against his 320,000? Behind my chair stood Eveline – blonde and tender and sweet as ever... She had gone pale... I turned to her... I lifted her up with my arms and set her on the gaming table... She closed her eyes and stood motionless like a statuette... Then I tore the silk garments from her body... and her shift... Naked she stood upon the table. And I cried: "Against your 320,000, I stake my wife and my girl, my beloved and my goddess... Agreed?" The skeleton grinned and caressed with its empty eyes the blooming flesh of the young woman's body... "Agreed," it bleated. Eveline stood motionless... We threw down our cards on the table... He had four aces. I saw how he threw his black cloak around Eveline and lifted her from the table... I heard him, in a metallic voice, order an automobile from the club servant... I rushed out into the black night. My fate is sealed... Soon the apple trees will bloom again... I will learn English at the Berlitz School... I have a gift for languages and will write for American newspapers and magazines... They are said to pay fabulously—really fabulously—$1,000 for an illustrated article... Well then... one must simply buy a Kodak and photograph everything... absolutely everything. $1,000—that's, let's see, in today's currency, 20,000 marks... Twenty articles, and I'll have Eveline back again. Ah, it's not as bad as it seems. Gambling—after all, that's the only way to cope with life and with fate. Even as an embryo, I had the habit of playing baccarat. When I came into the world after nine months—9, you must know, is the number of baccarat—I won in that way, with one coup, 1,000 marks, which I put aside to pay later for my volunteer military year... for my parents were simple people: my father a delicatessen dealer, my mother a candidate of philology... Shared interests brought them together—a holy sympathy of hearts. It was a love match, right out of the book. My mother nourished me at the breasts of science, which was considerably less exhausting than if she had used her own.

My father's method of education consisted in granting or withholding delicacies, carob pods, or American canned meat... Thus, practical life-wisdom and ideology kept the scales of justice balanced in my upbringing. At five years old, a comet struck my head, giving my skull a somewhat dented and flattened shape. At the same time, people saw in this sign from heaven that great things were destined for me. In my ninth year—9, remember, is the number of baccarat—Edward the Seventh of England lost India to me in a game of baccarat... I became Viceroy of India, a post I fulfilled completely until my thirteenth year. Thereafter, I returned the crown to His English Majesty. It was, by the way, only weakly gilded. Since then, I could not give up the game. But I kept losing—lost even my mind, which I had to pawn for 100 marks. For—to have luck, one must have money... and to have money, one must have luck. People want and should have happiness... Happiness is what costs a lot of money... An afternoon at jazz tea in the Paradise Bar—price: 100 marks. A dinner with Fern Andra—merely to be seen with her, at Hiller's or somewhere—price: 1,000 marks. A visit to Madame H. in Z. Street, where one meets a few boarding-school girls—price: 2,000 marks. And at the end, two hours in the gambling club called "Society of Younger Terrarium Enthusiasts"— price: who knows how many marks. Lend me 50 marks. I'll stake everything on my card. If I win, I'll buy myself a zebra or a spring cloud. Ah, the lovely money... People find epithets for money that are usually only used for women. Who would believe, seeing my patent-leather shoes and my creased creases, that I have no money? An elegant beggar—that's the worst. I'll go to a first-class hotel and live for a few weeks on credit... In a second-rate one, I wouldn't get any. It's a miserable life... Should I appear at the Corso Theatre as an eccentric dancer? Ah, the lovely money, and the lovely cards, and the lovely, lovely women—Diamond Queen... Spade Queen... Club Queen... and Heart Queen.

Part Twenty-Four:

Kaspar - A Tragedy

"Kaspar - A Tragedy" is an unpublished play that is copied from a manuscript.
"Kaspar" should not be confused with the 1912 play, "The Poor Kaspar."

Kaspar – A Tragedy

Characters:

The Farmer
The Farmer's Wife
The daughter of both, called Young Lady
Kaspar
The Maid
The Sexton
The Doctor
The Poet
The Jailer

Scene 1: In the Field

FARMER Finishing work, Kaspar

KASPAR Yes, sir

FARMER What are you waiting for?

KASPAR I don't know, sir.

FARMER Do you want to come with us or are you staying in the field?

KASPAR I'll stay, sir.

FARMER The farmer's wife puts milk and bread in your cupboard.

KASPAR Yes, sir

FARMER Good night, Kaspar

KASPAR Good night, sir

    FARMER exits.

KASPAR The sun is setting. My forehead feels cold. I know nothing. I can do
nothing. Oh, I...

    MAID comes

MAID I knew you were still in the field, pondering. Keeping yourself company.
It's going to be a hot night. Lightning is flashing everywhere.

KASPAR What do you want from me?

MAID You—you.

KASPAR You don't have much when you have me.

MAID A lot—a lot—I have everything.

KASPAR Don't believe it.

MAID I swear.

KASPAR Don't swear.

MAID My squirrel.

KASPAR You're making fun of my red hair.

MAID My red rider. My fiery head.

KASPAR I feel good when you kiss me. I lie quite still beside you. Don't upset me.

MAID Kaspar—

KASPAR Did you see the shooting star?

MAID Did you make a wish? What was it?

KASPAR It wasn't a shooting star, it was lightning. It flashed right through my heart.

MAID You—do you love the young lady, Kaspar. Is that true or not?

KASPAR I love no one. No human being and no animal.

MAID That's not true. You're not that godless. You secretly go to church, I've often seen it.

KASPAR It's so quiet in the church. And the windows are so brightly painted. And it smells completely different than in the goat shed.

MAID You take off your cap before every crucifix.

KASPAR Because there's a poor man hanging there on the wood, suffering greatly. I take off my cap before everyone who is in pain. Before every woman who is carrying a child. She bears double the pain.

MAID Kaspar, I'm having a child with you, you know it. I'm in my third month.

KASPAR Whoever fathers a child is a murderer.

MAID You seduced me in the hay.

KASPAR That's not true. I didn't seduce you. You didn't seduce me. It was the night.

MAID Don't forget to order the banns. I won't wait longer than four months for the wedding. It was a disgrace.

KASPAR Now—there's lightning again. And now it's thundering. The storm is approaching. Like a hot woman approaching you. Kiss me. Let the sky collapse above us. Now it's raining castles, it's going to be a wild night.

MAID Oh, you.

Scene 2: Farmhouse Parlor

MAID Leave me alone, farmer.

FARMER Don't be so prickly. We're both human: you and I.

MAID Go lie in bed with the farmer's wife. Do it with her.

FARMER But I'd just like to do it with you. You've got firm thighs and firm breasts. The farmer's wife is spreading out like a pancake.

MAID You shouldn't have smashed her eggs, then. (*laughs*)

FARMER Woman.

MAID Hush—the young lady is coming. (*exits*)

YOUNG LADY Father—

FARMER

YOUNG LADY I'm so restless. All these questions keep coming. I walk here and there. I find no peace.

FARMER Shall I get the doctor—

YOUNG LADY Oh, the doctor, what's he going to do? I know what to say sooner than he does. Hold on to your chest. And rest. And drink milk and eat eggs. And sleep, sleep a lot. Where is Kaspar? He put a forest herb in my soup yesterday, and I slept soundly like in a fairy tale.

FARMER Kaspar is in the field.

YOUNG LADY He's strong. He's digging up all the earth.

FARMER I have great joy and support in him. He thanks me for picking him up from the street.

YOUNG LADY He's an orphan. But I think he never had a father or mother. He fell to Earth from a star.

FARMER He doesn't look so heavenly, so starry. He has paws like a tiger. And— he'll probably chop down the thickest tree in the district all by himself.

YOUNG LADY Where is his mother? In the—

FARMER In the stable with the cows. Milking. But then she goes out into the fields to bring vespers to the farmhands and maids.

YOUNG LADY I'm looking for her in the fields, Father. I feel like walking a thousand miles today.

FARMER My angel!

First Scene

FARMER'S WIFE Kaspar –

KASPAR Farmer's wife –

FARMER'S WIFE Put the spade aside for once.

KASPAR It is not yet Vesper time.

FARMER'S WIFE I pardon you. Just do it.

KASPAR You are kind to me.

FARMER'S WIFE Come... here to me—into the shade. Sit with me.

KASPAR It's terribly hot.

FARMER'S WIFE Don't you want to love me? (*pulls him toward her*)

KASPAR I've always loved you, farmer's wife.

FARMER'S WIFE No one sees us here by the haystack. I'll lift my clothes, and you do it quickly. Heated love is the most beautiful.

KASPAR I'd gladly do it to please you, Peasant Woman, but the maid might take it badly; I'm promised to her.

FARMER'S WIFE Once is as good as never. And the maid won't find out.

KASPAR But there is someone else, before whose eyes I could not appear if I had sinned with you. And those eyes are like stars, and I would die if I saw them pale on account of me.

FARMER'S WIFE Who is it?

KASPAR The young lady.

The YOUNG LADY enters.

YOUNG LADY Mother, I'm as cheerful today as I haven't been in all these days. I picked forget-me-nots by the brook on the way and wove a garland and sang while doing it. I'll place it on your brown hair.

FARMER'S WIFE I am not worthy to be crowned; place the forget-me-not crown on Kaspar.

YOUNG LADY Kaspar already has a crown of gold. That's how his hair shines in the sun. Good day, Kaspar.

KASPAR Good day, Young Lady. I'm glad that you are so cheerful.

YOUNG LADY After all, it is summer and the birds sing and the flowers bloom and people—love.

KASPAR Show me how you do it, that you can love every creature.

YOUNG LADY This is how I do it. (*takes his head and kisses him on the forehead*)

KASPAR (*startled*) Young Lady.

FARMER'S WIFE Girl, you're not very clever. You'll mess with Kaspar's head.

KASPAR I am just the young lady's servant, farmer's wife.

YOUNG LADY Kaspar, when you're finished, you must come to the brook and carve me a willow flute. You must lull me to sleep... Music and sleep: they are my dearest siblings.

Scene 4: By the Stream

KASPAR I've caught a toad for you, Miss, do you want to play with it?

YOUNG LADY Show me, Kaspar. It sits quietly in my lap and looks at me with its golden eyes like... like... you, Kaspar.

KASPAR I wish I were a toad, Miss.

YOUNG LADY Being human isn't bad either. It's the same whether you're a human, a toad, a cloud, or a tree.

KASPAR I am a stream. Running away. Flowing.

YOUNG LADY I am a birch tree. Just slightly swaying.

KASPAR You are taking root: everywhere. Even in the rootless.

YOUNG LADY You have taken root in my heart, Kaspar.

KASPAR Miss!

YOUNG LADY Sing me a song, Kaspar.

KASPAR I'm going—where?
I came from—where?
Am outside and inside,
Am full and empty.
Born – where?
Chosen – when
I slept in the straw
With woman and man.
I deliver you,
And do you love me?
I sadden you,
do you sadden me?
I stand and fall,
I will be.
I am a universe
and am alone.
I was, I am.
So easy. So difficult.
I'm going—where?
I came from—where?

YOUNG LADY The willow caresses my forehead. Heaven smiles at me. I want to sleep. Play the willow flute, Kaspar.

> KASPAR *plays. The* YOUNG LADY *falls asleep. The* MAID *comes creeping.*

MAID Kaspar –

KASPAR Be quiet – the lady is asleep.

MAID Kaspar, you are playing a wicked game. You are deceiving me.

KASPAR Dear girl – that's not true. I sang the young lady to sleep.

MAID Only love that has been fulfilled sleeps so deeply.

KASPAR The young lady is ill.

MAID Not so ill that she can't spread her legs.

KASPAR You scold the young lady. She is as holy as a saint.

MAID We are all holy when we love. I love you.

KASPAR You love my weakness.

MAID I love your strength.

KASPAR When I'm with you for a long time, that's what you love. The young lady loves me senselessly, without purpose, just as I love the young lady. We are here, and so we love.

MAID Be careful, Kaspar, that nothing happens that could make you and me regret. I—hate the young lady. I am healthy. She is ill. I am hard. She is tender. I am evil. She is good. Day and night don't mix.

KASPAR Go—go—the young lady is stirring. Don't disturb her dream.

Scene 5: In the Field

FARMER Where is the girl?

FARMER'S WIFE By the stream. Kaspar is with her.

FARMER Matchmaker.

FARMER'S WIFE You lecherous goat. Sneaking after the maid. I once saw you grabbing her breasts and she slapped you in the face.

FARMER You old whore. You want Kaspar to mount you from behind like a dog. You're always in heat.

FARMER'S WIFE That's your fault. You can't do it without help anymore. If I don't work you with my hand.

FARMER Why didn't you give me a son? No heir? A sick child with death written all over his face?

FARMER'S WIFE I wonder what you got when you were with the soldiers in the big city.

FARMER Lying woman!

FARMER'S WIFE Man.

FARMER You won't defile my treasure, my sanctuary: my angelic maiden—

FARMER'S WIFE I love her no less than you. She's not a human being like you and me! That's why she can lie peacefully with Kaspar by the stream. Have no fear or misgivings.

FARMER She's—lying—with—Kaspar—by the stream?

FARMER'S WIFE What does it matter? Give her to Kaspar as his wife. You'll have an heir for the farm right away.

FARMER You're right to speculate on my death, that you'll marry Kaspar and you'll have your pleasure in your old age.

FARMER'S WIFE It wouldn't be a pity if you died.

FARMER Monster.

FARMER'S WIFE The maid is having a child with Kaspar, just so you know. He and she are getting married. He's already gone to order the banns.

FARMER Where is my angel so I can protect him?

FARMER'S WIFE Take care of yourself, farmer,

Scene 6: Village Church

The last notes of the organ fade away. The churchgoers leave the church: among them the DOCTOR, the FARMER, the FARMER'S WIFE, and the MAID. When the people see the MAID, there is whispering and finger-pointing. KASPAR, his head buried in his hands, has remained seated on the pew. The YOUNG LADY, last of all.

YOUNG LADY (*to the SEXTON in the gallery*) Hey, sexton—

SEXTON What is it?

YOUNG LADY You must do me a favor. Sexton, I'll do you one in return. You wanted to own the arias and cantatas by Bach and Haydn. I'll give them to you.

SEXTON Young Lady!

YOUNG LADY Play something for me.

SEXTON With pleasure, young lady.

YOUNG LADY Just for me, a heavenly, blissful music—just for me.

SEXTON What shall it be: something by Palestrina—

YOUNG LADY Nothing pious, nothing strict, nothing bitter, sexton—sweet, enchanting music: play me a minuet, a gavotte.

SEXTON Remember, young lady, this is a house of God.

YOUNG LADY And I am a child of man.

SEXTON If the pastor were to find out—

YOUNG LADY Priest or no priest, I stand with the good Lord. Play: I want to dance in his honor.

SEXTON (*shakes his head*) I'll do it to please you, because I respect you and know that your thought is not a bad one.

> *The SEXTON plays a cheerful gavotte. The YOUNG LADY spins lightly in the dance. KASPAR has raised his head and is watching her. She breaks off, breathless, clutching her chest.*

YOUNG LADY Ah, the air – it hurts.

KASPAR I would have liked to kneel like before the Holy Lady.

YOUNG LADY I danced – for you too, Kaspar.

KASPAR The doctor has forbidden any excitement for you. You are disobedient to him. You rage against your beautiful young life, which so many people enjoy, as if it were against a wayward foal.

YOUNG LADY I will die young – Kaspar, and that's why I will gladly die.

KASPAR Do you know what night it is today, young lady?

KASPAR Midsummer Night – the farmhands will light fires on the hills all around.

YOUNG LADY You have tears hanging in your lashes – why?

KASPAR (*lowers his head*) I saw how the people pointed at the maid, because she is pregnant by me, and I can't change it.—

YOUNG LADY Everything will be all right, Kaspar.

Scene 7: St. John's Night

Fires all around on the hills.

THE SERVANTS AND MAIDS We're twining the St. John's wreath. (*then exit, KASPAR stays behind with the MAID*)

MAID You have no more fire, Kaspar, you are cold as stone.

KASPAR There's enough fire burning on the hills.

MAID Come behind the bushes, I'm burning.

KASPAR I am burned away. Only ash now, I'm gray. Scatter me to the wind.

MAID If you don't love me tonight, I'll betray you.

KASPAR Your pregnant belly will find lovers enough. No one needs to fear he'll make a child.

MAID You still mock me in my misfortune, because I trusted your word. Shame on you, Kaspar, you are not an honest man.

> *One hears harmonica music.*

KASPAR I'm going. I must be among people, can't find my way. (*exits*)

MAID (*stays, then breaks into sobs.*)

> *The* YOUNG LADY *enters*

YOUNG LADY Why are you crying? Come, I'll caress you.

MAID Ah, Miss, you are kind to me.

YOUNG LADY Not kind enough. I am too weak to do you good. Why are you crying? Everyone is joyful on this night.

MAID Kaspar doesn't love me anymore. He's gone to the dancing girls.

YOUNG LADY He loves you. He doesn't know it.

MAID No, Miss, he loves you. And only you—he shouldn't love you.

YOUNG LADY Come, let's go to the dancing boys and girls. And if Kaspar dances with a strange girl, you dance with a strange boy.

> *Harmonica music. They exit. After a while:* KASPAR *enters with the* YOUNG LADY.

KASPAR Miss, I can't bear it any longer. You danced with me, and my head thunders as if a thousand storms were unleashed in it. Let a raging bull trample me to death, strangle me – I know I'm not even worthy of the death you've decreed – but redeem me from the depths of my ignorant being and my dull heart, my hellish heart that cries out to you, my heaven. I am the devil—yes, truly the devil – who loves you, angel, because you are full of what he is not: because you are good, beautiful, gentle. But he himself is a stinking beast. A snot-nosed one.

YOUNG LADY (*kneels before him*) Kaspar, I am your servant, do with me as you please. I kneel before your nameless torment in humility. For I am eternal bliss, but you are damned and shall be redeemed – through me –

Scene 8: Room

DOCTOR I always told the young lady: her weak lungs can't tolerate dancing. No excitement whatsoever. The heart is also affected. Only light diet. The stomach is also affected. What is one to do? The warning of science is not heeded.

FARMER The girl felt so light, so cheerful all these days. Just floated through the day. Sang like a swallow.

DOCTOR The euphoria well known to science! A very suspicious sign. The better a person feels, the closer they are to death. *Media in vita morte.*[17]

FARMER'S WIFE Oh God, we still owe her so much love.

DOCTOR Let's go to the patient, let's take her pulse. Is she coughing?

---

[17] In the midst of life, death.

FARMER A little.

DOCTOR Suspicious, highly suspicious. Closed tuberculosis usually all the more serious. (*exits*)

FARMER Let us make peace at her deathbed.

FARMER'S WIFE (*sobbing*)

FARMER I feel it: our happiness is dying. What remains for us: growing old together, the quiet evening. Death together.

> KASPAR *enters.*

FARMER Farmer's wife, Farmer.

FARMER'S WIFE Kaspar, you look deathly pale.

KASPAR Farmer – how is the young lady?

FARMER Not well, Kaspar.

KASPAR I – am – to blame, Farmer – for her suffering.

FARMER Don't talk nonsense, Kaspar. The young lady was always sick.

KASPAR I – am – to blame – Farmer – I can't say otherwise – I alone am to blame.

FARMER We are all to blame, Kaspar, because we were bad.

KASPAR I – alone – am to blame – I danced with the young lady – then the blood broke from her mouth.

> *The* DOCTOR *comes from the other room.*

DOCTOR If you want to see your child alive once more, come, Farmer, Farmer's wife.

> FARMER *and* FARMER'S WIFE *exit into the room –* KASPAR *remains motionless. The* MAID *enters.*

MAID Kaspar, forgive me: I danced with the servant from... the farm. We went into the forest—and he forced me— (*she collapses before him*)

> *A tender cry comes from the* YOUNG LADY *in the room*

Kaspar, come, say goodbye to me.

> KASPAR, *without having noticed the maid, exits.*

Scene 9: Courtroom

JUDGE Three years in prison with hard labor, revocation of civil rights. Next.

> *A convicted man exits. The next one steps forward.*

JUDGE Ten months in jail, three of which count as pre-trial detention. Next.

> *same as above*

JUDGE Seven years in prison with hard labor, a fine of 5,000 marks, revocation of civil rights for ten years. Next.

> *same as above*

JUDGE Death by hanging. Next.

> *same as above—Death by hanging. Next.*
>
> KASPAR *steps forward.*

KASPAR Pass judgment on me, Judge! I have sinned.

JUDGE Where do you come from?

KASPAR From life. And I want to enter death.

JUDGE What have you done? Theft? Robbery-murder? Rape? Category A, B, C... There's only a limited set of motives for human actions. Well?

KASPAR I did none of those.

JUDGE Then at least don't waste my time—get out of here, you're innocent. Next.

KASPAR I am guilty – guilty as no man has ever been.

JUDGE I've never seen anyone so eager to be judged. Why, and for what, should I sentence you?

KASPAR I killed a human being with my love.

JUDGE Nonsense. One kills with a knife, an axe, et cetera – but not with love. Love is not a weapon.

KASPAR I violated an angel with my embrace. My wicked kiss was her death. I am a thousand times more guilty than the poor thief who stole out of hunger, or the poor murderer who killed in despair. I killed out of the inborn hatred of evil for good.

JUDGE Nonsense. Some people are only good because so many are bad. The good are guilty of the evil.
Kaspar: I don't understand you. I killed the young lady, the farmer's daughter.

JUDGE You accuse yourself?
Kaspar: Yes.

JUDGE (*rings a bell. A* GUARD *appears*) Take him into custody pending clarification of the facts. – Next: twelve years of forced labor—

Scene 10: Prison Cell

KASPAR I've already been wearing down the soles of my shoes for a year. I like to suffer. No: I don't suffer at all. I like to work. Is it summer again? I think I sense, through the barred window up there, a scent of the chestnut tree in the yard.

GUARD No. 311: sweep the cell, empty the bucket. You have a visitor.

KASPAR A visitor? Whom? I haven't heard anything from the world for a year.

GUARD No. 311: (*unlocks the cell; lets a* MAID *in, carrying a small child in her arms.*)

MAID Good day, Kaspar. I got permission to visit you. Don't you want to say good day to your child?

KASPAR Good day, madam. Good day, child.

MAID Why are you so upset, Kaspar? Look at me: I am cheerful because I'm allowed to see you. And because I have good news: You don't need to stay in prison anymore. It was a terrible lie by a wicked person, that you were supposed to have killed the young lady. The farmer, the farmer's wife, and everyone testified for you, that you are a good man and not capable of such a crime.

KASPAR It cannot – be... The judge – and – I am guilty, did I not feel it myself in the deepest –

MAID Kaspar, one is guilty of the other. Who knows how much. Who knows what for. You have to live and work in life. Life is waiting. The plaice is steaming. The oxen are already standing restlessly at the plowshare, and the dog barks behind the lambs. Kaspar, look here at your child!

KASPAR takes the child into his arms.

KASPAR (*happily*) Upsadaisy – whoops – that's a strong lad – he will tear out trees like I did.

MAID Come, do you hear the prison bells ringing? I've sent for the pastor to come straight to the church: he is to marry us: you and me – and baptize the little child with the name of the young lady: Maria. Because that is the way it is going to be.

About the Translator

Jim Doss is a founding editor of the bi-annual journal *Loch Raven Review*. He was born and raised in the foothills of the Blue Ridge Mountains, and is a graduate of the University of Virginia. His work has appeared in numerous publications, both on the Internet and in print. Doss has published three books of poetry: *Learning to Talk Again* (2011), *What Remains* (2017), and *The Last Goodbye* (2024). He has also translated Georg Trakl's complete poems, *The Last Gold of Expired Stars*, Ernst Toller's autobiography, *A Youth in Germany*, and *Letters from Prison* in addition to a number of Ernst Toller's plays, and a poetry anthology entitled *Nine Holocaust Poets* (2024). He recently published two books of novels by Klabund: *Bracke and Six Other Novels* (2025) and *Borgia and Four Other Novels* (2025). He is a retired software engineer.

www.ingramcontent.com/pod-product-compliance
Lightning Source LLC
Chambersburg PA
CBHW030633020726
47493CB00006B/1699